Expanding Approaches to Bible Translation

Biblical Performance Criticism Series
Orality, Memory, Translation, Rhetoric, Discourse

David Rhoads, Kelly R. Iverson, and Peter S. Perry, Series Editors

The ancient societies of the Bible were overwhelmingly oral. People originally experienced the traditions now in the Bible as oral performances. Focusing on the ancient performance of biblical traditions enables us to shift academic work on the Bible from the mentality of a modern print culture to that of an oral/scribal culture. Conceived broadly, biblical performance criticism embraces many methods as means to reframe the biblical materials in the context of traditional oral cultures, construct scenarios of ancient performances, learn from contemporary performances of these materials, and reinterpret biblical writings accordingly. The result is a foundational paradigm shift that reconfigures traditional disciplines and employs fresh biblical methodologies such as theater studies, speech-act theory, and performance studies. The emerging research of many scholars in this field of study, the development of working groups in scholarly societies, and the appearance of conferences on orality and literacy make it timely to inaugurate this series. For further information on biblical performance criticism, go to www.biblicalperformancecriticism.org.

Books in the Series

Holly E. Hearon & Philip Ruge-Jones, eds.
The Bible in Ancient and Modern Media

James A. Maxey
From Orality to Orality: A New Paradigm for Contextual Translation of the Bible

Antoinette Clark Wire
The Case for Mark Composed in Performance

Robert D. Miller II, SFO
Oral Tradition in Ancient Israel

Pieter J. J. Botha
Orality and Literacy in Early Christianity

James A. Maxey & Ernst R. Wendland, eds.
Translating Scripture for Sound and Performance

J. A. (Bobby) Loubser
Oral and Manuscript Culture in the Bible

Joanna Dewey
The Oral Ethos of the Early Church

Richard A. Horsley
Text and Tradition in Performance and Writing

Kelly R. Iverson, ed.
From Text to Performance: Narrative and Performance Criticisms in Dialogue and Debate

Annette Weissenrieder & Robert B. Coote, eds.
The Interface of Orality and Writing: Speaking, Seeing, Writing in the Shaping of New Genres

Thomas E. Boomershine
The Messiah of Peace: A Performance-Criticism Commentary on Mark's Passion-Resurrection Narrative

Terry Giles & William J. Doan
The Naomi Story—The Book of Ruth: From Gender to Politics

Bernhard Oestreich
Performance Criticism of the Pauline Letters

Marcel Jousse, Edgard Sienaert, ed.
Memory, Memorization, and Memorizers: The Galilean Oral-Style Tradition and Its Traditionists

Margaret E. Lee
Sound Matters

Thomas E. Broomershine
First-Century Gospel Storytellers and Audiences

Margaret E. Lee & Bernard Brandon Scott
Sound Mapping the New Testament, Second Edition

Werner Kelber, ed.
The Forgotten Compass: Marcel Jousse and the Exploration of the Oral World

Peter S. Perry, ed.
Biblical Humor and Performance: Audience Experiences That Make Meaning

"Those of us who do our biblical studies work in African contexts understand just how important translation studies are, constituting a significant component of 'African biblical studies.' This edited collection of essays enables us to understand just why translation studies are so important, combining emerging theory with particular practices and intersecting biblical textual orientations with a focus on orality and performance. Translation in general and biblical translation in particular is more complex and includes more than we have envisaged. This interdisciplinary volume, both as a product and a process, summons us to delve more deeply into translation."

—GERALD O. WEST,
Professor Emeritus, School of Religion, Philosophy, and Classics,
University of KwaZulu-Natal, Durban, South Africa

"This timely collection is a must-read for anyone seeking to understand the growing multimodal movement in Bible translation. As each new author takes their turn, they open our eyes to a broader perspective that not only integrates sign language and oral translations but puts them center stage. As with all good performances, the book challenges us to think afresh: confronting long-cherished assumptions about values and processes, and even the nature and purpose of Bible translation."

—PHIL KING,
Director of International Translation Services, SIL Global

"Despite the accelerating advances in translation studies, Bible translation has been relatively stuck in a linguistic conceptualization of what the Bible is and how it should be translated across cultures. This book is ground-breaking in its attempt to challenge narrow perspectives on Bible translation, using recent developments in translation studies, multimodality, semiotics, and biblical performance criticism. Maxey has successfully brought ten contributors with unique academic and professional backgrounds to pose key questions about experiencing the materiality of Bible translation. This is a must-read for scholars, Bible translators and anyone passionate about Bible engagement in different modalities."

—SAMEH HANNA,
Global Translation Consultant, United Bible Societies

"By viewing Bible translation beyond its interlinguistic dimension as a modern-day performance of ancient biblical traditions, this volume succeeds in a novel way to move biblical performance criticism within the milieu of a sophisticated theoretical approach of multimodal translation. Modes combine forces to excel for specific purposes. As a project of ten collaborators on intersemiotic Bible translation challenging the great divide between oral and written, the essays follow a recent trend in translation studies."

—JACOBUS A. NAUDÉ AND CYNTHIA L. MILLER-NAUDÉ,
Senior Professors, University of the Free State, Bloemfontein, South Africa

"The book's engagement with multimodality, materiality and performance in relation to Bible translation processes is a welcome broadening of the field and a contribution to scholars working in the field of Bible translation, including Bible translators."

—HEPHZIBAH ISRAEL,
Senior Lecturer in Translation Studies, University of Edinburgh

Expanding Approaches to Bible Translation
Multimodal Perspectives

Edited by
JAMES A. MAXEY

CASCADE *Books* • Eugene, Oregon

EXPANDING APPROACHES TO BIBLE TRANSLATION
Multimodal Perspectives

Biblical Performance Criticism 21

Copyright © 2025 Wipf and Stock Publishers. All rights reserved. Except for brief quotations in critical publications or reviews, no part of this book may be reproduced in any manner without prior written permission from the publisher. Write: Permissions, Wipf and Stock Publishers, 199 W. 8th Ave., Suite 3, Eugene, OR 97401.

Cascade Books
An Imprint of Wipf and Stock Publishers
199 W. 8th Ave., Suite 3
Eugene, OR 97401
www.wipfandstock.com

PAPERBACK ISBN: 978-1-667-7128-2
HARDCOVER ISBN: 978-1-667-7129-9
EBOOK ISBN: 978-1-667-7130-5

Cataloguing-in-Publication data:

Names: Maxey, James A., editor.

Title: Expanding approaches to Bible translation : multimodal perspectives / edited by James A. Maxey.

Description: Eugene, OR: Cascade Books, 2025. | Biblical Performance Criticism 21. | Includes bibliographical references and index.

Identifiers: ISBN 978-1-6667-7128-2 (paperback). | ISBN 978-1-6667-7129-9 (hardcover). | ISBN 978-1-6667-7130-5 (ebook).

Subjects: LCSH: Biblical translation. | Bible—Translating. | Translating and interpreting. | Performance—Religious aspects—Christianity. | Oral tradition.

Classification: BS449 E88 2023 (print). | BS449 (ebook).

VERSION NUMBER 05/20/25

JPS Tanakh: The Holy Scriptures: The New JPS Translation according to the Traditional Hebrew Text. Jewish Publication Society, 1985.

The Holy Bible, New International Version®, NIV® Copyright © 1973, 1978, 1984, 2011 by Biblica, Inc.™ Used by permission. All rights reserved worldwide.

Scripture quotations marked NRSVue are taken from the New Revised Standard Version Updated Edition. Copyright © 2021 National Council of Churches of Christ in the United States of America. Used by permission. All rights reserved worldwide.

Contents

Preface | vii

List of Abbreviations | viii

List of Contributors | ix

1. Introduction | *James A. Maxey* | 1

2. Engaging Multimodal Social Semiotic Dimensions of the New Testament in Translation | *Holly Hearon* | 18

3. Biblical Translation, Performance, and Re-Translation in Local Communities | *Peter S. Perry* | 44

4. Multimodality and Performance: Creole Translation and Identity | *Marlon Winedt* | 70

5. Labyrinths of Meaning: Unstable Signs in Urban Spaces | *Matt Valler* | 94

6. Increasing Communication Bandwidth: From Multimodal Translation Process to Four Revised Qualities of Bible Translation | *Sebastian Floor* | 122

7. Re-Translating a Contested Performance Tradition | *Nathan A. Esala* | 153

8. Echoing Forward, Echoing Back: Thick Translation, the Song of Songs, and the Performance of Cultural Exchange | *Becka Mara McKay* | 185

9. Performance in Sign Language Bible Translation | *Isela Trujillo* | 203

10. Translating What Is (not)(un)Said | *Richard W. Swanson* | 229

Preface

It has been forty years since I began this journey of Bible translation. At that time, it all appeared so straightforward to me: linguistics, communication theories, exegetical methods, translation principles, theological underpinnings, and ideological motivations. These past forty years have enlarged my understanding of Bible translation. This growth is in many ways the result of people who have expanded my thinking and commitments. From the Vuté community in Cameroon to my professors and fellow students during my doctoral studies at Lutheran School of Theology at Chicago and Catholic Theological Union, from biblical studies scholars whom I encountered at conferences such as Society of Biblical Literature to Translation Studies scholars with whom I engaged during my years in Italy. And to the Bible translation guild that has encouraged and challenged me—from my early years at Lutheran Bible Translators where I spent more than a decade learning an oral language and doing NT translation in central Cameroon, to the Nida Institute at American Bible Society where we developed a global research and training program, to my current time at Seed Company where I'm asked to leverage the many networks developed over my career. All these experiences, circumstances, and associated people have helped me to see the ever-expanding topic of Bible translation. This book demonstrates part of this expansion and demonstrates the vastness of possibilities of both the subject and the people involved in Bible translation.

Abbreviations

ACN	accuracy, clarity, and naturalness
BPC	Biblical Performance Criticism
BT	Bible translation
CBBT	Church-Based Bible Translation
CBS	Contextual Bible Study
DPP	Decolonial Pedagogies Project
ETEN	Every Tribe Every Nation
FIA	familiarization, internalization, and articulation
JBL	*Journal of Biblical Literature*
MMT	multimodal translation
MTL	[superscripted L] Masoretic Text Leningradis
OBT	Oral Bible Translation
QA	quality assurance
TS	translation studies
TUAA	trustworthy, understandable, appropriate, and appealing

Contributors

NATHAN A. ESALA is a biblical scholar, translator, performer, pastor, and activist. Nathan earned his MDiv from Concordia Seminary in 2001. Joining Lutheran Bible Translators in 2002, Nathan was *translated* to Ghana, Africa, where he served as a Bible translation advisor in the Komba Bible project for ten years. In Ghana, Nathan learned how to become more human. He continued that process as a research associate at the Ujamaa Centre at the University of KwaZulu-Natal (UKZN). In 2021, Nathan earned his PhD in religion from UKZN. He is the author of *Biblical Translation as Invasion in Postcolonial Northern Ghana* (2024). Nathan works for Seed Company as the Coordinator for Strategic Alliances.

SEBASTIAN J. FLOOR is a Dutch-born South African currently living in Cape Town. He and his wife Karen served for twenty years with SIL in Mozambique and from 2009 to 2019 served as regional director for Southern Africa, first with Wycliffe South Africa and then with Seed Company. He is a translation consultant since 2001 and now serves in that role with Seed Company. He is part of the ETEN Innovation Lab on Quality Assurance and since 2021 has led a working group called Psalms That Sing involved in promoting the translation of the psalms in poetic format. He has earned a PhD at Stellenbosch University on theme analysis and information structure in biblical Hebrew, and he is especially interested in biblical theology, pragmatics and discourse, biblical key concepts, and missiology.

Contributors

HOLLY HEARON is T. J. and Virginia Liggett Professor of Christian Traditions and New Testament Emerita at Christian Theological Seminary (Indianapolis). She has published numerous chapters and articles on oral storytelling and communication practices in the first-century Mediterranean world, most recently "Communication in Context: Jesus Movements and the Construction of Meaning In the Media World of the First Century," in *Bridges in New Testament Interpretation* (2018), and "The Materiality of the Bible as Performance," in *Aspects of Performance in Faith Settings: Heavenly Acts* (2019).

JAMES A. MAXEY is director of Strategic Alliances at Seed Company. He has two other books in the BPC series: *From Orality to Orality* and *Translating Scripture for Sound and Performance* (co-edited with Ernst Wendland). Besides numerous journal articles, he has contributed the following chapters: "Alternative Evaluative Concepts for the Trinity of Bible Translation" (2016) and "Translating Sacredness: Performance Translation from a Hospitality Perspective" (2024).

BECKA MARA MCKAY is a poet and translator who earned her MFA in creative writing from the University of Washington and her MFA in literary translation from the University of Iowa, where she also earned a PhD in comparative literature. Publications include poetry: *A Meteorologist in the Promised Land* (2010), *Happiness Is the New Bedtime* (2016), and *The Little Book of No Consolation* (2021), and translations of Israeli fiction: *Laundry* (2008), *Blue Has No South* (2010), and *Lunar Savings Time* (2011). She is professor of translation and creative writing at Florida Atlantic University, where she is also director of creative writing and faculty advisor to the literary journal *Swamp Ape Review*.

PETER S. PERRY, PhD, is pastor of St. John's Lutheran Church, Glendale, Arizona, affiliate Associate Professor of New Testament for Fuller Seminary, and administrator for www.BiblicalPerformanceCriticism.org. He is author of *Insights from Performance Criticism* (2016) and editor of *Biblical Humor and Performance* (Cascade Books, 2023) and is working on projects on embodied cognition and rhetoric.

RICHARD W. SWANSON is professor of religion (emeritus) at Augustana University. He has written several books, all of which have the phrase "provoking the gospel" in the title. His most recent project was the creation of a play (with Grace Ahles and Hanna Beshai). The title of the play is *This Is My Body*, a phrase that shows up in sacramental theology and in every #MeToo story you have ever heard.

ISELA TRUJILLO is from Mexico and joined United Bible Societies in 2009 and prepared the Greek-Spanish Interlinear of the New Testament with Elsa Tamez (2011). Later, she worked for the Mexican Bible Society (2012) and collaborated with various indigenous Bible translation projects in Mexico and the Central America region. After receiving training in Sign Language and Deaf culture, she became a translation consultant for Sign Language projects in 2017. At present, she works primarily with Sign Language Bible translation projects for Latin America and the Caribbean region. Her academic background is in linguistics (PhD 2012, MA 2008), biblical sciences, and social anthropology. Her research interests are sociolinguistics, Bible and intercultural studies, Sign Languages and Deaf culture.

MATT VALLER holds a PhD in translation studies from Queen's University Belfast and an MA (with distinction) in aspects of biblical interpretation from the London School of Theology. His current research advances a New Materialist theory of translation, specifically in relation to place. Matt founded Labyrinth in 2015, and has since designed interactive storytelling experiences in London; Melbourne; New York; Washington, DC; and Barcelona, among others. Recent publications include: "Taking the Measure of the Mississippi: Translation, New Materialism, and the Negotiation of Boundaries" (2024) and (with Piotr Blumczynski) "Reassembling the Ruins: Revisiting Latour's Concept of Translation in Modernity's Growing Aftermath" (2024).

MARLON WINEDT, educated in theology, philosophy, and Bible translation in the US and the Netherlands, has dedicated thirty-five years to Bible translation. As a global translation advisor for the United Bible Societies, he works across the Caribbean and Americas. Marlon has published several articles in *The Bible Translator*, including "Translation as Performance and Engagement: Performing Philemon from a Modern Caribbean Perspective" (2015) as well as other journals and is a researcher in biblical exegesis, performance criticism, and Creole studies. Marlon is a native of the island of Curaçao where he is based and also serves as a pastor and adjunct professor for several institutes.

1

Introduction

JAMES A. MAXEY

Location of This Book Within the Biblical Performance Criticism Series

Since 2009 the books in the series of Biblical Performance Criticism (BPC) have demonstrated a significant range of research in the general area of biblical studies with the distinguishing feature being oral performance. Bible translation (BT) is an area of research and practice that belongs within the range of these discussions of BPC.[1] Translators of the Bible benefit significantly from the research of biblical scholarship in general and in turn contribute to biblical scholarship via the insights gained from translation. Likewise, practitioners of BT contribute to BPC as they experiment with translating the Bible beyond print.

Performance is often used as a broader term for orality within BPC, tapping into earlier classical, anthropological, and historical orality studies. During its relatively short lifespan, BPC has addressed the relationships of orality with the written. Outside of this series, biblical scholars have nuanced this relationship and even critiqued BPC's views of the dominant influence of orality in antiquity. A second critique has been directed at BPC's validation of modern-day performances as a means to investigate historical performances. In a sense, a new great divide has

---

1. Two previous volumes on Bible translation in the BPC series: Maxey, *From Orality to Orality*; Maxey and Wendland, *Translating Scripture for Sound and Performance*.

developed in biblical studies regarding performance where historical research of communication is pitted against heuristic performances today.[2] Translation in many ways represents a modern-day performance as it demonstrates the heuristic insights by translating ancient biblical traditions.

In the great divide debates of historical and modern performances, we find that translation becomes another window into this perceived duality.[3] The general position of this project is that these so-called great divides are challenged with the concept of multimodal translation. The assertion is that throughout human history, communication has always been multimodal. It is not necessary to choose between oral and written as universally preferred or dominant, or any of the many other modes of communication. Multimodality does not mean that all modes do the same thing for communication. As we will see in the following chapters, certain modes excel for certain contexts and purposes. We see this happening in our current digital age, for example, where images, sound, writing, and much more combine forces in particular ways for particular purposes of communication. Bible translation has demonstrated this multimodal nature as it has been expressed early on through oral compositions accompanied by performative features such as gestures that in time led to other composites of communication through material objects (manuscripts and codices), alphabetic writing, images and illustrations, joining forces to record and perform biblical traditions.

The practice of multimodality has a long history, but a sophisticated theoretical approach to it is relatively recent. Even more recent is the engagement of multimodality with translation studies.[4] And even more recent, perhaps only just appearing in a published book form here, Bible translation theorists and practitioners begin to articulate multimodal Bible translation.[5] Most of the chapters in this volume did not start with

---

2. Others have addressed both critiques elsewhere. Hurtado, "Oral Fixation and New Testament Studies?"; Perry, "Biblical Performance Criticism"; Iverson, *Performing Early Christian Literature*; Elder, *Gospel Media*.

3. History of Bible translation is an important research area but is not in focus in our current project. Several studies provide a variety of historical insights, including Noss, *History of Bible Translation*.

4. Boria et al., *Translation and Multimodality*.

5. Others have also addressed this subject in conference papers or journal publications, for example: Floor, "Search for a Seamless Integration"; Winedt, "Bible Translation as Incarnation"; Naudé and Miller-Naudé, "Meaning-Making Processes in Religious Translation"; Maxey, "Beyond Print/Oral Translation."

a self-conscious presupposition of multimodality. But the seemingly disparate ways in which Bible translation was being expanded could all be encompassed, sometimes in hindsight, from a multimodal perspective. A few of the chapters tackle this theory head on while others let it sit more below the surface.

Project Description

The range of topics in this volume is broad as is the social locations of the authors. Some come from a professional guild of Bible translators. Several contributors are organizationally attached to one of the many Bible translation agencies that exist around the world.[6] These are the ones whose day job it is to wrestle with Bible translation. But there are other contributors who have done Bible translation their whole careers without naming it as such until more recently. Oftentimes, these are people who come from the biblical scholarship guild. Other authors come from translation studies. These contributors have practiced and theorized about translation and have sometimes done so with biblical material but not exclusively. All these contributors have participated in some type of translation seminar in the in the Emilia-Romagna region of northern Italy in the 2010s. Several of the contributors participated in a series of four seminars on intersemiotic translation. It was here that we researched and explored translation from a semiotics perspective. And it is here that we first came together to challenge the assertion that translation was restricted to words. Our thinking has expanded since those research seminars yet the chapters in this book owe a significant amount to those seminars and the discussions, formal and otherwise, that took place over the past fifteen years.

Authors and Audiences for This Project

Who is the anticipated audience for this book? Given the publisher and the series, there are some expected audiences, such as biblical scholars and those who are interested in performance. But the title suggests that we are anticipating this book will help those involved in Bible translation. These chapters do not compile a how-to manual—despite that there are many practical examples of how Bible translation takes place today in

---

6. Many of these Bible translation organizations are members of the Forum of Bible Agencies International, https://forum-intl.org.

diverse settings. The authors of these chapters are practitioners, but they are also theorists. Pedagogically, there is need for something between this book and a manual for multimodal translators on the ground.[7] Whereas all the chapters are written in English, not all the contributors claim English as their first language. This should encourage readers who might likewise identify. As some have said, the ideas and practice of performance with biblical material have been around for centuries, but it's only recently that the academic researchers and publishing houses of the West have recognized their viability. Maybe the material in this book will provide opportunities for existing practitioners to have greater confidence in what they have already been doing.

Timing of This Project

Why this volume now? Bible translation is at risk of being understood in an increasingly narrow way. This might come from biblical scholarship that wants to assert that Bible translation is limited to the act of linguistic transposition, from one verbal language to another. The false assertion is that there is "translation proper" and then other translation-like activities that are all well and good, but they are not translation. Other words are used instead of translation for these other activities: adaptation, Scripture engagement, transcreation, etc. The assertion of this volume is that translation, including Bible translation, is larger than what we have historically thought. The complex modes with online and social media communication today have underscored that translation is more than words and it's even more than media.[8]

A second reason for this volume now is that there are currently a lot of activities being done with BT and orality without sophisticated theoretical foundations. These new methodologies can be generalized as Oral Bible Translation (OBT).[9] In many ways, this book presents diverse

---

7. Perhaps there is sufficient material here to develop seminars and course syllabi for capacity building of translators.

8. There is some overlap between mode and media with regard to Bible translation as demonstrated by Merz, "Bible Translation in Theory and Practice." I would argue, however, that a focus on media does not explain the meaning-making process of modality, especially from a social science perspective as does multimodal translation.

9. The following is only a sample: Faith Comes by Hearing, "Oral Bible Translation"; https://spoken.org/oral-bible-translation/; Word for the World, "Hearing the Word." It was reported at the OBT Global Gathering in July 2024 that there are over eight hundred OBT active projects currently. An example of a more sophisticated approach

examples that expand the discussion beyond orality and also presents an underlying theory that is more encompassing than what OBT offers.[10] By over-emphasizing or isolating orality, a neglect of other modes involved in communication can become a restriction to translators, especially when ideological assertions such as oral-only communities are made. These self-imposed limitations can constrain practitioners from leveraging other existing modes of communication in translation methods and resources. As we will see, multimodality offers a communication theory that can help avoid simplified notions of transfer of meaning from one medium to another without any change. Take for example a text translated for print that is then read aloud and recorded and calling this an oral translation. Or the converse, taking an orally translated text and transcribing it and calling this a written translation. Multimodality provides clarity that modes have particular capacities and constraints which enhance that mode but cannot be transferred directly to other modes without respecting how each mode comes with various affordances and constraints.

A third reason for the timing of this volume is the work being done in recent translation studies research. Translation is explored as a process that can be found in human communication, where communication theories assert that translation is part of a semiotic process that is involved in meaning making. Translators will become better equipped in the translation processes when they understand better how communication involves semiotic processes. The general notion of the expansion of what translation is becomes fundamental to this volume, hence the title, *Expanding Approaches to Bible Translation*.

Expansion of Translation and Closing the Gaps

The expansion of how translation is defined beyond linguistics is matched by a definition of Bible beyond a book.[11] This is not meant as a theological assertion. Limiting Bible to a book is challenged in this project

to OBT is Frost, Mustin, and Beal, "Attaining Quality in Oral Bible Translation."

10. A critique of OBT from a multimodal perspective was presented at the 2023 Bible Translation Conference with the paper Maxey, "From Mono to Multimodal Translation."

11. Using Bible without the definite article, the, is meant to remind the reader that the use of Bible here is intended to be conceptual in an attempt not to predetermine its mode or media.

where Bible is expressed in a variety of modes and media. Some would be tempted to suggest that each of these is a derivation from the original book with alphabetic writing as the primary mode. This does not match our historical research nor our theoretical underpinnings. Such culturally dominant ideologies as equating Bible with a book problematizes defining Bible. This leads to the assertion that Bible translation reveals itself as contested space with both Bible and translation being conceptually expanded. We are aware that such expansions and contestations can be provocative.

The combination of performance and translation suggests a significant contribution from both fields of study. Each of these asserts a certain fundamental human capacity along with claims that each discipline crosses over to other disciplines not so much in an interdisciplinary fashion but in what has been called transdisciplinarian.[12] Transdisciplinarity questions an Enlightenment categorization of primary concepts such as translation and performance. Although this theoretical assertion merits pursuit, here is not the place. But if this claim is accurate, then discussions about performance and translation in general and BT in particular should not be peripheral. Whether we conceive of this activity as translation as performance or performance as translation or some other relationship between the two, translation-performance plays a central role in human experience, including Bible. Suffice it to say that both are essential to this current project and translation-performance as transdisciplines can be said to inform this whole project.

There remain significant gaps in research and dialogue related to multimodal Bible translation. Biblical scholars are preoccupied with their historical research whereas translation studies scholars often exhibit a type of allergy to discussions of sacred text translation. Bible translation contributors are often required to produce quantifiable results for their agencies and find it difficult to find time and permission to interact with those outside the BT guild. The result is a type of ghettoization where questions, experiences, and pursuits for knowledge are not shared. This volume is a gesture toward trying to close the gaps between these three areas of research and practice.

I would suggest these chapters demonstrate an even broader contribution that joins Bible translation, biblical and translation studies under

---

12. Arduini and Nergaard, "Translation"; Marais, *(Bio)Semiotic Theory of Translation*; Marais, *Translation Beyond Translation Studies*; Carlson, *Performance*; Schechner, *Performance Studies*.

a heading of what I would call global Bible translation studies. Global Bible translation studies would be the result of these disciplines (and others) dialoguing in ways that they seldom do. Each of these disciplines would need to demonstrate a disposition of expansion in order for global Bible translation studies to gain traction. Examples of such expansion include (but are not limited to): Bible translation would need to be considered under a broader heading of Sacred Text Translation to embrace the commonalities of other sacred text traditions. Translation would need to embrace a concept of translation beyond translation proper that limits translation to words. Biblical scholarship would need to embrace the human agency behind and in front of the written text as well as the materiality of other modes and the social shaping of all such materiality. The intersection of these disparate disciplines (and others) can potentially come together as global Bible translation studies.[13]

Beyond a Book to a Process

This project has attempted to shift the focus beyond a product to a process. From the start, the goal was to be interactive throughout the process of research and writing. Quarterly online meetings were set to get to know the other contributors and to update each other on their particular topic, their challenges, and their aspirations. Early abstracts, outlines, and drafts of each of the contributions were made available to the other authors on a platform that permitted interaction with the material through comments, Q & A, etc. This was not easy. Our academic training and experience have conditioned us to understand that research and writing for publication is a solo journey. It's often only in the final stage that an editor provides feedback to an author, and if the project is multi-authored, the authors seldom have access to the other authors' material prior to the pre-publication version. Our attempt in this project was to create a community of researchers to dialogue together toward a common goal. As the instigator of this project, I will be the first to admit that this proposed method failed at times, but there were some successes. It's hard work to change our habits, dispositions, and methods.

As mentioned above, this project was started as more than a pursuit of a published book. One of the aspirations is that the raw material of

13. Many other established disciplines would contribute to such dialogue, such as ethnomusicology, ethnopoetics, theater studies, semiotics, cultural studies, film studies, folklore studies, etc.

prepublication drafts and author interactions would be available to the general public. Given that these interactions appear online, with multimedia capacities, this online platform can provide things to the reader beyond the published book. It might be as simple as viewing YouTube videos of performances. Or it might be a thread of discussion of a particular section of a chapter that helps the reader appreciate the debates and growth of ideas in the making.[14]

For most of the people involved in Bible translation today, there is a general instrumentality to it. Vision and mission statements discuss Bible translation as a means to an end. For many of the agencies, this is articulated in terms of life change. Although the book contributors come from various backgrounds, including religious views, I think we would all agree that our experience with this project has contributed to some changes for us. These might not be articulated in the ways that are often cited on websites and marketing material. I would suggest that this project is highlighting the process itself that includes interaction with people. This interactive process reflects our understanding of what translation and performance are and what they can do.

Key Terms and Concepts

Throughout this book, various key terms are used. Oftentimes the chapter author will define the term when they use it. In other projects, there is sometimes a glossary of terms at the end of the book. For this project, I want to say a few words in this introductory chapter about what I consider to be key terms or concepts related to this project. Do I think that one size fits all with each of the authors? No. I'm steering away from suggesting that I'm giving definitions of terms. I also want to say that I am openly borrowing from my colleagues in this project (and perhaps from others who are not involved in this project) as I describe these terms. Where possible, I will name the people who have helped me better understand the terms. In other words, I'm trying to create a type of open access of terminology used in this book that is not proprietary in nature. I have already mentioned most of these terms above, but here is the short list: performance, translation, semiotics, multimodal.

---

14. Early drafts of chapters with comments from the project collaborators along with YouTube recordings of Zoom meetings of collaborators as well as other related material to the project can be found at https://expandingapproachesbt.pubpub.org.

Performance

Performance is broader than orality. Richard Schechner's descriptions of performance encompass all social aspects of life, nuanced by numerous disciplinary lenses.[15] Peter Perry refines Schechner's description for BPC by stating: "[performance is] a communication event re-expressing traditions before an audience."[16] In BT, performance participates in constructing and sustaining (and sometimes deconstructing or disrupting) biblical traditions. For those who presuppose writing for translation, performance is what is understood as what is done after a stable text is translated. However, in this volume, it is sometimes difficult to differentiate performance and translation. Sometimes we are translating a performance; sometimes the translation becomes a way to perform an identity. At other times, we (re)translate to perform a different function than a previous tradition. Nathan Esala gives us some excellent examples of how Bible (re)translation can perform alternative identities.

Translation

Translation studies has approached defining and describing translation in many ways.[17] These definitions and descriptions range from etymological and linguistic comparisons to philosophical descriptions.[18] The following are some ways that this book's contributors have discussed translation. Richard W. Swanson uses the imagery of carrying across with the term translation.[19] Matt Valler borrows from translation studies' use of negentropy to describe how translation is an open and not a closed system, whereby translation is viewed as a creative generative act. He goes on to assert, "Conceptualizing Bible translation as a translational experience offers an alternative to the dominant strictures of language translation."[20] Becka McKay underscores that translation consists of a series of translation choices, with the translator leveraging her agency in

---

15. Schechner, *Performance Studies*.
16. Perry, "Biblical Performance Criticism," 5.
17. Bassnett, *Translation*.
18. Tymoczko, *Enlarging Translation*; Marais, *(Bio)Semiotic Theory of Translation*; Blumczynski, *Experiencing Translationality*.
19. For a discussion of this metaphor and others related to translation, see Blumczynski, *Experiencing Translationality*.
20. Valler, "Labyrinths of Meaning," 107.

selecting translation strategies. Bible translation is a special part of general translation as it is understood as a part of Sacred Text Translation. Communities invest a sacred value into their traditions that are ascribed to rituals, songs, or other performances, as well as to texts. Questions about what a good translation is, as Sebastian Floor poses, become more complex when what is translated is not a written text. Translation studies' suspicion of such sensitive and established subjects as original text or the assertion of translation equivalence creates tensions within BT. Several contributors question what it is that we are actually translating, if it's not words or texts. Related to this general concept of translation is re-translation. Several of our contributors discuss their work more as re-translation that is not limited to a chronological second or successive translation but more of an ideological reshaping of earlier translations.

Semiotics

Semiotics is used here as an iterative process of meaning making, or as Matt Valler's definition of semiosis as the "ongoing, processual movement of meaning through signs." This process is expanded when social contributions are taken into account. Social semiotics, therefore, is the study of how social elements shape meaning-making processes. Holly Hearon provides a helpful overview of a particular approach to this topic where social semiotics challenges established thoughts in BT about textual meaning and its stability. How one thinks about meaning making shapes how we understand the role of translation and how communication happens. In everyday speech, semiosis is about signs. Isela Trujillo and Marlon Winedt provide us with the insights they have gathered from their experiences with working with Sign Language translators. Their presentations provide concrete examples of the social aspects of semiosis where materiality is integral in communication: paper, computers, paintings, bodies, etc. Equally important, social semiotics examines how people use materials in making meaning. An excellent example of this is how the human body itself contributes to meaning making in embodied performance, as several of our contributors observe.

Multimodal

One way to think about modes is as the five human senses: sight, hearing, smell, touch, and taste, as Sebastian Floor suggests. One can also assert that each of these human senses can be broken down into more detailed modes that leverage various semiotic resources. Sight can involve sign Language but also alphabetic writing, for example. Holly Hearon provides a definition: "'Mode' refers to a material resource employed by a sign-maker in the realization of meaning ... [with] 'multimodality' to the weaving together of multiple modes in the realization of a meaningful whole."[21] The assertion in this project is that human communication involves several modes simultaneously in complex meaning making. They work with each other and do not need to be in competition with each other while oftentimes a particular mode is more apt in certain social settings than others. The social aspect of semiotics informs our understanding of multimodality in that social elements shape what, how, and why various mode complexes are used in society. When it comes to BT, multimodality expands our thinking about translation involving more than translating words. We see this historically when we research oral performances or storytelling such as Jesus' parables. But it doesn't stop there; manuscripts and medieval illuminated Bibles or modern-day books with covers, print fonts, maps, footnotes, glossaries demonstrate multimodal communication. With social media today we experience a flurry of multimodal with sound, (moving) images, text, and the tactile mediation of devices.

Chapter Authors and Topics

Beyond this introductory chapter, there are nine chapters. Perhaps they can stand alone, but I would like to think that they cannot. They require the other chapters to bolster them up. Some are more theoretical, others more methodological, others can barely be recognized as Bible translation to the traditional eye. Each of the chapters merits consideration of how they expand our understanding of what Bible translation is. It is our contention that these chapters belong in a series on Biblical Performance Criticism because they carry forward the notions of biblical scholarship and performance in a particular way. They are not your typical biblical scholarship, nor are they your typical Bible translation or translation studies scholarship. The title suggests they are examples of Multimodal Bible Translation. They demonstrate that there is more going

---

21. Hearon, "Engaging Multimodal Social Semiotic Dimensions," 28.

on here than some tired divide of written vs. oral or historical vs. modern performances.

Below I provide some background of each author while also providing some aspects of their chapter. The order of the chapters is not random, but the borders blur between theory and practice.

- *Engaging Multimodal Social Semiotic Dimensions of the New Testament in Translation*

    Holly Hearon co-edited the first volume in the Biblical Performance Criticism series, *The Bible in Ancient and Modern Media*. Holly participated in several intersemiotic translation seminars in Italy where she demonstrated a capacity to contribute from her areas of expertise and dialogue with translators, semioticians, and scholars from other disciplines in creative and constructive ways. Holly is perhaps the first of our group to research multimodality and demonstrates the breadth of her understanding of this social semiotic approach and ways that it can inform a number of other disciplines including Bible translation. Holly's contribution in this project lays the theoretical groundwork for this project as we discuss the practice of multimodal communication from a social semiotic perspective.

- *Biblical Translation, Performance, and Re-Translation in Local Communities*

    Peter Perry has invested significantly in Biblical Performance Criticism with several ground-breaking publications on the subject and multiple performances of biblical material and is administrator for the BPC website.[22] Peter has expanded the theoretical reach of BPC and in many ways has introduced the subsequent theoretical phases of BPC through his publications. Peter's chapter connects social semiotic multimodality to BPC and expands our understanding of BT by showing how it affects multilingual communities in the USA who maintain connections with their community via social media. Oftentimes BT is understood as some activity "over there" and we forget the richness of linguistic and cultural diversity in our own contexts. Immigration,

---

22. Perry, *Insights from Biblical Performance Criticism*; Perry, *Biblical Humor and Performance*; Perry, "Biblical Performance Criticism"; https://www.biblicalperformancecriticism.org.

refugees, and identity issues are all a part of today's world and are demonstrated in the congregation Peter explores in Arizona where multilingualism and multimodality are an inherent part of their community.

- *Multimodality and Performance: Creole Translation and Identity*

    Marlon Winedt's history with Bible translation is extensive as he's participated in many different roles as translator, consultant, teacher, and researcher. Marlon is actively involved in performance of biblical materials for local communities. He demonstrates a deft understanding of multimodality as presented by theorists such as Gunther Kress and Theo van Leeuwen. Marlon's chapter demonstrates the hybrid nature of identities, linguistics, and translation. His Caribbean roots inform his assertions that translation of any sort—including Bible translation—is an articulation of identity and that questions of identity are always embodied and contested. Marlon's choice of subject matter is Philemon as he explores timely issues of performance and addresses both biblical and social experiences of slavery and their implications for translation and beyond.

- *Labyrinths of Meaning: Unstable Signs in Urban Spaces*

    Matt Valler exhibits a wide breadth of translation experiences both within and outside of Bible translation. He is an advocate for re-reading and re-translation as an act of identity formation and expression of agency. As someone from the UK, Matt's engagement in "hacking" historical sites in urban settings around the world (in this chapter, the National Mall in Washington, DC, and the Alamo in Texas) demonstrates his research creativity and discipline as he provides insightful commentary to what are considered well-known cultural spaces, many with biblical foundations. Matt's current scholarly endeavors demonstrate that he is a theoretician whose voice in translation studies will be articulate and expansive in ways that might provide opportunities for the field of Bible translation to rethink what translation is, question stability of meaning, explore translation beyond interlingual texts, and interrogate presuppositions such as original and distinction of translation from interpretation.

- *Increasing Communication Bandwidth: From Multimodal Translation Process to Four Revised Qualities of Bible Translation*

  Sebastian Floor is one of several respected Bible translation consultants in this book project. His experience as a Dutch citizen who has lived his entire life in southern Africa shapes his commitments to Bible translation as he facilitates access to the Bible to communities in the languages and media of their preference. Sebastian exhibits his abilities to move from theory to the practical application of various methods through several multinational translation projects, most recently with the Psalms That Sing project where communities translate and experience the Bible in numerous modes and media.[23] Such practical commitments have led Sebastian to see the need to expand the criteria used to evaluate translations. Previous criteria presupposed a written translation and communication model; Sebastian explores criteria that can be used with written translations but beyond to multimodal translations.

- *Re-Translating a Contested Performance Tradition*

  Nathan Esala engages in both the struggle and solidarity required from activists involved in Bible translation today. Nathan demonstrates his deep knowledge of biblical scholarship while negotiating Bible translation as a social action and its relationship with marginalized communities. Nathan emphasizes that Bible translation is not a one-and-done activity but that it requires re-translation that shifts according to the agents, audiences, and purposes. Nathan peels back the layers of the historical translations of sections of Ruth that unveil gaps that reveal translators wrestling with the text throughout history. Nathan continues his explorations with contemporary performances of Ruth where such translation gaps are also found and explored with communities in northern Ghana in a pursuit of co-liberation.

- *Echoing Forward, Echoing Back: Thick Translation, the Song of Songs, and the Performance of Cultural Exchange*

  Becka McKay has a background in Hebrew language—both modern and biblical. Becka is an extensively published poet whose

---

23. www.psalmsthatsing.org.

writing abilities are evident in her chapter that also exhibits a deep understanding of the history and current views of Hebrew Bible translation. Her training, expertise, and experience in translation studies establishes her as an important voice that can contribute to the literary translation of the Bible. Becka's creativity and commitment to social action are evident as she struggles with seemingly everyday linguistic choices to have significant social trajectories in translation. Her introduction of "thick translation" helps us think through translation strategies as we provide hearers and readers the necessary backgrounds to appreciate the translation choices made.

- *Performance in Sign Language Bible Translation*

  Isela Trujillo's capacities as a linguist and translation consultant from Mexico are on exhibit in her important contribution of Sign Language translation. For those of us who are from hearing communities, we are often ignorant of the intricacies of Sign Language communication, including translation. Isela opens to us this world and demonstrates that deaf communities contribute not only to our understanding of translation in general but especially Bible translation. The process, choices, and questions of Sign Language translation offer important insights into those who are eclipsed by thinking only in verbal and aural ways. Isela demonstrates how Sign Language translation is arguably the most powerful demonstration of performance and an ideal example of multimodal translation.

- *Translating What Is (not)(un)Said*

  Richard W. Swanson leverages his long career as an educator and especially his provocative demonstrations of theater translation and performance of biblical materials. Richard's commitment to an interpretive community of actors, dramaturgs, directors, and others is on display as he explores the translation of provocation that requires more than a translated script but an interpretive cast and audience. Richard's participation in past intersemiotic translation seminars in Italy is evident as he articulates what other theater translation practitioners concur about the heuristic negotiation of meaning constructed in communities and audiences. Richard's examples from Greek antiquity and the Gospel of Mark provide clear examples of theater translation that negotiates the indeterminacies of scripts and performances.

Conclusion

This book is one part of a two-year project that began with the provocative invitation of David Rhoads as founder and first editor of the BPC series. As is typical with both performance and translation, the way has been circuitous toward the publication of this book which is simply a point on a long road of discovery. The camaraderie of the group of the ten of us is another result of this project which might very well result in yet unforeseen collaborations and echoes of interactions that we have had during our time together. But hopefully the expansion of ideas and practices will not remain within the topics of this book and the collaboration of the contributors. Our wish is that those who access this material will take these ideas and examples and expand them into their own contexts for purposes that are beneficial to communities around the world.

Bibliography

Arduini, Stefano, and Siri Nergaard. "Translation: A New Paradigm." *Translation* 1 (2011) 8–17.

Bassnett, Susan. *Translation*. London: Routledge, 2014.

Blumczynski, Piotr. *Experiencing Translationality: Material and Metaphorical Journeys*. London: Routledge, 2023.

Boria, Monica, et al., eds. *Translation and Multimodality: Beyond Words*. London: Routledge, 2019.

Carlson, Marvin. *Performance: A Critical Introduction*. London: Routledge, 1996.

Elder, Nicholas A. *Gospel Media: Reading, Writing, and Circulating Jesus Traditions*. Grand Rapids: Eerdmans, 2024.

Faith Comes by Hearing. "Oral Bible Translation." www.faithcomesbyhearing.com/what-we-do/oral-bible-translation.

Floor, Sebastian. "The Search for a Seamless Integration of Orality and Literacy in Bible Translation: Some Perspectives from Southern Africa." Unpublished paper presented at the 2011 Bible Translation Conference, Dallas, TX.

Frost, Joshua, Nikki Mustin, and Heather Beal. "Attaining Quality in Oral Bible Translation: A Guide to Effective Practice." *Journal of Translation* 20.2 (2024) 21–62. https://doi.org/10.54395/JOT-FMBOBT.

Hurtado, Larry W. "Oral Fixation and New Testament Studies? 'Orality,' 'Performance' and Reading Texts in Early Christianity." *New Testament Studies* 60 (2014) 321–40.

Iverson, Kelly. *Performing Early Christian Literature: Audience Experience and Interpretation of the Gospels*. Cambridge: Cambridge University Press, 2021.

Marais, Kobus. *A (Bio)Semiotic Theory of Translation: The Emergence of Social-Cultural Reality*. London: Routledge, 2019.

———, ed. *Translation Beyond Translation Studies*. London: Bloomsbury, 2022.

Maxey, James A. "Alternative Evaluative Concepts to the Trinity of Bible Translation." In *Translating Values*, edited by Piotr Blumczynski and John Gillespie, 57–80. New York: Palgrave Macmillan, 2016.

———. "Beyond Print/Oral Translation: A Hospitality Approach to Performance." Presentation at Oral Bible Translation Conference, Rockville, VA, October 3, 2018. https://www.youtube.com/watch?v=Qx73Khbp2cI.

———. "From Mono to Multimodal Translation: Beyond OBT to MMT." Unpublished paper presented at 2023 Bible Translation Conference, October 14, 2023, Dallas, TX.

———. *From Orality to Orality: A New Paradigm for Contextual Translation of the Bible*. Biblical Performance Criticism 2. Eugene, OR: Cascade, 2009.

———. "Translating Sacredness: Performance Translation from a Hospitality Perspective." In *(Re)-Gained in Translation: Bibles, Histories, and Struggles for Identity*, edited by Sabine Dievenkorn and Shaul Levin. Berlin: Frank & Timme, 2024.

Maxey, James A., and Ernst R. Wendland, eds. *Translating Scripture for Sound and Performance*. Biblical Performance Criticism 6. Eugene, OR: Cascade Books, 2012.

Merz, Johannes. "Bible Translation in Theory and Practice." *The Bible Translator* 72.2 (2023). https://doi.org/10.1177/20516770221150806.

Naudé, Jacobus A., and Cynthia L. Miller-Naudé. "Meaning-Making Processes in Religious Translation Involving Sacred Space." In *Translation Beyond Translation Studies*, edited by Kobus Marais, 197–218. London: Bloomsbury, 2022.

Noss, Philip A., ed. *A History of Bible Translation*. Rome: Edizioni di Storia e Letteratura, 2007.

Perry, Peter S. *Biblical Humor and Performance*. Biblical Performance Criticism 20. Eugene, OR: Cascade Books, 2023.

———. "Biblical Performance Criticism: Survey and Prospects." *Religions* 10.2 (2019) 117. DOI: 10.3390/rel10020117.

———. *Insights from Biblical Performance Criticism*. Minneapolis: Fortress: 2016.

Schechner, Richard. *Performance Studies: An Introduction*. 3rd ed. London: Routledge, 2002.

Tymoczko, Maria. *Enlarging Translation, Empowering Translators*. Manchester: St. Jerome, 2007.

Winedt, Marlon. "Bible Translation as Incarnation of the Word of God: Transformational Power Through Form and Meaning." *The Bible Translator* 72.2 (2021) 220–40.

The Word for the World. "Hearing the Word: An Introduction to Oral Bible Translation." Feb. 6, 2023. https://www.twftw.org/post/hearing-the-word-an-introduction-to-oral-bible-translation.

2

Engaging Multimodal Social Semiotic Dimensions of the New Testament in Translation

Holly Hearon

"Language and meaning in social contexts are always multidimensional."[1]

WHEN WE SET ABOUT translating the New Testament, what is it that we are translating? If we put aside our theological assumptions about the nature of the text, our answer will likely focus on "words." After all, take away the words, and there is nothing left to translate. Yet there is more to it than that. Akma Adam observes that the notable capacity of words to facilitate communication has prompted the idea that words possess special properties, making them uniquely appropriate for the articulation of meaning.[2] The result is that we have become fixated on words to the exclusion of other meaning-making (semiotic) resources.[3]

Increasingly, however, studies in communication have observed that "meaning" does not reside solely in words, but is generated through the combined effects of multiple semiotic resources.[4] Gestures, touch, eye

---

1. Hodge, *Social Semiotics for a Complex World*, 14.

2. Adam, "Interpreting the Bible at the Horizon," 162. Isela Trujillo notes the negative impact that emphasis on oral words has had on Deaf people (see her essay in this volume, "Performance in Sign Language Bible Translation," 203–28).

3. Semiotic resources are "the actions, materials and artifacts we use for communicative purposes"; these may be physiological or technological (van Leeuwen, *Introducing Social Semiotics*, 285).

4. Adami, "Social Semiotic Multimodal Approach," 375; Tuominen et al., "Why

movements, physical proximity, rhythm, color, layout, symbols, and so forth are interwoven with words to construct a sign complex that expands meaning beyond what is signified by words alone.⁵ A banal example from a North American context serves to illustrate. Consider the linguistic sign "really." If speaking, we can add an eyeroll and employ tone of voice to signal that we highly doubt how "really real" something is. It is the non-linguistic semiotic resources that reverse the lexical meaning of "really." If writing, we can combine non-linguistic resources such as italics, punctuation marks, and emojis (*really!?* 😬) to produce a different meaning. The italics add emphasis, while the exclamation point and question mark communicate a state of excitement, tinged with uncertainty. The emoji adds an important clarification, signaling that the sign complex references anxiety rather than jumping up and down with hopeful anticipation. In both cases, "meaning" derives not from the word "really" on its own, but from the combined effect of the semiotic resources employed.

A challenge when translating the New Testament is that we are so focused on words that we easily overlook the multiple semiotic resources that are co-present in the production of meaning. This is in part because we simply may not recognize the resources that are being employed. In other instances, our privileging of words may overshadow the co-presence of non-linguistic resources. Learning to identify the multiple semiotic resources that are co-present in a text is only the beginning, however. A still greater challenge is understanding how they work together to create meaning potential, in the making of the sign and in translation.⁶ This, in turn, may challenge assumptions we have about the nature of texts. And this cannot help but challenge how we think about translation.

In this chapter, I explore the challenges above through the lens of multimodal social semiotics.⁷ A strength of multimodal social semiotics is that it focuses both on the materiality of representation and on

---

Methods Matter," 1–2.

5. Jewitt, "Introduction to Multimodality," 15; Kress, *Multimodality*, 79, 157.

6. Kress, "Transposing Meaning," 32.

7. Multimodal social semiotics bears similarities to several theoretical and methodological approaches employed by biblical scholars, yet a search on "key words" reveals that few biblical scholars (to date) have self-consciously engaged multimodal social semiotics. Among those who have, see Al-Ameedi and Ghitheeth, "Multimodal Discourse Analysis of Image-Biblical Verses"; Apostel, "Death is Sleep"; Clivaz, "Bible in the Digital Age"; Floor and Harmelink, "Multimodality in Bible Translation"; Hearon, "Social Semiotic Multi-Modal Approach"; Hearon, "Music as a Medium of Oral Transmission"; Hearon, "Materiality of the Bible as Performance."

theoretical dimensions of meaning-making.[8] The two are viewed as part of a whole.[9] I confine my discussion to the New Testament simply because this is my area of expertise. A further caveat: I am neither a translator nor a semiotician, although I have engaged both translation and multimodal social semiotics in my work. My goal in this chapter is to expand our understanding of the nature of New Testament texts, with the hope of raising questions and insights that may prove useful for the task of translation, broadly conceived of as performance.

Materiality and Meaning

Mainstream linguistics theories of the twentieth century, observes Gunther Kress, viewed linguistic systems as abstractions that were coherent and stable.[10] In contrast, "A multimodal social-semiotic approach to *representation* . . . puts the emphasis on the *material*, the *physical*, the *sensory*, the *bodily*."[11] Shifting our attention from "words" to "materiality" requires a different way of thinking about texts. From a multimodal social semiotic perspective, "text" refers not to words on a page, but to any materially composed (i.e., multimodal) meaningful whole.[12] "Material" refers not just to what we can touch and feel, but to what can be engaged by any of the human senses: sight, smell, sound, taste, touch.[13] Some of these materials are enduring; for example, cut stone or linguistic symbols inked on paper. Others are ephemeral, such as facial expression or vocal inflection. Words, whether written or spoken, are material resources that may be employed, along with other material resources, to construct a text; yet a text may be devoid of words.

---

8. Social semiotics emerged as a discipline with the publication of Michael Halliday's study, *Language as Social Semiotic*. In *Spoken and Written Language*, Halliday began to observe the differing semiotic potentials in written and spoken language. Building on the work of Halliday, Gunther Kress and Theo van Leeuwen introduced the language of multimodality in *Reading Images: The Grammar of Visual Design*, followed by *Multimodal Discourse: The Modes and Media of Contemporary Communication*.

9. Kress, "Discourse Analysis and Education," 208; Kress, *Multimodality*, 105.

10. Kress, *Multimodality*, 105.

11. Kress, *Multimodality*, 105, cf. 76–78. Italics original.

12. Adami and Pinto, "Meaning-(re)making in a World," 73.

13. Kress, "Semiotic Work," 52.

"Materiality" is inextricably linked to "meaning" because, as Kress notes, unless the "conceptual" is "made material" we cannot "get at it."[14] Thus, meaning and materiality are not separate entities, but are regarded as an integrated whole, what in social semiotics is called a "sign."[15] To put it another way, a sign is the bringing together of a meaning with a form that can mean it.[16] Meaning, however, does not reside in the sign per se; rather, it resides with the sign-maker, who selects the material forms that best give realization to what it is the sign-maker wants to communicate.[17] Each material resource employed contributes in some distinctive way to the realization of the sign-maker's meaning by drawing attention to what it is the sign-maker wants to emphasize.[18] Yet, meaning is not *solely* determined by the sign-maker; it also is determined in part by the one who *interprets* the sign, based on what material resources they recognize and how they ascribe meaning to them through the filters of their contexts and experiences.[19] These ideas will be developed further below.

Before proceeding, however, it will be helpful to pause and explore how the relationship between materiality and meaning re-orients our approach to New Testament documents with a view to translation. There are two avenues to explore: one is the materiality of the text, constituted by linguistic symbols on an analogue or digital "page"; the other is the materiality described within the narrative world of the individual documents. In both, the sign-maker has latitude to control what materiality is employed. We will look briefly at these two avenues, focusing on Acts 13:14b–17 for illustrative purposes.

> And on the Sabbath day they went into the synagogue and sat down. After the reading of the Law and the Prophets, the officials of the synagogue sent them a message, saying, "Brothers, if you have any word of exhortation for the people, give it." So Paul stood up and with a gesture began to speak: "Fellow Israelites and others who fear God, listen. The God of this people Israel chose our ancestors and made the people great during their stay

14. Kress, "Discourse Analysis and Education," 211.
15. Kress, *Multimodality*, 61; Hodge, *Social Semiotics for a Complex World*, 34.
16. Kress, *Multimodality*, 108.
17. Kress, *Multimodality*, 116.
18. Jewitt, "Introduction to Multimodality," 15; Adami, "Social Semiotic Multimodal Approach," 372.
19. Kress, "Transposing Meaning," 32, 35; Kress and Mavers, "Social Semiotics and Multimodal Texts," 173.

> in the land of Egypt, and with uplifted arm he led them out of it. (NRSVue)

The human senses are our point of entry into the text.[20] Beginning with materiality of the text, much of what we encounter engages the sense of sight. There are lower- and upper-case letters and spaces between words, which are arranged in a linear fashion running from left to right. The words are framed by punctuation marks, while quotation marks signify direct discourse. A single font color (black) is employed, and the font type is Times New Roman. If you are reading this in book form, the lines of words will be arranged in a single column on the page; if you are reading this on a digital device, you may have the latitude to alter the design by making the linguistic symbols larger or smaller or changing the color of the screen on which they appear.

The sense of touch is also engaged. If you are holding the book, you feel the texture of the paper and the weight of the book. If you are reading in braille, you experience the sensation of raised bumps on stiff paper. If you are engaging the text through a digital device, you will access the text by touching keys or a screen and arranging its size and placement on the screen to suit your needs or preferences.

The sense of sound may be engaged if the text is read aloud, either by an artificially created voice or a living voice. This introduces additional material potentials through the resources of intonation, pitch, rhythm, accent, volume, voice quality, and so forth. And finally, the sense of smell may be engaged. If you are reading the book, it may possess a distinctive smell that will vary depending on whether the book is brand new or has absorbed years of dust on a shelf.

From a multimodal social semiotic perspective, this extensive, but by no means exhaustive, description of the materiality of the text highlights several important things. First, materiality places controls on how we engage texts. We may or may not have the latitude to alter aspects of a text. (Consider the difference between having a text read to us vs. reading a text aloud ourselves.) Second, texts draw on conventional communicative patterns that are grounded in social values, contexts, and practices. For example, academic books employ a similar design, font, font color, and quality of paper, while books for children aged one to three

---

20. There is by no means a universal experience of how human senses are perceived or employed in engaging materiality. I write from the perspective of a North American not living with a disability. See Floor, "Increasing Communication Bandwidth," 122–52, in this volume, for additional comments on the role of the senses.

are generally small and square, have pages of cardboard, and employ different fonts that may be of multiple colors. This materiality shapes both our expectations about what we are engaging and our response to the content. Precisely because these patterns are conventional, the meaning-making process is, at a certain level, obscured by normativity. Yet because normativity is dependent on context and social practice, it contributes in significant ways to meaning. Third, there is, nonetheless, the potential for variation. A sign-maker may exclude, alter, or exploit some of these material dimensions to emphasize aspects of the meaning they want to express. For example, the sign-maker might change the font from Times New Roman to "handwriting-Dakota," exchanging the formality of the former for an informal font that is suggestive of personal intimacy and, perhaps, a sense of being made privy to exclusive information. Fourth, meaning is dependent on not only the construction of signs, but also the interpretation of signs. Signs are not always stable or coherent. Finally, the sensorial experience generates an affective as well as cognitive response to the text, magnifying the role of the interpreter.

In the narrative world of Acts 13:14b–17 materiality is mediated through words. The linguistic choices made by the sign-maker give realization to participants, processes, and circumstances: what social semiotics calls "experiential meaning."[21] In creating this narrative world, the sign-maker has even greater latitude to limit what materiality is present, and, consequently, the materiality to which the interpreter has access. Even so, the interpreter continues to participate in meaning-making process.

Entering the narrative world of Acts 13:14b–17, we immediately become conscious of how the sign-maker is directing our seeing and hearing. We see (and don't see) the interior of a synagogue; this suggests that the significance of the space is social rather than physical. The reference to a reading from the Law and the Prophets underscores the social over the physical: it is an activity associated with synagogues, yet we do not see the scroll, nor see who is reading, nor hear the words read. What is omitted, then, is just as important as what is included. What is included is sufficient to signal that this is a place where the words of God are spoken and heard. By omitting the seeing and hearing of the reading from the Law and the Prophets, however, the sign-maker signals that the words (of God) are those we hear spoken (by Paul) to those who are gathered

---

21. O'Halloran, "Historical Changes in the Semiotic Landscape," 100–101; Nørgaard, *Multimodal Stylistics of the Novel*, 44–45.

in the synagogue ("fellow Israelites"; "those who fear God"). By directing us to hear Paul referencing God's decisive action in "choosing," "making great," and "with uplifted arm" leading the Israelites out of Egypt, the sign-maker signals that a new deliverance is upon them.

There are five references to movement; we will focus only on three: they sat down; the officials of the synagogue sent them a message; Paul stood up. The one other reference to Paul and those with him sitting down is in Acts 16:13: "On the Sabbath day we went outside the gate by the river, where we supposed there was a place of prayer, and we sat down and spoke to the women who had gathered there." The similarities to Acts 13:14b–17 are striking, as are the differences.[22] Absent from Acts 16:13 is a reference to standing up; rather they speak with the women while sitting. In Acts 13:14b–17 we see Paul and his companions sit down and, after receiving an invitation from the leaders of the synagogue to address "the people," we see Paul stand up. On a surface level these combined actions create a storyline. They also give realization to the formality of the setting and social relationships within the space that is "synagogue." The "leaders of the synagogue" have authority to invite guests to address "the people," in this way honoring the guests (welcomed as "brothers"), while also emphasizing their role as leaders. When Paul stands up, he "gestures with his hand" (κατασείσας τῇ χειρί). This gesture is used when addressing a group or crowd (cf. Acts 12:17; 19:33; 21:40) to signal that one is about to speak. Combined with Paul's use of a formal address (to "mature male brothers" [ἄνδρες ἀδελφοί]), the sign-maker constructs, through materiality, an oratorial figure, "Paul."

There is much more that could be said about these few verses, but this is sufficient to illustrate some of the ways materiality is employed in a linguistic text to give realization to the sign-maker's meaning. Paul's speech will continue through v. 42. The space dedicated to the speech can distract us from the significant realization of meaning effected through physical place, gesture, sound (or lack thereof), and actions. Focusing on the introductory verses shows that "meaning" includes not only verbal content, but spatial relationships, social relationships, and social processes, which, although described with words, are conveyed without words. Further, while the various expressions of materiality work together within the narrative to create an integrated, meaningful whole, we see that each

---

22. It is important to state that women were not excluded from nor isolated within the ancient synagogue (Brooten, *Women Leaders in the Ancient Synagogue*, 101–35).

material expression offers its own distinctive emphasis or insight so that meaning is constructed layer upon layer.

The analysis of materiality and meaning within the narrative-world-of-the-text is easily recognized as bearing similarities, in particular, to narrative criticism, rhetorical criticism, and performance criticism. One could argue, even, that there is nothing new here. Yet I suggest that four important insights are gained from attending specifically to the relationship between meaning and materiality. First, what is conceived cognitively is dependent on materiality if it is to be communicated to others; it is materiality that gives realization to meaning. Second, by drawing attention to "materiality" we are reminded that meaning making extends beyond words; indeed, meaning can exist (e.g.) in gestures and actions. Attending to non-linguistic materiality is essential to comprehending totality of meaning. Third, meaning is both expressed through and perceived by means of the body. Thus, materiality offers the possibility of moving beyond the false duality of mind and body to recognize that "meaning" comprises both mind *and* body, affect *and* cognition, an integrated whole.[23] Fourth, the relationship between materiality and meaning focuses attention on agency. Meaning is constructed materially by a sign-maker who *selects the materials* to give realization to the thoughts, ideas, questions they want to communicate to others.

Authorship, Agency, and Meaning Making

When we think of written texts, we tend to think in terms of authors/authorship. Questions concerning authorship focus on *who* is writing: e.g., their gender, social status, affiliations, and how they have been shaped by their social and cultural contexts. There is an implicit assumption (which may or may not be correct) that answering these questions will offer insight into textual meaning. Multimodal social semiotics shifts attention from authorship to agency: i.e., *action undertaken to produce an effect.*[24] This invites questions about access to and the selection of material resources, how these materials function to give realization to the sign-maker's meaning, and how this meaning shapes the social and cultural structures that constitute "context." While drawing a distinction

23. Kress, *Multimodality*, 83.

24. As notions of "author/authorship" become increasingly complex with the advent of the internet, the language of "agency" may prove to be a helpful alternative. Such a discussion is beyond the scope of this chapter.

between "authorship" and "agency" is somewhat contrived (authors, after all, exercise agency), I believe it is helpful in two regards: first, it turns our attention to questions that focus explicitly on meaning-making activity, and second, it guards against the creation of fictive authors.

The latter is particularly important where authorship is uncertain or unknown. Consider: while names designating authorship have been assigned to the New Testament documents, it is not clear whether any of these persons in fact authored the texts bearing their names (excepting, of course, the genuine letters of Paul). Even if we believe the names to be those of the authors, we know little about any of these persons; in the case of Paul, we know only what he chooses to reveal about himself for his meaning-making purposes. While third- and fourth-century legends may tell us something about how Christians remembered these individuals, they are of little help in gaining insight into the relationship between authorship and "meaning." Rather, they risk the danger of promoting a "cult of personality" in which a figure's fictive character and biography is read into a text by an interpreter or translator. In contrast, analysis of agency avoids this potential pitfall by focusing directly on the material realization of meaning. This, in turn, draws our attention to the production of meaning as an *act of communication*.

Communication is a process involving multiple steps. As described by Kress, it begins when an individual or group experiences a prompt within their social environment that generates in them a desire to engage the world.[25] Kress calls this first impulse "representation": a thought or idea, as yet, not realized materially. A transition from "representation" to "communication" takes place when the individual (or group) employs semiotic resources to give material realization to the "meaning" they wish to convey. As an act of communication, this material expression ("sign") is designed to gain the attention of an interlocutor.[26] It is only when an interlocutor *responds* to the "sign" that a communication exchange can be said to have occurred.[27] This response need not necessarily result in the creation of a new sign; it requires only that the interlocutor *engage* the initial "sign"/prompt.[28] Engagement is understood as filtering the received "meaning" through the interlocutor's own interests, values, needs,

---

25. Kress, *Multimodality*, 33, 49.
26. Kress, *Multimodality*, 51, 155.
27. Kress, *Multimodality*, 54.
28. Kress, *Multimodality*, 54.

and experiences in order to determine what is most relevant, useful, or important and framing these selected elements in relation to the interlocutor's social contexts and circumstances.[29]

Critical, here, is recognizing that in a communication exchange, agency is exercised *not only by the initiator* of the first sign, *but also by the interlocutor who interprets* the sign.[30] Kress observes that a meaning-making sign is "always both a 'full' representation of the sign-maker's *interest*" and, at the same time, "only ever a partial account of some entity or phenomenon when seen from a different position."[31] This suggests that the same sign complex can support variable meaning, because meaning resides not primarily in materiality but in agency. An exception would be where meaning has been fixed by social practice/power over time. Yet, potentially, such a meaning could be challenged at any time. This leads David Machin to describe communication exchanges as struggles over definitions of reality.[32] The question at stake is whose reality: the sign-maker's or the interlocutor's? In such a contest, notes Kress, the distribution of power will not be equal: setting the ground is different from making selections based on the terms established by the ground.[33] Further, the ability to access specific material resources for meaning making will be dependent on each agent's financial, social, and cultural power.[34]

Multimodality, Agency, and Meaning Making

"In a *sign* something to be meant is brought together with a *form* which can mean it."[35] The relationship between the two is not one of equivalence, but of aptness.[36] Earlier, *form* was spoken of in terms of materiality; here we expand the discussion by exploring "materiality" in relation to mode

---

29. A "frame" defines the world that is to be engaged, marking its temporal and spatial limits (Kress, *Multimodality*, 149). I propose that it marks social and cultural limits as well.
30. Kress, *Multimodality*, 35–37. Kress contrasts his understanding of communication with that of the sender–message–receiver model associated with Saussure and others (Kress, *Multimodality*, 33–34; 63–66).
31. Kress, "Transposing Meaning," 35.
32. Machin, "Need for a Social and Affordance-Driven," 331.
33. Kress, *Multimodality*, 37.
34. Kress, *Multimodality*, 28.
35. Kress, *Multimodality*, 108. Italics original.
36. Kress, "Transposing Meaning," 30.

and multimodality. "Mode" refers to a material resource employed by a sign-maker in the realization of meaning; "multimodality" to the weaving together of multiple modes in the realization of a meaningful whole. Jewitt describes this weaving together as *orchestration*.[37] To realize a piece of music, for example, choices must be made regarding what instruments to include based on the qualities and capabilities of each instrument, and the effects and affects that can be created when their various resources are combined. To realize meaning, a sign-maker similarly makes choices regarding what modes to employ based on the effects and affects they can create when combined.[38] Since each mode will carry only a part of the meaning, the sign-maker must consider what semiotic work is being done by each particular mode.[39]

While all modes exhibit materiality, not all materiality functions as a mode. Kress describes "mode" as a joint project of:

- the potentials inherent in the material;
- a culture's selection of features from the bundle of potentials;
- and the shaping over time (by members of) a society of the features selected.[40]

Through this cultural process modes take on meaning-making capacities, that express something about the world, about social relationships/positioning, and about texts.[41] To more fully grasp the "what" and "how" of modes, it will be helpful to explore briefly each component of the "joint project." What will become evident is that the relationship between the three components is fluid rather than hierarchical or linear.

The Potentials (Affordances) in Materiality

All manner of materiality possesses distinctive resources for giving material representation to meaning; Kress calls these resources "affordances."[42]

---

37. Jewitt, "Introduction to Multimodality," 15.
38. Kress, "Semiotic Work," 54.
39. Jewitt and Henrikson, "Social Semiotic Multimodality," 150; Kress, *Multimodality*, 96.
40. Kress, *Multimodality*, 80. See also Kress, "Transposing Meaning," 24.
41. Bezemer and Jewitt, "Multimodal Analysis," 184; Adami, "Social Semiotic Multimodal Approach," 373.
42. Kress, *Multimodality*, 8, 114. The term "affordances" is distinctive to Kress.

A comparison of written words and spoken words illustrates this. Both modes employ linguistic resources (lexis, syntax, and grammar), but the two modes each offer different affordances. Speech exhibits affordances such as pitch, intonation, intensity, vocal quality, accent, rhythm, and silence: all aural affordances.[43] In contrast, writing employs visual affordances such as spatial arrangement, position of elements in a framed space, size, color, shape, and icons (e.g., circles, lines, dots).[44] Speech may be woven together with visual modes such as gesture, facial expression, action, posture, and so forth to emphasize different aspects of "meaning," while written words may be woven together with visual modes such as image, color, design, or symbols to the same end. In choosing which mode(s) to employ, a sign-maker must assess the affordances and limitations of each mode to determine which will be most effective in realizing the sign-maker's meaning within a given social and cultural context.[45]

Two popular sayings demonstrate the tension between affordances and their limitations. Consider: "a picture is worth a thousand words" and "a picture can express a thousand words, but a few words can change its story." The affordances of pictures and written words are similar: both employ color, shapes, and lines in spatial arrangements. Yet they differ in how they employ spatial relationships, and this places limitations on how they can express "meaning." In a picture, the colors, lines, and shapes are presented in a spatial arrangement that is experienced simultaneously. Simultaneity allows the viewer to "read" the spatially arranged colors, shapes, and lines in an order of their own determination, and to make connections between them based on the viewer's interests and ideas.[46] The reason a picture is worth a thousand words is precisely because of the affordance "simultaneity"; the totality of the experience is expansive, non-linear, allowing the viewer to make multiple connections in a single moment.[47] In contrast, the colors, lines, and shapes of written words are arranged in a grammatically and syntactically governed order along a line, unfolding meaning sequentially over time.[48] Words can change the story of a picture because their sequential affordance interrupts the effects

---

43. Bezemer and Kress, "Writing in Multimodal Texts," 171.
44. Bezemer and Kress, "Writing in Multimodal Texts," 171.
45. Nathan Esala, "Re-Translating a Contested Performance Tradition," 153–84 in this volume, offers further discussion of modes and limitations.
46. Kress, *Multimodality*, 81.
47. Machin, "Need for a Social and Affordance-Driven," 328.
48. Bezemer and Jewitt, "Multimodal Analysis," 184–85.

and affects of simultaneity, giving priority to the sign-maker's ordering of the spatial relationships, rather than that of the viewer. Nonetheless, it is possible for a picture to give the lie to words: for example, when words proclaiming universal prosperity are juxtaposed with images of mass poverty. In multimodal communication events, the modes selected may convey similar, or very different, or even contradictory meanings.[49]

The capacity of modes to arrange spatial and/or temporal relationships between people, events, and objects prompts different ways of perceiving and experiencing the world.[50] In the examples above, the modes employed are oriented toward spatial arrangements, on the one hand, and temporal relations, on the other. In other cases, modes may combine both dimensions. Music, for example, can be given material realization as a musical score (which is oriented toward spatial relationships) or in performance (which is oriented toward temporal relationships). In fact, attention to both spatial and temporal dynamics are necessary for the realization of meaning in music. The same is true for dance, gestures, and actions, where spatial relationships are revealed in movement through time. The affordances (and limitations) of modes prompt sign-makers to move in certain directions in the realization of meaning, particularly when these affordances take on status as cultural conventions.[51]

Cultural Selection of Affordances

"What a community decides to regard and use as mode is mode."[52] The shift from materiality to mode occurs when a culture cultivates selected affordances to realize, support, or resist cultural values, knowledge, meanings, valuations, structures, and institutions. The determinative factor here is affordance—what the materiality can do.[53] Consider Tibetan Buddhist sand mandalas. Tibetan monks use colored sand to create intricately designed visual images that will be swept away upon completion. "Sand," in this cultural context, functions as a mode because it aptly gives

---

49. Hodge, *Social Semiotics for a Complex World*, 17.
50. Kress and Mavers, "Social Semiotics and Multimodal Texts," 174.
51. Bezemer, "What Modes Can and Cannot Do," 8; Kress, *Multimodality*, 76, 120.
52. Kress, *Multimodality*, 87.
53. So Bezemer: "affordances include both inherent material properties and social and cultural conventions, that is, they refer to prior semiotic work that was done with materiality by a specific community in response to their needs and demands" ("What Modes Can and Cannot Do," 8–9).

material realization to a cultural acknowledgment of impermanence. In contrast, other cultural contexts use oil-based or acrylic paints on canvas to create portraits intended to preserve a living person's image for posterity. Here the paint functions as a mode because it aptly gives material realization to a cultural emphasis on immortality.

Kress observes that use of modes and their affordances varies across cultures in part because individual cultures value, develop, and employ the senses differently.[54] Some cultures encourage physical closeness, including physical touch, while others foster physical distance and restraint from touching. Thus, two different cultures may each employ the mode we think of as "gesture," but will draw on affordances of "gesture" differently: in one case, taking advantage of bodily movements that narrow the distance between persons (e.g., direct eye-contact; stepping in closer; using arms and hands to touch or embrace); in the other, fostering bodily movements that maintain physical distance (e.g., avoiding eye-contact; stepping back; keeping arms and hands in one's personal space zone). In other instances, cultures may use different senses to realize a similar meaning: for example, where one employs the mode of speech, another may employ gesture, and so forth.[55] Anyone who has traveled outside their cultural context has likely encountered confusion at some point over differences in how cultures value and engage the senses. There may be instances where we have missed a cultural cue altogether because we simply have not recognized the mode being employed. Differences in modal use also may arise when a group lacks access to certain senses. Deaf communities have developed grammatically and syntactically complex visual Sign Languages that draw on gesture, facial expression, and spatial arrangements to communicate complex meanings.[56] Those who do not have access to eyesight engage affordances (such as echolocation) that are available through the other senses and of which those with eyesight may have no knowledge or experience.

Within some cultures, the use of certain modes and their affordances may be circumscribed by group. In complex social systems that exhibit a high degree of specialization, certain groups may employ a particular mode because it serves the meaning-making needs of that

---

54. Kress, "Semiotic Work," 56.
55. Kress, *Multimodality*, 84.
56. Trujillo, "Performance in Sign Language Bible Translation," 205–6.

group. For example, "fonts" function as a mode among graphic designers.[57] While others may be aware of fonts, they do not need to access this mode for their meaning-making purposes. In other cases, group identity may exert formal or informal boundaries around the use of modes or particular modal affordances. In this volume, Marlon Winedt writes that in the complex social and cultural contexts of the Caribbean, orality is an important mode of cultural expression among the Creole.[58] Calypso music, reggae, and oral poetry give material realization to "meaning" in the forms of social commentary, political critique, and preservation of communal wisdom. Although orality is not exclusive to the Creole, its use with distinctive genres and in specific cultural contexts to build communal identity distinguishes its function as mode here from that of other cultural contexts in the Caribbean.

The affordances of modes also may be selected for the purposes of resistance meaning making. In the United States, the hair of black Americans has been often subjected to scorn by white Americans. A response within black communities has been to turn hairstyling into a cultural expression of dignity, beauty, and status, resisting the meaning ascribed by the dominant culture.[59] A different form of resistance may be expressed through acts of cultural defacement. Writes Sharon Daniel (building on the work of Michael Taussig): "Defacement is a gesture of desecration—a transgression of a symbolic order that reverses and undoes the thing transgressed. Defacement is also embellishment: destruction that contextualizes and illuminates."[60] So, for example, Daniels describes embellishing US flags made in prison factories with embroidered texts identifying ways the criminal justice system has violated the constitutional rights of prisoners.[61] These acts of resistance demonstrate the use of modes to both deconstruct and reconstruct cultural meaning at particular moments in time.

---

57. Kress, *Multimodality*, 87–88.
58. Winedt, "Multimodality and Performance," 73–74.
59. See DeLongoria, "Misogynoir: *Black Hair Identity Politics," 39–49.
60. Daniel, "Materializing a Gesture of Resistance," 287.
61. Daniel, "Materializing a Gesture of Resistance," 287.

Modes and Their Affordances Shaped Over Time

Among the forces that shape modes over time is the tension inherent in efforts to bring meaning together with materiality. Kress describes this tension as "ceaseless semiotic work with and against the potentials and the resistances of the materials for the making of meaning."[62] This semiotic work involves a constant testing of materiality, pushing it to the point where it resists and working with it to uncover the full range of its affordances. So, we learn, in sand is discovered an affordance that aptly expresses the ephemeral, while a hand gesture conveys meaning that words fail adequately to express. Modes lean toward adaptability rather than fixedness. An individual's semiotic repertoire, observe Adami and Pinto, changes constantly as they encounter new signs and participate in new interactions that test the limits of their existing repertoire.[63]

Among the forces that shape modes over time are changes in social practices and requirements.[64] Sometimes these changes occur by fiat, sometimes through a slow process of erosion. Consider the case of gloves. Today we generally give gloves little thought, but in the years surrounding the turn of the twentieth century, it was averred, "Watch a woman putting on her gloves and you will find out more about her than you could in several months of ordinary discourse."[65] The affordances of gloves offered a rich vocabulary for expressing status and character among the upper and middle classes in England. The two World Wars, however, brought about changes in social practices that, in turn, altered the meaning-making affordances of gloves. The materials and resources that went into making gloves were now required for other purposes, thus gloves were less accessible as a semiotic resource. Further, appearing in new kid gloves could be viewed as unpatriotic, attaching to the wearing of gloves a potentially negative meaning. The World Wars also brought about changes in social requirements. Activities that had previously required the wearing of gloves declined and were replaced by women's entry into war-time work and civilian occupations, which in turn brought

---

62. Kress, "Discourse Analysis and Education," 28.
63. Adami and Pinto "Meaning (re)making in a World," 85.
64. Kress, *Multimodality*, 82.
65. "What Her Gloves Tell" (*The Dundee Courier and Argus*, Thursday, 2 April 1896, 6), quoted in Vincent, "Gloves in the Early Twentieth Century," 194.

about changes in women's fashions. By the 1950s gloves had become associated more with utilitarian purposes than ideas of social fitness.[66]

Technology, also, is a primary factor in shaping modal affordances over time. Leden and Machin observe in connection with this that modes have a fundamental dependency on each other: for example, writing is always realized through typography and spatial arrangements.[67] A change in the affordances of one necessarily brings about changes in the others. Early New Testament documents were initially handwritten on papyrus scrolls in scriptura continua, that is, in a stream of letters with no space between words. Fairly early on, codices came into use alongside of scrolls, possibly because they were able to accommodate multiple texts in a single volume.[68] This, in turn, would have brought about changes in community access to and use of these texts. Illuminations began to be introduced around the fifth century, eventually becoming a fine art that enhanced the beauty and value of manuscripts, introducing social distinctions among them. It wasn't until the medieval period that an aerated script, which introduced spacing between words and an increase in grammatical markings, began to be used.[69] By the thirteenth century it had brought about a small revolution in how books were engaged, leading to the practice of private study.[70] In the fifteenth century the invention of the printing press brought about a technological revolution. It reduced the cost of book production and purchase, enhanced design potentials, and vastly expanded direct access to the printed text of the Bible. This, in turn, began to increase literacy among the masses. The next technological revolution of equal (if not greater) impact occurred in the twentieth century with the invention of computers. The rapidly expanding world of digital media has generated an exponential expansion in affordances and expanded New Testament texts far beyond book form, which, in turn, has brought about changes in access to the texts and their use within Christian communities and elsewhere. Peter Perry, in this volume, observes that the idea of *Lek Jot* is being separated from the iconic book among Sudanese Dinka.[71]

---

66. Vincent, "Gloves in the Early Twentieth Century," 197–201.
67. Leden and Machin, "Doing Critical Discourse Studies," 327.
68. Hurtado, *Earliest Christian Artifacts*, 88.
69. Saenger, *Space Between Words*, 26, 32.
70. Saenger, *Space Between Words*, 264–65.
71. Perry, "Biblical Translation, Performance, and Re-Translation," 58.

Summary

Modes are the material means (physiological and technological) by which sign-makers give realization to meaning. They emerge within specific cultural contexts and serve the beliefs, valuations, and practices of that culture in particular times and places. The analysis of modes and their multimodal functions provides a method for breaking down complex signs into their various modal affordances to better understand how each affordance makes a distinctive contribution to meaning.[72] These functions are not universal, but culturally specific. Modes will change over time in response to a culture's changing communication needs and technological developments, as well as challenges to cultural practices, valuations, and beliefs.

The cultural specificity of modes means that while they exist across cultures, we can never assume that they are used in the same way, that they communicate the same thing, or that they serve the same cultural values, beliefs, and practices.[73] To understand the cultural function of modes, it is necessary to examine them within the theoretical frame of social semiotics, which seeks "to understand how modes are produced by and contribute to cultural settings" and "to get at their social function and meaning potential in the communicative landscape."[74] This is particularly important when we turn to translation, where multiple agents are engaged and negotiations across time, geographies, social systems, and cultures are required to carry over meaning from one modal complex to another.

Agency, Multimodal Social Semiotics, and New Testament Translation

All New Testament texts are multimodal, whether an oral tradition, a second-century fragment of papyrus, Codex Sinaiticus (fourth century), Wettstein's *Novum Testamentum Graecum* (1751), a Harper Collins study Bible, a Sign Language performance, a biblical storytelling event, a film, or a webpage.[75] Each new translation/"performance" involves the

---

72. Adami and Kress, "Introduction: Multimodality, Meaning Making," 234.

73. Tomalin, "Multimodal Dimensions of Literature," 142; Adami and Pinto, "Meaning (re)making in a World," 72.

74. Jewitt and Henrikson, "Social Semiotic Multimodality," 146.

75. Nathan Esala, writing in this volume, begins with the assumption that biblical

transposition of meaning across modes.⁷⁶ Transposition is not achieved by copying or imitating the multimodal signs of the source material; the cultural specificity of modes makes one-to-one correspondence between modes across cultures and time impossible.⁷⁷ Rather, transposition requires undertaking a process of re-semiotization through the creation of new signs.⁷⁸ As a result, translating for new social and cultural contexts requires that "meaning" be realized through different multimodal signs from those of the source text.⁷⁹ Because the new signs offer a different "take" on the world, a reverse translation will never come up with, exactly, the same source text.⁸⁰

This is one of the reasons Adami and Pinto argue that when translators focus only on words, they are (implicitly or explicitly) operating under two false assumptions. The first is that nonverbal modes do not require translation because they are universally recognized and share universal meaning.⁸¹ As has been shown, modes are, by definition, generated within and for specific cultural contexts. Paul's reference to being led by Christ in triumphal procession (2 Cor 2:14), for example, can easily be misconstrued without knowledge of the larger cultural context, leading to misappropriation.⁸² The second false assumption is that when nonverbal modes are replaced by linguistic modes, there is no effect on intermodal relations and meanings.⁸³ As we have seen, however, "meaning" is dependent on the distinctive contribution of each modal affordance to the sign complex. The replacement of one mode with another

---

texts have circulated through various performance events in different times and places; in each performance, new elements are linked to the cultural form and some elements disappear. As a result, each biblical story bears traces of multiple versions. "Re-Translating a Contested Performance Tradition," 157–59, 165.

76. Kress, "Transposing Meaning," 36.

77. Kress, "Transposing Meaning," 37; Bezemer, "What Modes Can and Cannot Do," 16; Bezemer and Kress, "Writing in Multimodal Text," 183, 184.

78. Iedema, "Multimodality, Resemiotization," 42; Kress and Mavers, "Social Semiotics and Multimodal Texts," 173.

79. Tomalin, "Multimodal Dimensions of Literature," 138; Kress, "Transposing Meaning," 36.

80. Adami, "Social Semiotic Multimodal Approach," 375; Kress, "Transposing Meaning," 38; Bezemer and Kress, "Writing in Multimodal Texts," 175.

81. Adami and Pinto, "Meaning-(re)making in a World," 78.

82. See discussion in Matera, *II Corinthians*, 70–75, where he argues that Paul sees himself as a captive, not as a conquering hero.

83. Adami and Pinto, "Meaning-(re)making in a World," 78.

alters intermodal relationships and the material expression of "meaning." Peter Perry, writing in this volume, observes that some Sudanese Dinka speakers have a particular concern for how the reading of biblical texts sounds. When a reader replaces one word with another in translation, the mode "sound" is replaced with a linguistic mode "word." The result is that the reading no longer *sounds* like Bible to this audience, because the translator has not recognized the role that sound, tone, and pitch play in constituting "Bible."[84] This raises the important question: "if meaning is achieved through intermodal relations that are culturally specific, how can we assume that the target audience can access such meaning when only one of those modes is translated?"[85]

To get at the multiple affordances that are at play in the meaning-making process manifested in a text, it can be helpful to ask questions, for example: What do we know about the cultural setting and its communication practices? What prompt in the social context might the text (i.e., the sign complex) be responding to? What purpose might it be intended to serve? Do these suggest anything about the point-of-view of the sign-maker or their role within the cultural setting(s)?[86] What non-verbal modes are identifiable in the multimodal sign complex that is the text? How do the various modal affordances work together to construct "meaning" and what distinctive emphases does each affordance bring to that "meaning"?[87] What range of meanings might these modal affordances offer an interlocutor and what interpretations might emerge based on an interlocutor's affinity spaces/communities?[88]

Rather than narrow the meaning of the (multimodal social semiotic) text, these questions expand the interpretive possibilities. As Sebastian Floor (in this volume) observes, "meaning" is not limited to the words of the text; there is meaning making also in the mind of the interlocutor (translator).[89] This is an important reminder that "meaning" is never wholly "fixed," because the cultural and social contexts in which it is materially realized are constantly shifting, requiring on-going re-semiotization. Adami vividly describes this process as "situated, dynamic,

---

84. Perry, "Biblical Translation, Performance, and Re-Translation," in this volume, 57, 63.

85. Adami and Pinto, "Meaning-(re)making in a World," 78.

86. Adami and Pinto, "Meaning-(re)making in a World," 84.

87. Bezemer, "What Modes Can and Cannot Do," 15.

88. Adami and Pinto, "Meaning-(re)making in a World," 77.

89. Floor, "Increasing Communication Bandwidth," 134.

relational, and emergent in actual instances of interaction with others, with texts, and the environment."[90]

It is here that the agency of the translator comes to the fore. We often think of translators as dispassionate, less interested, fully dedicated to submitting to the ground established by the initiator of the source text. Yet from a social semiotic point of view, a translator is never wholly uninterested nor ever completely passive in their role as a meaning-making sign-maker. Three aspects of translation in particular highlight the translator's agency. The first of these is foregrounding.[91] In the move across cultural contexts, the available range of modes and their potential meaning-making capacities (affordances) change. It falls to the translator to determine which modes to employ, and which aspects of "meaning" to emphasize using the affordances of the selected modes.[92] The result can move in different directions depending on the purpose of the translation. For example, Isela Trujillo, in this volume, tells us that Sign Languages are high-context languages that require significant visual information to convey speech or narration. This is often supplied by foregrounding inferences in the source text through Signing.[93] Richard W. Swanson, in his chapter, proposes that performance (one medium of translation) is, above all, provocation (resonating with Machin); modal selection and foregrounding, therefore, will focus on destabilizing power structures in and outside the text that seek to control "meaning."[94]

A second aspect that draws attention to the translator's agency concerns social relations. This refers not to social relations as they are manifested in the text but to the repositioning of the relationship between the sign-maker and interlocutor as a result of choices in materiality and modality.[95] These choices direct who has access to "meaning" (i.e., social practices around media), how they have access (i.e., protocols of engagement), and how "meaning" is determined (i.e., social practices around meaning-making). Several essays in this volume touch on this aspect of translation. Trujillo and Winedt note that the translators of written texts can remain anonymous; in contrast translators in Deaf communities are

90. Adami, "Social Semiotic Multimodal Approach," 374.
91. Bezemer and Kress, "Writing in Multimodal Texts," 186.
92. Bezemer and Kress, "Writing in Multimodal Texts," 175.
93. Trujillo, "Performance in Sign Language Bible Translation," 209.
94. Swanson, "Translating What Is (not)(un)Said," 240.
95. Bezemer and Kress, "Writing in Multimodal Texts," 186–87.

physically visible and therefore known.[96] This does not mean the translator is always physically present, yet when they are this introduces still other potentials for interaction and the production of "meaning."[97] Matt Valler and Nathan Esala both promote the idea of communal translation. For Esala, it is a way of strengthening communities' relationship to the text; for Valler, it offers the possibility of translations that are open-ended, unfinished, contested.[98] Digital media provide still a different angle on this with websites that are, on the one hand, the work of a single agent, or, on the other hand, communal works, which may or may not be anonymous. They can allow for interaction, or close off interactive capabilities.

The third aspect of translation that highlights the translator's agency concerns the transmission of cultural values. As has been noted repeatedly, modes are culturally determined and serve cultural ideas, valuations, and practices. As a result, cultures, modes, and meaning are entangled in ways that are not always easy to distinguish. This creates a number of challenges for translators. One translator may argue that it is necessary to preserve the cultural values manifest in a text in order to understand actions, attitudes, and events as well as for the sake of narrative coherency. While a plausible argument for historical accuracy, it is complicated when "truth" claims are ascribed to the "text." When this happens, arguments for historical accuracy must face a counter argument: i.e., that this (intentionally or unintentionally) reifies specific cultural values, beliefs, and practices that do not necessarily have anything to do with the truth claims of the text. Examples include patriarchalism and kyriocentrism, which, when conflated with "truth" are imposed on cultures where these are contested values/practices. Esala cautions that contemporary practices of translation also often serve (neo-)colonial paradigms, re-enforcing aspects of modern colonialization that have roots in the practices of ancient empires, which in turn have informed biblical ideas of G-d.[99] Although there is no room to untangle this conundrum here, Becka McKay, in a later chapter, offers "thick translation" (textual annotation) as one possible way to (at least) give interlocutors access to the multiple

---

96. Trujillo, "Performance in Sign Language Bible Translation," 210; Winedt, "Multimodality and Performance," 78–79.

97. Trujillo, "Performance in Sign Language Bible Translation," 210; Winedt, "Multimodality and Performance," 78–79.

98. Esala, "Re-Translating a Contested Performance Tradition," 172–73; Valler, "Labyrinths of Meaning," 119–20

99. Esala, "Re-Translating a Contested Performance Tradition," 171

layers of meaning that can otherwise disappear in translation. I suggest that multimodal social semiotic dimensions of text, while a source of these complications, also offer the very resources needed for negotiating the complex relationship between cultures, texts, social practices, and "meaning." These multimodal social semiotic resources are neither ancillary nor incidental; they are essential.

Conclusion

Returning to the question with which we began—"When we set about translating the New Testament, what is it that we are translating?"—my hope is that "words" no longer feels like an adequate answer. The response "a social semiotic multimodal text" may hardly seem like a welcome alternative (amply demonstrated by the universal reaction I have received to the title of this chapter). Yet broken down into its constituent parts, it aptly describes three dimensions of any text, the New Testament or otherwise, that must be accounted for in translation: (1) it is social = it is a communication event, involving a sign-maker and an interlocutor within a temporally, geographically, and culturally bound social system; (2) it is semiotic = it is an act of signification (meaning-making), involving agency on the part of at least two individuals (a sign-maker and an interlocutor/interpreter); (3) it is multimodal = it gives material realization to meaning through the combined work of multiple modes and affordances: i.e., semiotic (meaning-making resources) that have emerged over time within specific cultural contexts and which are employed by meaning-making agents.

Translation of the New Testament presents peculiar challenges. This is, in part, because we do not possess any original manuscripts of the New Testament, and therefore have no access to a single source text. More significantly, it is because what we do possess is material evidence of an endless cycle of communication exchanges. Each exchange has involved at least one sign-maker and one interlocutor, each of whom has been an active agent in the construction of "meaning." Where, then, does "meaning" reside? It cannot be said to reside solely with the initial sign-maker. To repeat Kress: the initial sign is "always both a 'full' representation of the sign-maker's *interest*" and, also, "only ever a partial account of some entity or phenomenon when seen from a different position."[100] Does it re-

---

100. Kress, "Transposing Meaning," 35.

side, then, with the interpreter? This would be to ignore the initial prompt and interactive character of communication. Does it reside within the communication exchange? If this is the case (and I propose that it is), then four realizations come into view: first, that what we are translating is dynamic rather than stable/coherent because it is constantly being transposed; second, that a range of meaning potentials exists that only more or less represent the realized meaning of the initial sign-maker as interpreted by an interlocutor; third, that "meaning" is linked to struggles to (re)define "reality" in constantly shifting social and cultural contexts; and fourth, that translators are not passive participants, but active, meaning-making agents in this process.

Bibliography

Adam, A. K. A. "Interpreting the Bible at the Horizon of Virtual New Worlds." In *The Bible in Ancient and Modern Media: Story and Performance*, edited by Holly E. Hearon and Philip Ruge-Jones, 159–73. Biblical Performance Criticism 1. Eugene, OR: Cascade Books, 2009.

Adami, Elizabeth. "A Social Semiotic Multimodal Approach to Translation." In *The Routledge Handbook of Translation Theory and Concepts*, edited by R. Meylaerts and K. Marais, 369–88. London: Routledge, 2023.

Adami, Elizabeth, and Gunther Kress. "Introduction: Multimodality, Meaning Making, and the Issue of 'Text.'" *Text and Talk* 34 (2014) 231–37.

Adami, Elizabeth, and Sara Ramos Pinto. "Meaning-(re)making in a World of Untranslated Signs: Towards a Research Agenda on Multimodality, Culture, and Translation." In *Translation and Multimodality: Beyond Words*, edited by Monica Boria et al., 71–93. London: Routledge, 2020.

Al-Ameedi, Riyadh Tariq Kadhim, and Hayder Hameed Ghitheeth. "Multimodal Discourse Analysis of Image-Biblical Verses." *Turkish Journal of Computer and Mathematics Education* 12 (2021) 2646–52.

Apostel, Lilith. "Death Is Sleep: The Pervasiveness of a Material and Multimodal Conceptual Metaphor in Ancient Egypt." *Journal of Cognitive Historiography* 6 (2020–21) 65–107.

Bezemer, Jeff. "What Modes Can and Cannot Do: *Affordance* in Gunther Kress's Theory of Sign Making." *Text and Talk* 44.4 (2023). https://doi.org/10.1515/text-2022-0055.

Bezemer, Jeff, and Carey Jewitt. "Multimodal Analysis: Key Issues." In *Research Methods in Linguistics*, edited by Lia Litosseliti, 180–97. London: Continuum, 2010.

Bezemer, Jeff, and Gunther Kress. "Writing in Multimodal Texts: A Social Semiotic Account of Designs for Learning." *Written Communication* 25 (2008) 166–95.

Brooten, Bernadette J. *Women Leaders in the Ancient Synagogue*. Brown Judaic Studies 36. Atlanta: Scholars, 1982.

Clivaz, Claire. "The Bible in the Digital Age: Multimodal Scriptures in Communities." In *Digital Humanities and Christianity: An Introduction*, edited by Tim Hutchings and Claire Clivaz, 21–45. Berlin: de Gruyter, 2021.

Daniel, Sharon. "Materializing a Gesture of Resistance." *Forum: Art, Process, Protest* 3 (2018) 285–97.

DeLongoria, Maria. "Misognoir: *Black Hair Identity Politics and Multiple Black Realities." *Africology: The Journal of Pan African Studies* 12 (2018) 39–49.

Floor, Sebastian, and Bryan Hamerlink. "Multimodality in Bible Translation: Could It Contribute to Quality Assurance?" In *Quality in Translation: A Multi-Threaded Fabric*, edited by Stephen Watters and Reinier de Blois, 127–55. Dallas: SIL Pike, 2023.

Halliday, M. A. K. *Language as Social Semiotic: The Social Interpretation of Language and Meaning*. Baltimore: Arnold, 1978.

———. *Spoken and Written Language*. Oxford: Oxford University Press, 1985.

Hearon, Holly. "The Materiality of the Bible as Performance." In *Aspects of Performance in Faith Settings: Heavenly Acts*, edited by A. Rosowsky, 188–210. Newcastle: Cambridge Scholars, 2019.

———. "Music as a Medium of Oral Transmission in Jesus Communities." *Biblical Theology Bulletin* 43 (2013) 124–34.

———. "A Social Semiotic Multi-Modal Approach to Communication Practices in Early Christianity." *Journal of Early Christian History* 4 (2014) 44–67.

Hodge, Bob. *Social Semiotics for a Complex World*. Cambridge: Polity, 2017.

Hurtado, Larry W. *The Earliest Christian Artifacts: Manuscripts and Christian Origins*. Grand Rapids: Eerdmans, 2006.

Iedema, Rick. "Multimodality, Resemiotization: Extending the Analysis of Discourse as Multi-Semiotic Practice." *Visual Communication* 2 (2003) 29–57.

Jewitt, Carey. "An Introduction to Multimodality." In *The Routledge Handbook of Multimodal Analysis*, edited by Carey Jewitt, 14–27. London: Routledge, 2009.

Jewitt, Carey, and Brett Henrikson. "Social Semiotic Multimodality." In *Handbuch Sprache im multimodalen Kontext*, edited by N. M. Klug and H. Stökl, 145–64. Berlin: de Gruyter, 2016.

Kress, Gunther. "Discourse Analysis and Education: A Multimodal Social Semiotic Approach." In *An Introduction to Critical Discourse Analysis in Education*, edited by Rebecca Rogers, 205–26. London: Routledge, 2011.

———. *Multimodality: A Social Semiotic Approach to Contemporary Communication*. London: Routledge, 2010.

———. "Semiotic Work: Applied Linguistics and a Social Semiotic Account of Multimodality." *QILA Review* 28 (2015) 49–71.

———. "Transposing Meaning: *Translation* in a Multimodal Semiotic Landscape." In *Translation and Multimodality: Beyond Words*, edited by Monica Boria et al., 24–28. London: Routledge, 2020.

Kress, Gunther, and Diane Mavers. "Social Semiotics and Multimodal Texts." In *Research Methods in the Social Sciences*, edited by Bridget Somekh and Cathy Lewin, 172–79. London: Sage, 2005.

Kress, Gunther, and Theo Van Leeuwen. *Multimodal Discourse: The Modes and Media of Contemporary Communication*. New York: Oxford University Press, 2001.

———. *Reading Images: The Grammar of Visual Design*. London: Routledge, 1996.

Leden, Per, and David Machin. "Doing Critical Discourse Studies with Multimodality: From Metafunctions to Materiality." *Critical Discourse Studies* 16.5 (2019) 497–513. DOI: 10.1080/17405904.2018.1468789.

Machin, David. "The Need for a Social and Affordance-Driven Multimodal Critical Discourse Studies." *Discourse 7 Society* 27 (2016) 322–34.
Matera, Frank. *II Corinthians: A Commentary*. New Testament Library. Louisville: Westminster John Knox, 2003.
Nørgaard, Nina. *Multimodal Stylistics of the Novel: More Than Words*. Routledge Studies in Multimodality 25. New York: Routledge, 2019.
O'Halloran, Kay L. "Historical Changes in the Semiotic Landscape: From Calculation to Computation." In *The Routledge Handbook of Multimodal Analysis*, edited by Carey Jewitt, 98–113. London: Routledge, 2011.
Saenger, Paul. *Space Between Words: The Origins of Silent Reading*. Stanford, CA: Stanford University Press, 1997.
Tomalin, Marcus. "The Multimodal Dimensions of Literature in Translation." In *Translation and Multimodality: Beyond Words*, edited by Monica Boria et al., 134–57. London: Routledge, 2020.
Tuominen, Tina, et al. "Why Methods Matter: Approaching Multimodality in Translation Research." *Linguistica Antverpiensia, New Series: Themes in Translation Studies* 17 (2018) 1–21.
Van Leeuwen, Theo. *Introducing Social Semiotics*. London: Routledge, 2005.
Vincent, Susan. "Gloves in the Early Twentieth Century." *Journal of Design History* 25 (2012) 190–205.

3

Biblical Translation, Performance, and Re-Translation in Local Communities

PETER S. PERRY

IN THIS CHAPTER, I use Biblical Performance Criticism (BPC) as conceptual framework, analytical criteria, and practice to describe and analyze how a specific community, Emmanuel Sudanese Lutheran Fellowship in Glendale, Arizona, communicates biblical traditions. The description of BPC here is brought into dialogue with social semiotic communication theory as proposed by Gunther Kress.[1] The goal of this analysis is (1) to support the work of Bible translators in improving translation theory and practice, (2) to encourage funding and institutional support for revising the Dinka Bor New Testament and completing a translation of the Hebrew Bible, and (3) to persuade Bible translation (BT) agencies to play a supportive role in bringing Dinka speakers together to discuss Dinka language and orthography. Since 2013, I have been privileged to serve as supervising pastor for Emmanuel. They have graciously invited my participation and have taught me about Dinka language and culture. Thanks are due to more people in the community than I can name here, but I offer special gratitude to Solomon Machar Kuch and Ayak Chol who met with me to discuss this chapter, give feedback, and check my Dinka translations. Unless noted, all translations are my own, errors included.

---

1. Kress, *Multimodality*; Kress, "'Partnerships in Research'"; Bezemer, "What Modes Can and Cannot Do."

Biblical Performance Criticism

Biblical Performance Criticism (BPC) reconceives how the Bible is understood, analyzed, and used, including:

1. Reframing the biblical materials within the ancient communication cultures of Judaism and early Christianity, which may be characterized by oral-scribal, group-oriented, and agrarian values, attitudes, and behaviors and not visual-print, individual-oriented, and industrial values, attitudes, and behaviors of the post-Gutenberg world. Within BPC, people speak of "biblical traditions" rather than "texts," because many moderns consider a "text" an object independent of a community while a manuscript in the ancient world was an expression of traditions within a community.

2. Analyzing specific events communicating these traditions and how meaning is made through the interaction and interrelation of at least five aspects (performer,[2] audience,[3] situation,[4] biblical traditions,[5] and media[6]) and not independently. Whole

---

[2] By "performer," we mean a broad category that includes any person who re-presents a biblical tradition, that is, someone who communicates traditions not for the first time. This person otherwise might be called a lector, reader, storyteller, translator, preacher, teacher, blogger, or so on. This "re-presentation" may be multi-sensory, for example, both visual and auditory, and multi-dimensional, for example, a YouTube video may be a two-dimensional representation of a three-dimensional event over time as well as multimodal, since a YouTube video may display text, static images, and dynamic video.

[3] An "audience" is one or more persons who are experiencing the performance event.

[4] By "situation," we mean anything that may shape the way the performer performs and the audience experiences the performance. This may include the shape, size, lighting, and material of the room, for example, performing in a dimly lit cave will change both the performer's decisions and the audience's experience. It also may include the actual relationship dynamics of the audience, the performer, and people outside the performance. It may also include the larger social, economic, and political dynamics that may cause a performer to consciously or unconsciously emphasize one thing over others or for an audience to interpret part or the whole performance in relation to the "situation."

[5] The "text" is often the most available, albeit partial, expression of traditions, but "traditions" refers to a larger network of ideas that are transmitted by a group of people. A physical manuscript represents one resource used to express these ideas, but we shouldn't assume it was the only one used by a group. "Traditions" is always plural since there are always multiple traditions at work in any community.

[6] By "media" of a performance, I mean the technology of communication (e.g.,

performance events, understood as dynamic systems, are the focus of analysis.

3. Foregrounding the ways these traditions are embodied in community. Since a communication event is a multi-sensory event experienced by multiple people, analysis is grounded theoretically and phenomenologically in actual experiences of sight, sound, smell, touch, even taste, by embodied people in relationships formed by memory, emotion, culture, and socioeconomic power dynamics.

4. Embracing many methods, since each offers unique insights into aspects of the communication event; for example (this list is illustrative and not exhaustive): historical criticism illuminates situations in which a text was composed, written, and communicated; narrative criticism opens up the text and the way traditions are told as stories; each variant described by textual criticism unlocks another way audiences experienced the text; rhetorical criticism exposes the strategies of moving, instructing, and engaging the audience; cognitive linguistics root language in psychology and neurology to describe how human beings communicate, whether in ancient or modern cultures; translation studies brings both theoretical foundation and real-world communication experience across cultures; and so on. People involved in BPC each bring different disciplinary preferences and strengths and learn from each other how to best integrate each discipline's insight into analysis of performances. To summarize: BPC is inherently multi- and inter-disciplinary.

Because BPC reframes biblical materials as people communicating traditions, it is perhaps more accurate to think of BPC as a reconceptualization more than a research agenda. With a focus on embodied communication, BPC is people- and relationship-centered, and so may be more helpfully described as a movement more than a method. There is a wide variety of areas and goals among those interested in BPC. As a movement, BPC practitioners are involved in biblical studies, Bible translation, biblical storytelling, and/or leadership in Christian and Jewish congregations,

---

in-person gathering, codex, video), or what Kress more precisely defines as "the conditions and means for *disseminating* meaning" (*Multimodality*, 34). While "media culture" has long been a topic in BPC, I have usually subsumed it under "situation" or as a part of the inquiry process, but now see it as an irreducible aspect of the performance event. See Perry, "Embodied Cognition."

and while some engage in BPC as a critical (that is, systematic analytical discipline), not all do.

This description of BPC coheres well with social semiotic theory as proposed by Gunther Kress.[7] Space only allows a suggestive sketch. "Semiosis," or meaning making in Kress's description, is a continuous social process of meaning making. Kress shifts from a linguistic to a multimodal framework for meaning making. Like other kinds of semiotic theories, Kress describes sign-makers as interested agents who make signs with particular signifiers to express meaning (the signified). Kress helpfully describes the multimodal and social aspects of this process that fit with claims of BPC:

1. "Multimodality" refers to the domain of potential socially shaped resources for making signs. Language is only one kind of resource, which can be used in a variety of modes, such as writing and speech. A sign-maker selects the modes and their affordances based on the fitness for the purpose, what Kress calls "aptness."[8] Multiple modes may be used together in complex ensembles.[9] For translators, especially those working in Sign Language, video, and other multimodal digital media, this analytic framework seems essential. In a live, face-to-face performance, BPC practitioners would say that a performer selects visual modes (e.g., gestures, facial expressions, eye direction, props), auditory modes (tone, volume, and other prosody) that also include spatial (proximity, orientation) and temporal possibilities (movement, tempo, and pause), that fit the performer's perception of the purpose of the performance and its potential effects on their audience.[10]

2. "'Materiality' is inextricably linked to 'meaning,'" as Holly Hearon describes elsewhere in this volume.[11] Signs are always material, that is, they exist in space and time and are perceived through senses.

---

7. We need to distinguish Kress's social semiotic theory from others, e.g., Michael Halliday's, on which Kress depends.

8. Kress, *Multimodality*, 156.

9. Kress, *Multimodality*, 169.

10. Kress, *Multimodality*, 86–87, answers the question, "What is a mode?" by offering both social and formal criteria that make it impossible to abstract a mode from a particular group: "*socially*, what counts as a mode is a matter for a community and its social-representational needs. What a community decides to regard and use as a mode *is* mode" (86, emphasis in original).

11. Hearon, "Engaging Multimodal Social Semiotic Dimensions," 21.

The sound of a voice is material, as is the gesture of a hand or a printed page. Too often discussions of communication are abstract and disembodied. People make meaning not only with concepts but with specific materiality, such as sound or color or shape and their embeddedness in embodied relationships.[12] As demonstrated below, BPC is concerned with all the material aspects of the event and their interrelationships, for example, the shape and size of the book, the way it is held in front of the audience, the relationships and responses of the audience, and so on.

3. Meaning making cannot be abstracted from actual sign-makers and the social processes of sign production. The temptation, which Jeff Bezemer believes even Kress fell prey to, is that scholars want to be able to generalize in order to reach definitive and universal conclusions.[13] Or, as Marlon Winedt argues in his chapter, there is a seductive tendency toward an idealized or utopian account of what happens in translation rather than a realistic account of "how power, ideology, and culture influence meaning-making."[14] Since all meaning making is socially shaped and therefore contingent, the best we can do is aggregate data for particular groups in particular times and places to suggest such social meaning makings are "conventional."[15] While translators may want their translation to be used to replicate the same set of meanings for all audiences, as I illustrate below, it is not possible. In BPC, we exercise this epistemological humility by describing "performance scenarios" as thickly as possible using interdisciplinary methods and resources.

4. Existing signs are continuously reused by sign-makers into new signs. This "ceaseless *social (re)making* of a set of cultural resources"[16]

---

12. Kress, *Multimodality*, 78.
13. Bezemer, "What Modes Can and Cannot Do," 15.
14. Winedt, "Multimodality and Performance," 71.
15. Bezemer, "What Modes Can and Cannot Do," 16: "I can, with each analysis of a sign making event, aggregate our understanding of conventions for making meaning with certain sets of material resources, i.e., of the ('preferred,' 'common') use of modes in specific periods, spaces, and social networks." He concludes, "I believe that this can be achieved—producing plausible, situated accounts of sign making, and documenting norms and conventions for specific communities of sign makers," which should give encouragement to BPC scholars describing ancient and modern performance scenarios.
16. Kress, "'Partnerships in Research,'" 242. Emphasis in original.

fits the way BPC defines "performance" as a re-presentation of traditions. BPC insists that every performance is somehow dependent on prior performances, so all meaning making is in some way continuous from one to another. Yet, each performance is still a new event, and so is also in some way discontinuous with previous events. As I show below, every reading of the Dinka New Testament is a new meaning-making event, even when using the same physical object and expressing the same words from the page.[17]

As I have described elsewhere,[18] BPC seems to be deployed in three ways: (1) analytical, through which scholars aggregate historical data about past communication events, (2) heuristic, through which scholars perform and analyze actual interactions of performer, audience, situation, traditions, and media to give insight into ancient performances, and (3) practical, through which lectors, preachers, teachers, YouTube commentators, and others analyze the every-day, ordinary performances of biblical traditions.

This project is an example of the practical mode of BPC. Every Sunday at Emmanuel Sudanese Lutheran Fellowship, a lector stands to read the Dinka Bor translation of the New Testament (*Lek Jot de Yecu Kritho*). There are informal conversations about how to improve the effectiveness of these readings. Although the participants would not label it such, those conversations are an example of the practical mode of BPC, analyzing performances of biblical traditions in order to optimize the impact of these readings. This paper is an attempt to formalize that analysis as an example to Bible translators and others and encouragement to allocate of energy, expertise, and money for Dinka speakers to translate the Hebrew Bible, to re-translate *Lek Jot*, and to support orthographic reform. It is my hope that leaders of BT agencies will be persuaded of the value of such efforts for other language groups.

This exhortation for re-translation of *Lek Jot* should be heard within a larger movement toward decolonializing Bible translation and empowering local communities. As described below, the social dynamics around *Lek Jot* continue to replicate the effects of colonial power relationships

---

17. While I have focused here on convergences between BPC and social semiotics, let me also mention topics for future dialogue: the role of the audience, interaction between audience and performer, and how misunderstanding and overinterpretation occur, just to name a few.

18. Perry, "Biblical Performance Criticism."

that disempowered local communities. Elsewhere in this volume, Nathan Esala gives an example of Contextual Bible Study (CBS) as a way to empower local communities in translation activities. Building on the work of Deborah Shadd, he argues for the logic of liberation to motivate and structure re-translation rather than the colonial logics of progress or challenge.[19] Or, as Gerald West puts it, re-translation offers an opportunity for exposing the epistemic and economic foundations of colonial practices and also, "for the capacity of such [re-]translations to reconfigure and reinvent the ideo-theological and social space of African post-colonies, offering biblical re-translated resources for community based participatory development."[20] This chapter is a small attempt toward that goal.

A Brief Introduction to the Dinka Bor Translation of the New Testament (*Lek Jot de Yecu Kritho*)

The translation of the New Testament that is used by Emmanuel Sudanese Lutheran Fellowship in Glendale, Arizona, is the Bor dialect of Dinka (Jiëŋ) used around the town of Bor, about two hundred kilometers north and downstream on the White Nile River from the capital of South Sudan, Juba.[21]

The New Testament translation (*Lek Jot*) was begun in 1905 by Englishman Archibald Shaw (1879–1956).[22] Shaw, a missionary of the Christian Missionary Society, was the only one of seven missionaries who stayed and learned the language well and spent the rest of his life promoting the Dinka people and language. Selections in Dinka Bor from the NT were produced in 1908. The Gospel according to Luke was translated with the assistance of catechumen Alier E. Kut and published in 1915. Philip Anyang Agul, Gordon Apec Ayom, and Paulo Barac Macok were instrumental in translating and revising the remainder. The whole NT was published in 1940.[23]

Emmanuel members admire *Lek Jot*'s creative translation. As they compare it with English translations, they give credit to Shaw for inspired

---

19. Esala, "Re-Translating a Contested Performance Tradition," 153–84.
20. West, "Moffat's seTlhaping Translation," 7.
21. Idris, "Modern Developments," 7–8.
22. See also Deng, *Piööc*, 20–23; and briefly Idris, "Modern Developments," 19.
23. YouVersion, "Lek Jot de Jecu Kritho 1940."

choices. For example, διὰ συνείδησιν θεοῦ (1 Pet 2:19) communicates the idea of a conscience formed by God that leads one to endure when suffering unjustly. Translators rendered this, "ne nyiny nyic en Nhialic piɔu," or when back translated, "through knowing knowledge in God's heart," a clever turn of phrase with alliteration not found in Greek that adds to its aural impact in Dinka.

The multimodal social experiences of translators are implied by the influence of other languages, including English, Hebrew, Greek, and Arabic. Proper nouns, such as Γαλιλαία "Galili" (John 2:1), Φαρισαῖος "Parithai" (John 3:1), and so on, are transliterations influenced by English translation and pronunciation. The English word "adopt" is shortened to dɔp, perhaps reflecting the way the English speakers suppressed the initial *a* and final *t*, to translate Acts 7:21 and Rom 8:15, 23, 9:4. The Greek text of Acts uses ἀνατρέφω ("I nurture, grow up") and Romans uses υἱοθεσία ("sonship"), but the KJV (and its descendants) translate some form of "adopt" for each, which suggests that translators followed the KJV and the way the English word "adopt" was pronounced.

English was not the only influence on word choice and pronunciation. βασιλεύς was translated using the transliteration of the Hebrew מֶלֶךְ, *melek*. Ἡρώδης ὁ βασιλεὺς was translated according to both Hebrew phonemes and the way English translators pronounced the rough *eta* as if the Hebrew guttural *heh*: "Kerod melek" (Matt 2:1). Some names are often transliterated directly as pronounced in Greek, for example, Greek city names such as ἐν Ἐφέσῳ, "ne Epetho" (Rev 2:10), or ἐν Περγάμῳ, "ne Pergamo" (Rev 2:12), suggesting no influence of the English pronunciations "Ephesus" or "Pergamum." Greek names that combine sounds not used in Dinka are modified, such as the combination of *s* and *m* sounds ἐν Σμύρνῃ becomes "ne Thumurna" (Rev 2:8), adding a *u*-sound between *s* and *m* sounds to make the name easier to say for a Dinka speaker.

Arab hegemony in northern Sudan that was reinforced and institutionalized by English colonial rule[24] is evident in Arabic loanwords in Dinka, most notably, the word كنيسة (Dinka *kanitha*) used to translate ἐκκλησία. One passage where this multi-lingual soundscape is most evident is in the introduction to Christ's messages to the seven congregations of the book of Revelation. For example, "Gare malaika [Hebrew] de kanitha [Arabic] tɔ ne Epetho [Greek]," back translated "Write to the angel of the congregation in Ephesus" (Rev 2:1), reflects the cultures that

24. See brief history in Abdelhay, Makoni, and Makoni, "Colonial Linguistics." On the imposition of Arabic, see Idris, "Modern Developments," 12–18.

promoted these languages and their power that performed traditions with and on the Dinka people.

Dinka Phonology and Orthography

Lek Jot struggles to orthographically represent three independent dimensions of the Dinka phonological system: tone, vowel length, and vowel quality.[25] Using the language of social semiotics, Dinka speech utilizes these three aspects of the mode of speech as semiotic resources to make meaning.[26] However, the current mode of printed Dinka text does not have sufficient graphic resources (such as tone markings) and does not utilize available resources consistently (such as repetition of vowels or diaresis) to assist readers and speakers. Space does not allow us a detailed discussion of tone, vocal length, and vocal quality; since Emmanuel members concern themselves with vocal quality in their preparation, I give a brief discussion below.

Vowel quality (modal or breathy) distinguishes lexemes and inflected forms and are not marked in *Lek Jot*. In the early twentieth century, breathy forms were not marked.[27] The use of diaresis (called *kït ë yäu* in Dinka) to indicate breathy vowel quality began in 1978 by Job Dharuai Malou, developing writing resources for teachers.[28] For example, the common singular noun *nyin* (eye) is only distinguished from the plural *nyïn* (eyes) by the breathy quality of the *i* sound. Consider (back translation to right):

Lamba de guɔp, yenekee nyin. Yen na piath nyindu, ke guɔpdu ebɛn abi ya meer. (Matt 6:22)	The lamp of the body, it is the eye. So, if healthy is your eye, your whole body will be full of light.

25. Ladd, Remijsen, and Manyang describe seven different phonological parameters when studying the Luanyang dialect. Ladd, Remijsen, and Manyang, "On the Distinction," 663; Remijsen, "Tonal Alignment." Deng, *Piööc*, 6–10, only discusses vowel length and quality. See the proposal for morphophonemic spelling by Gilley, "Morphophonemic Orthographies."

26. The difficulty of representing tone, vowel quality, and length in writing shows they are distinct modes. See Kress, *Multimodality*, 79.

27. Nebel marked them in boldface in his 1948 grammar of the Rek dialect (*Dinka Grammar*). Gilley, "Morphophonemic Orthographies," 6–7, uses the term "creaky" instead of "modal."

28. See Lual and Malou, *Thuɔŋjäŋ athör tueŋ ë kuen*. For additional citations, see Idris, "Modern Developments," 20.

A reader must additionally process each instance of nyin: are these singular or plural? A pause placed before the first nyin in Matt 6:22, if performed as a cue for suspense (perhaps with eyes raised or other signal appropriate to the audience), could build anticipation to the question: what is the lamp of the body? However, when the audience picks up signals that the reader is struggling to disambiguate the text, the impact is lost and the ethos of the reader is diminished, affecting the overall impact of the reading on the audience.

Materiality and Media

Social semiotic theory helps better integrate how a particular medium of communication and its modes are selected and shaped culturally and are an irreducible aspect of every performance. "Media culture" here refers to the set of behaviors, attitudes, values, and relationships that emerge in a specific group of people in relationship to particular media. While "media culture" is not a phrase used in social semiotic theory, it helpfully correlates to material and social constraints.[29] Especially relevant here is Emmanuel's media culture around the printed book *Lek Jot* in relationship with hymns learned by memory in Kakuma and printed in the hymnal. The discussion below illustrates a key point of social semiotics, that social groups are in a continuous process of using and re-using available semiotic resources to produce new material forms to accomplish their goals and interests (recall that sound, tone, volume, gestures, and embodied responses are "material"). To narrowly assume an isolated, fixed semiotic "product," such as the physical object *Lek Jot*, is to misunderstand and to misrepresent how groups communicate traditions.

The particular contours of Emmanuel's media culture around *Lek Jot* were shaped by experiences in the refugee camp in Kakuma, Kenya. Kakuma was established in 1992 in northwestern Kenya to house the "Lost Boys of Sudan." Most of the leaders of Emmanuel were children and teenagers in the camp. There, they were evangelized by Anglican missionaries, who taught them songs with dancing. Dinka evangelists, catechists, and worship leaders emerged over the years, many of whom form the leadership core of Emmanuel today. Many songs used words and phrases from *Lek Jot*. It is difficult to overstate the importance of these multimodal experiences—textual for only the few catechists with

---

29. Kress, "'Partnerships in Research,'" 239–60. For further discussion of identifying constraints, see chapter by Esala in this volume.

a printed text, but visual, aural, and kinesthetic modes interrelated for most participants. Repeated experiences of singing with dancing created deep memories of the songs—and the biblical passages. Some learned to read Dinka in order to share passages from *Lek Jot* in worship and in catechesis.

When using *Lek Jot* as a material object, Emmanuel members engage specific resources for meaning making, including status and power granted to its wielder along with other potentials for performance. The 1959 printing of *Lek Jot* (the most recent edition) measures 17.8 centimeters tall by 8.9 centimeters wide by 1.9 centimeters thick. As a hand-sized book with thin pages, it is both portable to be used anywhere and fragile to be protected. Copies are scarce, so possessing a copy identifies a person as a leader of the Christian community. Few could read Dinka, and so the ability to verbalize the text conveyed additional status that was enacted when a reader stood to read the book in front of believers gathered under a tree or outside a tent. Further, a speaker using a loud voice and projected tone was required to ensure everyone could hear without amplification. Now, even with amplification, readers and audience expect loud volume and projected tone! Finally, singing hymns that used phrases and words from *Lek Jot* shapes both the fluency and the interpretation of both a reader and the audience. Each of these aspects experienced in Kakuma continues to shape the media culture around *Lek Jot*.

Because of the power and status attached to the physical object, Emmanuel and other Dinka faith communities experience a paradox. On one hand, there is hesitation to revise *Lek Jot*. On the other hand, revision is inevitable and is informally happening now. Both the status of *Lek Jot* as well as social power dynamics seem to be involved. There is hesitation, suspicion even, for those who would revise *Lek Jot*, accused by some of "ruining the Bible." This seems to stem from the sacred status attributed to the Bible that is transferred to the *Lek Jot* translation itself. Even more, experiences of *Lek Jot* and the songs based on it are central parts of Christian identity formed in the crucible of Kakuma. To change *Lek Jot* may suggest a threat to core identity. Some challenge, "who gave you the authority to do that?" Those who offer revisions may not only be perceived as threatening identity but also claiming authority and become caught in dynamics of jockeying for position within not only the Dinka community but the larger South Sudanese community.

In addition, the media culture that has emerged around *Lek Jot* mirrors the status and authority granted by people of various languages to publishers who produce "authorized" translations of the Bible. While some can name Shaw as one of the translators (if not attributing the translation solely to him), the power dynamics of those involved in revisions of *Lek Jot* have been hidden.

The Rejaf language conference in 1928 played a major role in establishing Dinka orthography, which led to revisions during the translation of *Lek Jot*. Only missionary societies and British government officials participated in the conference that formalized the system. Abdelhay, Makoni, and Makoni note, "Not only were 'native voices' conspicuously absent, but the inconsistency and contradiction of participants' positions were also not foregrounded."[30] Although beyond the scope of this paper, clear linkage can be established between the current orthographic confusion in reading *Lek Jot* fluently and the confusion institutionalized through colonial power at the 1928 Rejaf conference (see Abdelhay and Idris for details). The choice of the Lepsius system (named after Egyptologist C. R. Lepsius, who published *The Standard Alphabet* in 1855) that used diacritics had been adopted by the Arua conference in 1918, and Shaw himself spoke at Rejaf in favor of the Arua system, in part because it could be typed on English typewriters[31] but also because he thought the additional characters of the International Phonetic Alphabet (IPA) would be too difficult for ordinary people.[32] (Ironically, because the orthography is inadequate, *Lek Jot* is difficult to use by ordinary people.) Shaw's voice was not the only one heard. Others championed the "new character" group (e.g., Westermann, James, Meinhof).[33] As a result, mixed recommendations emerged from Rejaf.[34]

30. Abdelhay, Makoni, and Makoni, "Colonial Linguistics," 347.

31. The technological considerations of typewriters and die-cast printing (both essential for the British Imperial bureaucracy) should not be underestimated in analyzing orthographic decision making in the late nineteenth and early twentieth centuries. For example, James notes, "Types with diacritics are less durable than others, because the dots get worn out, or knocked off in everyday wear and tear. The types are not easily distinguishable: and the printer makes frequent mistakes" ("Practical Orthography," 128).

32. Abdelhay, Makoni, and Makoni, "Colonial Linguistics," 351–52. Shaw here was following Lepsius in thinking diacritics were only necessary for the "European student" and not the "uncritical Native." See Meinhof, "Principles," 232–33.

33. Meinhof, "Principles," 229, argues, "Orthography remains a purely mnemotechnic aid to remembrance of the spoken word, in which, as a rule, the particularly characteristic sounds are taken out of the abundant examples that occur in a language, and letters employed to represent them."

34. As Tucker later observes, "The question of a standard orthography was never

Two points are salient for our discussion of the media culture of *Lek Jot*: the power yielded to the social status of the book and a confused orthography. First the colonial power dynamics that excluded Dinka speakers from decisions about the orthography of their language at the same time reified the book *Lek Jot* that encoded the authority granted by hidden colonial actors.[35]

These power dynamics are hidden from the users of *Lek Jot*: this particular book, its format, and its translation is now *Lek Jot de Bɛnydiitda ku Duluɛŋda Yecu Kritho*, "The New Message of Our Lord and Savior Jesus Christ."[36] As a result, *Lek Jot* is received uncritically as "authorized" and beyond revision. Disagreement over orthography among Dinka scholars and speakers today is a second factor in resisting official revision, even as the translation is modified informally by Emmanuel readers and probably by Dinka communities around the world.

The reality is that *Lek Jot* is being revised whether it "ruins Scripture" or is "authorized" or not. Despite its iconicity, it is not a fixed semiotic resource but is constantly being revised in its use in performance. Readers stand up at Emmanuel worship services and elsewhere and must interpret the text that is unmarked for vocal quality, vowel length, and tonal variation. Some lectors are re-writing the text ahead of their performance with notations to aid the fluency of their reading. In other words, revision of *Lek Jot* is happening inevitably wherever it is being used.

Although not in an institutional sense, these are "authorized" re-translations because the lectors are being selected by local leaders and their communities. Readers with fluency are asked to read more often;

---

really harmoniously settled at the Rejaf Conference, and it has its repercussions yet, especially where two or more missionary societies are engaged on the writing of one language" ("Linguistic Situation," 33). To be fair, Meinhof is surely correct that every orthography is inadequate to represent living speech, a fact central to performance criticism and a multimodal analysis. "Even the best writing is therefore only an imperfect means of reproducing living speech and the most careful orthography will have its defects. These must, however, be avoided in such a way that misunderstanding and confusion" (Meinhof, "Principles," 231). The point here is the power dynamics that excluded Dinka speakers from decision making, reified the inadequate system in *Lek Jot* and other texts and the power unconsciously yielded to the material book and the particular translation and orthography that it conveys. See brief comments in Idris, "Modern Developments," 19.

35. The primary topic of Abdelhay, Makoni, and Makoni, "Colonial Linguistics."

36. One should recognize this title as a translation of the English title of the King James Version, and the reification of *Lek Jot* as related and socially dependent on the reification of the KJV in many English speaking communities.

those who prepare ahead of time are more fluent; those who prepare by marking their own text have a higher level of preparation and so fluency. These readers are unofficially revising the translation of *Lek Jot*, as I describe further below.

Social media and the internet have added other modes to the existing textual and in-person modes, complicating Emmanuel's media culture in at least three ways that may indicate openness to revising both the conception of *Lek Jot* as well as the translation itself. First, Emmanuel services are streamed live on Facebook and watched both live and later by Dinka Bor speakers around the world. Online worshipers are not comparing the reading to a printed copy; like many worshiping in-person, they also likely do not have access to a printed copy and, even if they did with some basic literacy, may not be able to process the orthography quickly enough to follow along. Online worshipers express their affirmation and critique of the services (especially the music) both on Facebook posts as well as through personal texts and phone calls that spread through the network of personal relationships back to worship leaders. As a result, online worshipers are more interested in the quality of the reading and how it "sounds like Scripture," which suggests audience expect that the performance will evoke memories of previous readings, especially those from formative experiences in refugee camps and later worship experiences. Readers, interacting after services with those in-person and online, say they do not want to "look bad on camera" and want to read well. In other words, the fluency of the reader, the style of the reading, and the memories it evokes have greater prominence to many audience members than adherence to the as-written text. Because of live streams, the emphasis for the in-person audience is also shifting to the performance experience as a whole rather than simply the text.

Second, *Lek Jot* is now available as a digital text—a distinct medium from a printed book. The "text" is now separable from the object of the 1959 printed edition which is so readily identifiable, even if a person couldn't fluently read it. Some readers in Emmanuel worship services bring the book up front which carries the subtle memories and cues of an authoritative reading of the New Testament. However, more readers are now printing a page of text to read in front of the congregation. They are able to manipulate the font style and size to be more readable.[37] One reader told me that he is able to achieve better eye contact with the

---

37. On thinking about font style, size, and other aspects of visual design as semiotic resources, see Kress and van Leeuwen, *Reading Images*.

congregation when he prints it larger and doesn't have to interrupt the reading with flipping pages or struggling to read characters blurred by thin paper. As people see a letter-size page brought forward to read, the idea of *Lek Jot* is further separated from the iconic book.

Third, social media creates a durability over distance for the performance event that is similar to a mass-produced written text (identical repeatability), exceeding it even in some ways because it evokes multiple senses and memories of known people and experiences, but without the iconicity of the book. An object like *Lek Jot* achieves iconic status for a community or group of people through repeated and prominent ritual use.[38] As a part of post-Gutenberg print-media culture, the book is available around the world in exactly the same form, bonding Dinka Bor speakers around the common iconic text. Ritual repetition is possible on social media as a person, family, or group may view a particular service over and over anywhere in the world. They too are bonded in a common experience across distance that can receive repeated viewings just as the book can be engaged repeatedly, generating both continuity as well as discontinuity with prior experiences. I suggest, however, that the two-dimensional screen with its sights and sounds that evoke emotions and memories of community and past experiences is becoming the durable icon, not the book. While this allows for a new configuration of the conception of *Lek Jot* and the possibility of modifying the translation, it also signals a problematic future for the larger Dinka Bor community (and likely for many communities), especially younger members who do not have the memories of people and events (such as life in the refugee camps) that evoke emotional impact while watching a video. While the social media recording is repeatable, few actually give it repeat viewings and so it functionally is as ephemeral as an unrecorded worship service. As a result, the community once gathered in-person to hear *Lek Jot* read and interpreted in embodied relationships is displaced by distant individuals (sometime families) interacting with a screen.

Preparing Lek Jot to Read Aloud in Worship

Whether one wants to acknowledge it or not, *Lek Jot* is being revised to various degrees by every reader who must make decisions about how to perform the text. At the most basic level, each reader is interpreting the

---

38. On definition and development of iconicity, see Watts, *Understanding the Bible*, 1–14.

unmarked text to fluently express the vocal quality (breathy or modal), vocal length (one, two, or three vowel lengths), and intonation of each word and phrase. For example, when reading 1 Petero 2:19, the reader encounters the word "ekɔu":

> Kene ee lɔyum enɔŋ Nhialic te ye raan kemɛɛn gum, ke ci tau ne *ekɔu* te cin awac, ne nyiny nyic en Nhialic piɔu.

Like many words in this verse, "ekɔu" would be unintelligible without the breathiness of ɔ, which could be marked with diaresis as ɔ̈. Human beings experiencing any language system need only a moment to automatically discard a nonsense option.[39] But it does take a second for the reader to realize that the translator means "kɔ̈u," referring to a person's back, as in the region of the body where a load is carried. The reader takes a further microsecond to realize that, in context, the prefix *e* is a shortened form of the third person pronoun "ye," referring to the generic person "raan" in the previous clause. Even though only a short time, this can create a halting reading that does not aid a hearer's comprehension or the effects of the text that would be more clear with careful intonation and phrasing.[40]

Another reader, Ayak Chol, prepares his reading ahead of time. He copies the text from the digital version of *Lek Jot* available from youversion.com and adds diaresis to mark breathy vowels. As he marked breathy vowels in 1 Petero 2:19–25, he included a subscripted *y* to make the pronouns "ye" and "yen" more clear (even if the *y*-sound is suppressed) and arranged the text to make phrasing more quickly evident:

Këννë ee lɔyum ënɔŋ Nhialic,	This is pleasant with God
të ye raan këmɛɛn gum,	when one has suffering placed
kë cï täu në ᵧekɔ̈u të cïn awäc,	on his back if there is no mistake

---

39. Understanding error correction is an advantage of Relevance Theory. A hearer naturally enriches an utterance using memory, observations, ideas, and goals to predict the intention of the speaker. If a speaker makes an error in pronunciation, for example, a listener may automatically predict the speaker's intent even without explicitly correcting the utterance. See Wilson and Sperber, "Relevance Theory."

40. See "Peter Achiek Reading Rom 5" for an example of a reader who is disambiguating in real time. He repeats phrases to clarify pronunciation (e.g., initial phrase "Yen na ci wɔ") as well as making what seem to be spontaneous corrections ("wëëk" instead of "wɔ ke" in v. 6) inserting (e.g., "Beny" into v. 9 before "Nhialicic") and replacing words (e.g., "Kritho" instead of "Wende" in v. 10), although these insertions and replacements may reflect liturgical habits rather than clarifying emendations.

| në nyïny nyic ₍ᵥ₎en Nhialic piɔ̈u. | with knowledge known in God's heart. |

Marking breathy vowels, suppressing *y*-sounds, revising misleading vocabulary, and practice lead to a more fluent and fluid reading, and increases the probability of impact on the audience.[41]

Revising Vocabulary Under the Influence of Hymns and Liturgical Hymns

Readers also encounter words that are awkward in their literary context and pause, stumble, or outright change them. For example, the phrase "tim nom" is the translation given ἐπὶ τὸ ξύλον (1 Pet 2:24) and back translates "head of tree," where the "tree" is understood to be "the cross" (as NRSV translates). The trouble is that "tim nom" gives an incongruous image in Dinka of Jesus pierced with the top point of the tree, not crucified to the tree.[42]

As Chol prepared to read, his mind went to Dit 29 (he remembers the songs by their number in the hymnal), a familiar Christmas hymn, *Bäk ketku din ë Bethlekem*, which includes the phrase "Në Tön cï nöök në timkɔ̈u thou" ("Of Him who hung upon a tree"). Another hymn, Dit 66, *Nhialic anɔŋ riɛerdït*, came to mind with the line in v. 4, "Piëëtë guɔ̈p timkɔ̈u" ("body on the tree") "Timkɔ̈u" ("back of tree") summons the more appropriate image of Christ crucified on the side of the tree rather than the top. Chol's first thought were familiar songs; his song-shaped intuition was confirmed by a similar choice in Jɔn 19:31: "ne tiɛm ageer kɔu."[43]

Confirming the choice to change the text to tim kɔ̈u, Chol then remembered the familiar text of An ye Nhialic gam ("I believe in God" = the Apostles' Creed): "Yɔn piɛte yen ne tim kɔu." It is not surprising that readers and hearers would naturally default to known phrasing used often in liturgy and hymns. Revising awkward phrasing toward these

---

41. See Chol's reading of 1 Petero at "Ayak Chol-1 Peter2'19–25."

42. Similar awkwardness is found in Dutuuc (Acts) 5:30; This translation is also used in John 19:19, perhaps more appropriately referring to Pilate's inscription placed at the top of the tree (tiɛm ageer nom), but even this suggests the inscription may face up rather than out.

43. "Tim kɔu" is also used in Mathayo 27:40, 42 (par Mak 15:30, 32); Dutuuc (Acts) 10:39, 13:29; Galatai (Galatians) 3:13; Kolothai (Colossians) 2:14.

known patterns increases the impact and evokes the familiarity, emotions, and communal experience of singing and reciting the liturgy.

Recalling the discussion of ekɔ̈u in the previous section, the phonological connection between ekɔ̈u and kɔ̈u is hopefully obvious and the potential aural impact clear: Christ bears (ekɔ̈u) on his back (kɔ̈u) the cross (tim), as a burden. So, preparing to read aloud, Chol revised 1 Petero 2:24 to include the word choice that is lexically more appropriate as well as resonating with the emotional and communal memories of liturgical use and offering more potential for amplifying the concept "bearing a burden" through repetition of sounds.

Ee kareckuɔ jɔt ë ekɔ̈u në tim kɔ̈u,	He raised our sins and bore (them) on a tree,
buk thou në rëëcda ku buk ya pïir në lajik:	so free from our sins that we live by holiness:
wɔ cï dɛm në yum cennë e yup.	we are healed by his wounds.

Local Translation: An Example of 1 Samuel 16:1–13

Since there is not a complete Dinka translation of the Hebrew Bible, Emmanuel usually hears a reading from the Hebrew Bible each Sunday in English translation.[44] Occasionally, leader Solomon Machar Kuch translates a passage from the English NRSV into Dinka Bor. Kuch's translation choices, whether conscious or unconscious, reflect the expectation of performance before an audience and a particular style of *Lek Jot* and the Dinka liturgy.

First, Kuch's translation uses parataxis, joining sentences together with coordinating conjunctions, a common style of storytellers. In this case, *go* ("then") marks transitions between each event in the story. English translations do not indicate this. In English translations of 1 Sam 16, the *waw*-consecutives that create this effect in Hebrew are not translated, e.g., וַיֹּאמֶר יְהוָה אֶל־שְׁמוּאֵל is translated "The Lord said to Samuel" (NRSV) without acknowledging the *waw*-consecutive. Translators of the Greek Septuagint, however, reflected this storyteller's style (Καὶ εἶπεν κύριος

---

44. The Psalms are translated and included in the hymnal. Other fragments of the Hebrew Bible, typically chapters for common theological topics such Gen 1–2 for "creation," were translated and included in a thin volume *Lek Thëër*, of which I have seen a copy, but no one at Emmanuel now possesses.

πρὸς Σαμουηλ . . .). Parataxis is common in conversation and storytelling as it helps an audience process shifts from one event to another.⁴⁵

Second, parataxis is one among other signs to a knowing audience that the translation adopts a style that "sounds like" *Lek Jot*. For example, it is often noted that Matthew's Gospel in Greek removes parataxis from passages borrowed from Mark.⁴⁶ In the story of John the Baptist, Mark uses καὶ to shift to describe the people coming out to be baptized (Mark 1:5) which Matthew changes to τότε (Matt 3:5). *Lek Jot* uses *go* in both cases. Moreover, *Lek Jot* adds *go* to some of Matthew's narratives that do not use coordinating conjunctions in Greek or in English translations.⁴⁷ In other words, Kuch may have been motivated to transition to each event using *go* both because it "sounds like Scripture" (that is, the familiar experience of hearing *Lek Jot*) as well as a natural storyteller's impulse to help an audience mark and process transitions.

In other choices, Kuch told me he consciously imitated the Dinka liturgy and the translation of Old Testament texts used there, especially in the choice of "Yekoba" ("Jehovah") rather than "Bɛnydit" ("Lord"). The word "Yekoba" is seldom used in *Lek Jot* (e.g., Mark 12:29–30 when quoting Deut 6:4–5); almost everywhere κύριος is translated Bɛnydit.⁴⁸ Most songs also use "Bɛnydit," and "Yekoba" is rare. However, "Yekoba" is used in translations of Hebrew Bible texts, such as Joel 2:13 and Dit (Psalm) 143:2, in the Confession/Absolution liturgy recited every Sunday. "Yekoba" seems to evoke the sound and feeling of the Hebrew Bible as Kuch and the congregation have experienced it.

When Kuch read 1 Thamuel 16:1–13 on March 19, 2023, he told the congregation that it was his own translation.⁴⁹ The congregation made an audible noise that seems to express their surprise that he is reading it in Dinka and that it is his own translation. I interpret this rapid reaction as a sign of their appreciation and respect. However, epistemological humility requires: was that how people received it? What kind of authority does

---

45. Lohr, "Oral Techniques."

46. E.g., Powell, *Introducing the New Testament*, 177.

47. For example, the parable of the talents (Matt 25:14–30) has verses that begin without coordinating conjunctions in Greek (25:16, 21, 23) and *Lek Jot* uses *go* to begin each. For the seventeen verses in Matt 25:14–30, *Lek Jot* uses *go* eight times to begin a verse.

48. E.g., Matt 1:20, 24; 2:13, 15, and so on. Interestingly, in some places Nhialic ("God") is used instead of Bɛnydit, e.g., Matt 1:22.

49. See Kuch's performance of 1 Thamuel at "Solomon Kuch 1 Sam 16'1–13."

Kuch's translation have compared with *Lek Jot*? What questions were raised as they heard the translation? As they discussed it with others, what feedback did they receive?

By re-centering meaning making on the performance event and away from the written text in isolation, BPC prevents us from drawing definitive conclusions based only on scholarly observations (which are naturally biased to overprocessing because of our training) or the performer's self-reflection (which also may be focused on details that audience members overlook). Meaning is not made only in the minds of individual audience members, but also in the network of relationships and conversations that happen after the performance. If we want to know what a reading meant to the congregation, we have to ask!

In my informal conversations with a handful of people after the performance, most people were impressed that Kuch translated the text into Dinka. There was no awareness of issues of authority, only that translation of this passage had not been done before, that a translation in Dinka was better than no translation. They were appreciative, and their respect for Kuch grew. Specific details of the translation (e.g., use of *go* or "Yekoba") were not noticed by most.[50]

Worship leaders who are Dinka literate and generally well educated in biblical traditions could articulate that "Yekoba" sounded more like the Hebrew Bible and Bɛnydit sounded more like the New Testament. One, in fact, thought Yekoba was equivalent to Nhialic ("God") while Bɛnydit was equivalent to Jesus (which would not be accurate to translations of the Hebrew Bible, which would likely use Yekoba for the Tetragrammaton and Bɛnydit for *adonai*). In general, Kuch's translation choices "sounded like" authentic *Lek Thëër* ("Old Testament"), and so consciously or subconsciously was granted that status based on style and performance.

Performance Criticism and Local Translation

This chapter points to ways Biblical Performance Criticism (BPC) reconceptualizes the communication of biblical traditions, offers criteria for analyzing and improving performances in community, and advocates for local community's identity and culture.

---

50. A further question would be to the children, who are English-primary speakers. What did they think of hearing the Old Testament reading in Dinka rather than English? What did it mean to them?

First, local faith communities can adopt and adapt BPC's reconceptualization of the various ways biblical traditions have been communicated.[51] By reconceiving what the "Bible" is, away from a particular physical object to an embodied communication event, faith communities may be empowered themselves to re-translate texts in ways that best invites them into the stories of God's promises and people. Classes, Bible studies, and sermons using the insights from BPC and the many disciplines that feed into it will help people better represent the reality of how the Bible has been transmitted. For most of Christian history, the stories and texts of the Bible were experienced in a community, not a mass-produced object.[52] Accepting such a different conception of the Bible will take a pastoral touch and sensitivity to the ways authority has been located in a particular book, but over time will open deeper and more accurate understanding to how the traditions have been actually transmitted.

Second, BPC offers criteria to think about more effective communication. Because BPC analyzes embodied communication, it invites performers to think about effective volume, pacing, tone, pauses, eye contact, gestures, and movement. Once a person becomes aware of the impact of each of these aspects, there's no going back! If proclamation of the stories of the Bible are central to a community's identity, then how could its leaders not want to be the most effective communicators they can? BPC gives examples in writing and video to think about and try different ways of performing a text and observing one's own reactions to the effectiveness of each version, for example, following the CBS method described by Nathan Esala in this volume, Richard W. Swanson's *Provoking the Gospel*, the many volumes of Michael Williams and Dennis Smith's *Storyteller's Companion to the Bible*, or videos of performances of biblical passages (e.g., by David Rhoads or Phil Ruge-Jones).

Third, by foregrounding the audience, in this case, the gathered community in-person and online, BPC invites a performer to reflect with audience members about what makes an effective translation and

---

51. See the rich example of "contextual translation" in Maxey, *From Orality to Orality*.

52. For similar observations see, for example, Maxey, *From Orality to Orality*, 10–11, who observed among the Vuté in Cameroon, "First, a performer would present his or her story in an animated manner.... The audience responded in laughter, clapping and joining in with the performer's singing.... The next step was the writing down of the story.... This reduction to writing demonstrated the difficulty of expressing all that the performer had said and done. Instead of a multi-dimensional performance, there was a two-dimensional linear series of letters on a blackboard."

performance of it as well as simultaneous attention to the different media and their audiences. Informally, audience members are already discussing a reader's effectiveness; BPC gives examples and structure that could lead to more intentional small and large group discussions.

In a group gathered to discuss the reading of Scripture, readers and hearers engage explicitly in discussion of effects, emotions, and changed attitudes, values, beliefs, or goals. Participants in such groups may be asked to give suggestions for what would be more effective volume, pacing, gestures, and so on. In small or large groups, adults and/or youth may be invited to perform parts of the text themselves.

Fourth, BPC advocates for local identity and culture. Individuals performing passages in groups will provide other ways to learn and practice Dinka apart from literacy. For Emmanuel and many Dinka communities, few can read Dinka but most speak fluently. *Lek Jot* is a challenge to read fluently because of the orthographic challenges described above. However, by hearing and repeating a story or text with feedback from the group until internalized, every Dinka speaker can communicate biblical traditions. Internalization, or "learning it by heart," does not necessarily mean it is recited word-for-word or exactly with the same performance characteristics but that a person can embody the passage in a way that helps makes sense both to them individually and to the group. As the group helps one another internalize the text, they will naturally struggle with its language, cultural presuppositions, and meaning, and they will naturally have a deeper understanding of the text itself.

A concern of Emmanuel and other Dinka communities is teaching the language to children growing up with other primary languages. Most Emmanuel children are learning English as their primary language. BPC provides a conceptual framework and practice that helps parents and the faith community teach not only biblical traditions but also Dinka language and identity. By shifting the focus from the printed book and required technical skills to fluently vocalize it toward the communication event of a performance, children can quickly participate and learn language and stories that build confidence and interest. Over time, a child who learns to tell a story by heart, for example, 1 Thamuel 16, will be more interested in reading it from a printed text and possibly reading it in corporate worship.

Further, advocacy means exhorting BT agencies to engage local communities in re-translation. Communities such as Emmanuel are already re-translating *Lek Jot* every time it is being performed—either informally as a reader disambiguates or formally as a lector prepares a text for reading by correcting and updating it. Some of this work has begun. The Dinka Language Institute began in Egypt in 1995, and in 2000 the Dinka Language Institute of Australia was founded.[53] SIL included literacy programs for Dinka speakers in Khartoum from 1991 to at least 2004,[54] but these efforts have not engaged the Dinka diaspora and were likely disrupted by the Sudanese civil war. Further focus and resources will strengthen these efforts, as I suggest below.

Conclusions

This chapter has demonstrated that Bible translation cannot be conceived as a one-time event, complete when the printed edition is published. Translation is an ongoing, multimodal and social process, the ceaseless activity of communities that are formed around biblical traditions and reuse them in new performance events. Biblical Performance Criticism (BPC) illuminates how a particular translation such as *Lek Jot* is a part of a dynamic series of events, as Dinka Bor communities like Emmanuel around the world perform biblical passages weekly. Each of these communities is re-translating *Lek Jot*, and each reading is a performance event that can be understood and analyzed using BPC.

What will be the role of BT agencies? This author advocates that these organizations allocate resources of leadership, money, and expertise to support the ongoing translation in local communities such as Emmanuel. Three areas seem especially ripe for BT leadership: completing the translation of the Hebrew Bible, revising *Lek Jot*, and facilitating agreement on Dinka orthography.

1. *Lek Thëër*. Emmanuel is not the only Dinka Bor community that is eagerly awaiting a complete translation of *Lek Thëër* (Old Testament). BT agencies have the clout, money, and expertise to bring together Dinka Bor leaders and scholars from around the world to complete this work, which began with the Psalms and some lectionary texts but foundered in disagreement and lack of consensus. The situation has changed because of the civil war that resulted in scattering Dinka Bor people around the world, the creation of South Sudan in 2011, and continued political and tribal conflict

---

53. Idris, "Modern Developments," 23.
54. Idris, "Modern Developments," 22–23.

in South Sudan. Today, the diaspora of South Sudanese Christians around the world are looking for partners to support both the promotion of Christian faith and Dinka Bor identity and culture.

2. *Lek Jot.* As described in this chapter, the lack of marking vowel quality (breathy or modal) and inconsistent marking of vowel length increases the difficulty of fluently and effectively reading *Lek Jot.* Dinka Bor leaders from around the world, facilitated by BT agencies, could revise the translation to be at least more effective in marking vowels.

3. Orthography. Dinka scholars have been working toward a standard orthography that better represents the sound of Dinka phonemes and thus pronunciation of words.[55] BT agencies are well equipped with the resources to assist this task, which will strengthen these communities in their work to promote Dinka culture and identity. It is difficult to teach reading and writing Dinka when there are few resources, and there are few resources in part because there is not agreement about how Dinka words should be written.

Along the way for Bible translation and local faith communities, Biblical Performance Criticism is an aid. BPC is a theoretical framework to understand the task of communicating biblical traditions, analytical categories for describing the dynamics of the performance event, and practical guide for maximizing the transformative power of every performance.

Bibliography

Abdelhay, Ashraf, Busi Makoni, and Sinfree Makoni. "The Colonial Linguistics of Governance in Sudan: The Rejaf Language Conference, 1928." *Journal of African Cultural Studies* 28.3 (2016) 343–58. DOI: 10.1080/13696815.2016.1146129.

"Ayak Chol-1 Peter2'19–25 30Apr2023." Vimeo video. https://vimeo.com/840069263.

Alëu, Alëu Majɔk. "The New Muonyjang (Dinka) Script." https://pioockuthuongjangda.files.wordpress.com/2013/12/the-new-muonyjang-dinka-script.pdf.

Anai, Jok Gai. "Thuongjang Cidmende—A Rebuttal by Jok Gai Anai." Dec. 21, 2016. https://pioockuthuongjangda.files.wordpress.com/2016/12/thuongjang-cidmende-rebuttal-by-jok-gai-anai.pdf.

55. In 2004, Idris wrote, "A very important issue of current interest within the Dinka speech community, in Sudan and in exile, is the establishment of an adequate orthography and the promotion of literacy in the Dinka language for future use in society" ("Modern Developments," 7). Twenty years later, it is unclear what progress has been made.

Bezemer, Jeff. "What Modes Can and Cannot Do: Affordance in Gunther Kress's Theory of Sign Making." *Text and Talk* 44.4 (2023). https://doi.org/10.1515/text-2022-0055.

Deng, Manyang. *Piööc de Akeer ke Thoŋ de Jiëëŋ*. Osborne Park, Western Australia: Africa World Books, 2018.

Gilley, Leoma G. "Morphophonemic Orthographies with Fusional Languages." Paper presented at the Third International Workshop on Writing Systems, University of Cologne, Germany, September 23–24, 2002. https://www.sil.org/resources/publications/entry/7859.

Idris, Hélène Fatima. "Modern Developments in the Dinka Language." PhD diss., University of Göteborg, Sweden, 2004.

James, A. Lloyd. "Practical Orthography of African Languages." *Africa: Journal of the International African Institute* 1.1 (1928) 125–29.

Kress, Gunther R. *Multimodality: A Social Semiotic Approach to Contemporary Communication*. New York: Routledge, 2010.

———. "'Partnerships in Research': Multimodality and Ethnography." *Qualitative Research* 11.3 (2011) 239–60.

Kress, Gunther, and Theo van Leeuwen. *Reading Images: The Grammar of Visual Design*. London: Routledge, 1996.

Ladd, Dwight Robert, Bert Remijsen, and Caguor Adong Manyang. "On the Distinction Between Regular and Irregular Inflectional Morphology: Evidence from Dinka." *Language* 85.3 (2009) 659–70.

Lek Jot de Bɛnydiitda ku Duluɛŋda Yecu Kritho. Khartoum: United Bible Societies, 1959.

Lohr, Charles H. "Oral Techniques in the Gospel of Matthew." *Catholic Biblical Quarterly* 23 (1961) 403–35. http://www.jstor.org/stable/43711060.

Lual, Akoon Kon, and Job Dharuai Malou. *Thuɔŋjäŋ athör tueŋ ë kuɛn*. Maridi, Sudan: Institute of Regional Languages, 1995.

Maxey, James A. *From Orality to Orality: A New Paradigm for Contextual Translation of the Bible*. Biblical Performance Criticism 2. Eugene, OR: Cascade Books, 2009.

Meinhof, Carl. "Principles of Practical Orthography–I." *Africa: Journal of the International African Institute* 1.2 (1928) 228–36.

Nebel, P. Arthur. *Dinka Grammar (Rek-Malual Dialect) with Texts and Vocabulary*. Verona: Istituto Missioni Africane, 1948.

Perry, Peter S. "Biblical Performance Criticism: Survey and Prospects." *Religions* 10.2 (2019) 1–17. https://doi.org/10.3390/rel10020117.

———. "Embodied Cognition and Performance from a Performance Criticism Point of View." Paper presented at the SBL Annual Meeting, San Antonio, Texas, November 19, 2023.

"Peter Achiek Reading Rom 5 12Mar2023." Vimeo video. https://vimeo.com/840069634.

Powell, Mark Allan. *Introducing the New Testament: A Historical, Literary, and Theological Survey*. 2nd ed. Grand Rapids: Baker, 2018.

Remijsen, Bert. "Tonal Alignment Is Contrastive in Falling Contours in Dinka." *Language* 89.2 (2013) 297–327.

"Solomon Kuch 1 Sam 16'1–13 19Mar2023." Vimeo video. https://vimeo.com/840087287.

Tucker, A. N. "The Linguistic Situation in Southern Sudan." *Africa: Journal of the International African Institute* 7.1 (Jan. 1934) 28–39.

Watts, James. *Understanding the Bible as a Scripture in History, Culture, and Religion.* Hoboken, NJ: Wiley, 2021.

West, Gerald O. "Moffat's seTlhaping Translation as Invasion: Re-Translation Resources for Decolonization." *HTS Teologiese Studies/Theological Studies* 79.4 (2023) a8895. https://doi.org/10.4102/hts.v79i4.8895.

Westermann, D., and Ida C. Ward. *Practical Phonetics for Students of African Languages.* Oxford: International Africa Institute, 1933.

Williams, Michael E., and Dennis E Smith. *The Storyteller's Companion to the Bible.* Nashville: Abingdon, 1991.

Wilson, Debra, and Dan Sperber. "Relevance Theory." In *The Handbook of Pragmatics,* edited by L. R. Horn and G. Ward, 607–32. Oxford: Oxford University Press, 2006.

YouVersion. "Lek Jot de Jecu Kritho 1940." https://www.bible.com/versions/1800-lekjot-lek-jot-de-jecu-kritho-1940.

4

Multimodality and Performance
Creole Translation and Identity[1]

MARLON WINEDT

Multimodality: An Introduction

Gunther Kress and Theo van Leeuwen's seminal work, *Reading Images: The Grammar of Visual Design*, laid the foundation for analyzing visual communication from a social semiotic perspective.[2] They argue that visual elements in texts are not merely illustrative or decorative but carry meaning in their own right. The book introduces key concepts such as salience, framing, and modality, which aid in analyzing how visual elements contribute to the overall meaning of a text. They continued to develop the whole area of multimodality as an academic field. Social semiotics suggests that communication and representation involve multiple modes (like speech, gestures, visuals, etc.), each contributing to meaning. It studies how these modes are used in different contexts to convey meaning (semiosis). Moreover, all forms of communication are shaped by cultural, historical, and social factors, affecting how meaning is created in different modes. For example, gestures, voice tone, and eye

---

1. I would like to thank the editor, James Maxey, for his input to this chapter, which has greatly contributed to its improvement.
2. See also Kress, *Multimodality*.

movement all play a role in making meaning. The meanings created by one mode are intertwined with those made by others in a communicative event. Social semiotics also recognizes that these modes are shaped by the communities that use them, becoming more defined, and shifting in meaning over time. Modes use shared resources within a community that help convey meaning, reflecting different aspects of the world, relationships, and structured communication.

Their approach is interdisciplinary, drawing on linguistics, semiotics, communication studies, and education, to explore the multifaceted nature of meaning making. They emphasize the importance of understanding the roles that different modalities play in communication and how these modalities interact. This perspective encourages a more comprehensive understanding of texts and communications, recognizing the complexity of modern media and the diverse ways in which people make meaning. Social semiotics, as developed by Kress and van Leeuwen, is particularly relevant in today's media-rich environment. It provides tools for analyzing not only traditional texts but also digital media, multimodal literacies, and the dynamic landscapes of online communication. Their work also has implications for education, as it highlights the need to teach students not only about language but also about the wide range of semiotic resources they encounter daily. Bible translation has always moved across modalities but at times it has been hard for the church community and the theological community to acknowledge this.

By focusing on the social aspects of semiotics, Kress and van Leeuwen highlight how power, ideology, and culture influence meaning making. They encourage a critical engagement with texts, asking us to consider who is making meanings, for whom, and with what purposes. This critical perspective is invaluable in understanding the complex interplay of text, image, and sound in conveying messages and in shaping our interpretation of the world around us.

Their contributions to social semiotics and multimodality have opened up new avenues for research and practice, making their work essential for anyone interested in the study of communication, culture, and education and in Bible translation as one expression of translation studies.[3] Translation in general has historically been used as part of

---

3. I have expressed the need for a more hermeneutical turn in translation studies where the power relations are shown more clearly and identity can be expressed not only through translation content but through the very materiality of translation, in non-print forms, thus seeing multimodal translation as a seminal philosophical,

oppressive colonial mindsets and so it is natural for translation studies in a cultural turn to be informed by postcolonial studies. The combination of these foci—identity and power—accentuates that the translator can no longer be viewed as a neutral liaison between source and target texts but rather plays the role of a cultural mediator.[4] Indeed the very dominance of print media and writing has been to the detriment of the performance centeredness of communication in different cultures. But this can be said also of the church in the West in general and all of us who are historically part of it. The written form became the center of the Protestant movement. Thus, the word of God for many was equal to a printed book. This dominance is also seen in the specific case of the author's own cultural setting in the Caribbean. The supremacy of print and writing has dominated Caribbean churches to the degree that the format color and language of the assumed authoritative version or versions stifled the use of Creole languages in the church context and beyond.[5] The idealized pastor in some circles became a man of letters instead of a more culturally anchored narrator and performer. In addition, the female voice, often expressed through storytelling, was excluded from this religious expository discourse of Bible proclamation. The fact that Bible translation is an expression of identity does not negate the fact that there is a written source text from which one departs and which provides the terms of reference.[6] The goal of Bible translation is not a platonic idealized translation but a rich, muddled dialogue between source text and the people groups who

---

cultural, and theological concept. See Winedt, "Bible Translation as Incarnation," 220–40.

4. James Maxey is one of the key persons to introduce the world of Bible translation to the art and science of performance criticism at a most opportune time through his dissertation, later published as Maxey, *From Orality to Orality*. His emphasis on the "sensorial nature of translation," "translation as experience," and the fecund notion that translation is a type of performance and performance, in turn, is a type of translation, marked a significant advancement in the field.

5. Winedt, "Impact of the KJV," 185–203.

6. *Text* in this chapter refers to any kind of intended or unintended input, no matter the modality (written, aural, oral, visual, tactile) which can be used to construct meaning in a particular social context. So, there is not just "written text" but there are also oral, visual texts, tactile texts like in, respectively, oral storytelling, braille, Sign Language, or theater performance. The term "source text" is used here without any value judgment or in a historical church theological sense. It refers to the text which is chosen or accepted as the basis to produce the new multimodal text. The translator always needs to assume an "original" (a corresponding text) from which to translate in the act of translation.

identify with the text of translation. This at its core is an expression of an incarnational theology, as an expression of visual and performance culture. Multimodality gives validation to a deeply cultural phenomenon which has consequences for the validation of people groups and their way of appropriating the word of God in their context.[7]

Caribbean Creole Creativity: Non-Written Performance

If we start from the premise of multimodality that all communication is a form of social semiosis, thus having meaning in a social context, then it is necessary to focus on concrete examples of cultural identity in order to show how translation works as multimodality.[8] The example of the performance of the letter of Paul to Philemon from, within, and addressing the context of the post-plantation slave reality is our case in point.

Indeed, the significance of orality in the Caribbean context is rooted in the region's colonial history, where oral traditions served as a means of resistance and identity preservation among enslaved populations and indentured communities. Tula's revolt in 1795 is a seminal event in Curaçao's history, symbolizing the struggle for freedom and dignity against the backdrop of colonial oppression and slavery. Performance criticism as a methodological approach emphasizes the embodied, communal, and dynamic aspects of biblical text interpretation, offering new insights into their meaning and relevance.

The Caribbean region, a tapestry of diverse cultures and histories, has been profoundly shaped by the legacy of orality. This oral tradition, a cornerstone of Caribbean identity, has played a pivotal role in preserving history, shaping cultural norms, and fostering resistance against

7. There awaits quite some work to see how Bible translation can profit from multimodal studies. That is intricately related to a wider issue between the application of multimodality in translation studies. "While translation studies have made incipient, but significant, attempts in recent years to engage with the field of multimodal studies, this interest has not been extensively reciprocal. The re-positioning of translation as a process of cultural mediation that engages with multimodality not as a curious add-on, but as part of its normal operation, will go a long way towards making translation—and translation studies—more relevant to multimodality." Boria, *Translation and Multimodality*, 202.

8. Kress, "Transposing Meaning," 44, states that there is an issue with how to name translation from a semiotic perspective: "The world of meaning and of the making of meaning is in the process of a profound change: a paradigm change from a focus on language to a focus on meaning; a change from a focus on one to many means of making meanings evident; and a shift in disciplines from linguistics to semiotics."

oppression. The significance of orality in the Caribbean cannot be overstated; it is both a historical foundation as well as a living, breathing reality of contemporary society, influencing music, storytelling, and even the way history is remembered and taught.

Historically, orality served as a vital means of communication and preservation of culture among enslaved African populations in the Caribbean. Denied the right to read and write, slaves relied on oral traditions to maintain their heritage, pass down stories from generation to generation, and keep alive the memories of their ancestors. This oral culture became a form of resistance, a way to assert identity and humanity in the face of dehumanizing conditions. Tales of Anansi, the trickster spider from West African folklore, for example, morphed into a symbol of resistance and survival, illustrating the cleverness and resilience of enslaved people.

In addition to preserving history and folklore, orality in the Caribbean has been instrumental in the fight for freedom and dignity. The oral recounting of events like Tula's, the Curaçao slave leader, in 1795 has immortalized these acts of resistance, ensuring they remain a source of inspiration for future generations.[9] These stories, passed down through the oral tradition, serve as reminders of the enduring struggle against colonial oppression and the resilience of the Caribbean people. Additionally, the Haitian Revolution (1791–1804), led by enslaved Africans in the French colony of Saint-Domingue, stands as one of the most successful slave rebellions in history.[10]

The role of orality extends beyond historical preservation and resistance; it is also deeply embedded in the Caribbean's artistic expressions. Calypso music, reggae, traditional creole chants, and spoken word poetry, for example, are all rooted in the oral tradition. These genres not only entertain but also communicate social commentary, critique political systems, and tell the stories of the people. The oral nature of these art forms allows for immediate engagement with the audience, creating a dynamic space for interaction, reflection, and communal solidarity.

Orality and embodied performance also play a critical role in the education system and in the way knowledge is transmitted in the Caribbean. In many communities, oral storytelling remains a primary method of teaching history, morals, and life lessons to the younger generation. This method of teaching emphasizes the importance of listening,

---

9. Curaçao History, "Tula, Curaçao's National Hero."
10. James, *Black Jacobins*.

remembering, and passing on knowledge, thus ensuring the continuity of cultural traditions and values.

Furthermore, the Caribbean's oral tradition has influenced the structure and rhythm of the region's languages and dialects. Creole languages, which blend elements from African, European, and indigenous languages, are a testament to the hybrid nature of Caribbean culture, born from a history of colonization and cultural exchange. The oral nature of these languages, with their rich proverbs and sayings, reflects the vibrant, dynamic nature of Caribbean culture.

Créolité as Identity and Ideology

Both in the literary field as well as in the theological and the philosophical field there has been this growing notion of the concept of the Caribbean as a bricolage, a positive creative mix, called créolité by different authors. Thus, orality, embodiment, in the Caribbean, serves as a powerful tool for cultural preservation, resistance, and education. It is a testament to the resilience of the Caribbean people, allowing them to navigate the complexities of their history while forging a distinct identity. The oral tradition continues to influence all aspects of Caribbean life, from music and art to language and storytelling, ensuring that the voices of the past resonate in the present and guide future generations. Orality is mixed with performance, visual arts, the use of vivid colors to paint buildings, and the kinetics of the body to accentuate and express the vibrant cultural life of the region, throughout its history. From that perspective multimodality is not just analytical but existential and an expression of identity.

Orality and embodiment in the Caribbean are essential tools for cultural preservation, resistance, and education, reflecting the resilience of its people. Influencing all aspects of life, from music to storytelling, orality intertwines with performance and visual arts, preserving a dynamic cultural identity. Édouard Glissant, a Martinican thinker, significantly shaped the concept of créolité, emphasizing the Caribbean's hybrid identity over the Négritude movement's focus on pan-Africanism.[11] Glissant argued that Caribbean identity is composite, shaped by African, European, Indigenous, and Asian influences, celebrating diversity and challenging European norms. His vision of Caribbean unity through créolité profoundly impacted literature and cultural studies. To Glissant,

11. For an insightful article on Glissant's thought see Wiedorn, "On the Unfolding of Édouard Glissant's Archipelagic Thought."

interconnectedness became the basis for a philosophy of the world where *Tout-Monde* becomes creolized.[12]

As a Bible translator and one who accompanies translation teams across the Americas and Caribbean region in their métier and calling, my argument is that the link between text and identity in Bible translation is a necessary link because of the embodiment of any type of translation. Even the Gutenberg paradigm of printing is an expression of a particular period and culture in Europe where writing itself is its own social semiotic expressions. Moreover, historical translations like the King James Version, the Reina Valera, Segond, Almeida, etc. are all expressions of cultural linguistic and ecclesiastic identities in a sense. Multimodality in Bible translation will and should lead to an indigenous theology.[13] The voices of the thousands of cultures and languages need to be heard. The question is not only "What does God say to the nations?" but "What does God say to the church through the multiple voices of the global South?" An interesting multimodal project which attempts to canalize these voices in Bible translations is the internet platform TIPs (Translation Insights and Perspectives) where one can find a number of translation issues and the proposed solutions by translators in a number of languages, including from Sign Language and insights from illustrations and images of the Bible.[14]

---

12. Glissant deliberately uses *Tout-Monde*, the creolized French of his native island, instead of the Continental French *tout le monde*. Interestingly, his notion of "rhizomatic" interconnectedness mirrors the multimodal approach, as an epistemological, hermeneutical, and fertile fusion of modalities. Thus, *Tout-Monde* refers to the interconnectedness of all cultures, emphasizing global diversity, mutual influence, and constant cultural interaction, where no single worldview dominates, fostering rich global relations and dynamic identity formation. See Glissant, *Traité du Tout-Monde*. See also Nesbitt, *Caribbean Critique*.

13. The perspective of Kwame Bediako on the link between translation and theology as the cradle for the development of localized theology within the African context is universally applicable. Bediako, "Africa and Christianity."

14. The website is maintained by Jos Zetsche. The author is part of a multiagency advisory board. https://tips.translation.bible/. (From the website: "The Translation Insights & Perspectives [TIPs] tool collects these outstanding translation insights so they can be made available to everyone in the church as well as researchers and other interested parties.")

Examples of Performance Hermeneutics and Semiosis: Philemon

We have Philemon as an expression of identity in our own mother tongue Papiamentu[15] with English translation to underscore the importance of language in shaping identity and cultural memory, particularly in post-colonial contexts where language has been a place of resistance and affirmation. Over the course of time we developed a more nuanced understanding of biblical performance and its impact on audience interpretation, particularly within the context of Caribbean theological perspectives and cultural dynamics.[16] U-Wen Low reflects in an article on the English performance of Philemon in Denver 2022, which is very helpful in elucidating the technique and impact on at least part of the audience.

> At the SBL Annual Meeting in November 2022, participants in the Performance Criticism of Biblical and Other Ancient Texts (PC-BOAT) seminar experienced a performance of Philemon by Marlon Winedt, a Black Caribbean scholar (Winedt 2022). Winedt's performance was a simple one: in front of a group of scholars in a conference setting, he stepped in front of the assembled audience and delivered the epistle with occasional consultation of notes, without props or any other scene-setting. Winedt did not simply recite the text, but decided to fully embody Paul's oration, which he had translated himself. He pointed to audience members as Paul named members of the congregation, including them in the performance; he pitched his voice and used facial expressions to indicate irony and sarcasm. He used his own body to illustrate the text, most notably in verse 12 (which Winedt chose to translate as "as if I am ripping out my own insides to send back to you!"). Performing in front of a scholarly audience, Winedt's performance was able to draw out certain aspects of the text: firstly, humor, which Paul (via Winedt) uses to draw in and disarm his wider audience. Secondly, the sense of social responsibility which Paul leverages to coerce Philemon was highlighted as Winedt pointed to members of the audience and made them participants in the oration,

---

15. Creole Portuguese language relexified by Spanish and Dutch, spoken on the islands of Aruba, Bonaire, Curaçao, in the Southern Caribbean, of the coast of Venezuela.

16. Winedt, "Translation as Performance and Engagement." A recording of this performance can be found at Winedt, "Webcam Video."

including Paul's witnesses to the epistle in verses 23 and 24. Thirdly, Winedt chose to highlight Paul's sense of emotion and passion regarding Onesimus, raising his voice and gesticulating at appropriate points. Finally, Winedt's own social location as a Black Caribbean performing an epistle addressing slavery added a significant dimension to the text which I will go on to discuss.[17]

U-Wen Low's article furthermore explores the transition of interpretive responsibility from audience to performer through the embodiment of biblical characters. This process challenges traditional cognitive constructions of these characters by introducing variations in gender, ethnicity, tone, and action. Such performer embodiment can create dissonance for audiences, prompting them to confront their own assumptions about biblical texts. This shift emphasizes the role of performance in facilitating a shared, temporal experience of narrative engagement, where the performer's interpretation opens new avenues for understanding and interacting with biblical stories.

Both Low and I underscore the interpretative power of performance. If one compares the performance of the same text by David Rhoads[18] in English or by Cliff Barbarick[19] in Greek, one can immediately see how embodiment influences the message reception. I focused on engaging Caribbean audiences by contextualizing biblical narratives within their cultural and linguistic landscape. Low emphasizes the performer's role in shaping audience perceptions and challenging existing interpretations through embodiment. The integration of cultural nuances, particularly from the Caribbean perspective, highlights the importance of context in biblical performance. Thus, he states that my translation and performance of Philemon in a Caribbean Creole language not only make the text accessible but also resonate with the audience's cultural identity, thereby deepening their connection to the narrative. The cognitive dissonance experienced by audiences in response to performer embodiment

---

17. Low, "Who Tells the Story," §5.1.

18. In a 2008 article Rhoads explains the importance of oral tradition in early Christianity, emphasizing that New Testament letters, particularly Paul's Letter to Philemon, were originally intended for performance rather than mere reading. He highlights the cultural and rhetorical elements essential to understanding these letters as dynamic stories embedded within the early Christian community. Rhoads, "Performing the Letter to Philemon." See also Halcomb, "David Rhoads Performing Philemon."

19. Barbarick, "Philemon."

aligns with my goal of eliciting a hermeneutical appropriation of biblical texts. The approach seeks to challenge audiences, encouraging them to re-evaluate their understanding of biblical narratives within their contemporary and cultural context. Thus, we can see how the performance of Philemon serves to highlight the potential for biblical performance as an educational tool. By leveraging the dynamics of performance, educators can foster an environment that encourages critical thinking, cultural engagement, and a deeper exploration of biblical texts.

The performance of Philemon in Papiamentu has shown the author that there is a complex interplay between biblical performance, cultural identity, and audience engagement. It underscores the transformative potential of performance in interpreting biblical texts, offering a compelling approach to engaging contemporary audiences with ancient narratives. This synthesis not only contributes to the field of biblical studies but also offers practical implications for theological education, pastoral ministry, and intercultural communication within diverse communities. I did not realize how impactful my physical (racial) appearance as embodied identity could be until I read Low's description:

> In Winedt's performance,[20] we are presented with a dark-skinned Paul who is passionate, resourceful, and who is willing to use his social capital to achieve results for some measure of justice. This may confront an audience whose previous mental model of Paul may have been a white authoritarian leader, who was happy to be complicit in the ongoing oppression of Onesimus. Some interpreters may never have seen Paul in the way Winedt presented him, and may not have possessed the right frames to envision him thusly. Winedt's embodiment of the character therefore provides them with a new reference point, or data, which needs to be incorporated into or rejected by their existing mental models of the character.[21]

The aspect of embodiment and the accompanying dissonance it might cause is not necessarily willed or planned by the performer who can only embody what he or she embodies. In other words, except for when one deliberately uses certain types of clothing, masks, or makeup, the reality of one's own body can communicate a message beyond the intention of the performer. In this case, the performer likes the fact that an ethnocentric view of Paul might be a challenge just by the performer being who

---

20. Winedt, "Performing Philemon."
21. Low, "Who Tells the Story," §5.1.2.

he is. But the very fact that to the outsider (outside of the performer's ethnic group) the performer is perceived as kind of a "challenging Paul figure" shows how performance unveils biases, and not necessarily negative ones.

First my performances in Papiamentu used to focus on providing a concrete example that showcases the letter's emancipatory character through my interpretation and framing of Paul's request to Philemon regarding Onesimus. In my translation and performance of this letter into Papiamentu, I highlight the subtle yet powerful plea for Onesimus's freedom, transforming the letter into a call for emancipation within a modern Caribbean context.

Paul's letter to Philemon, on the surface, requests the forgiveness and welcoming back of Onesimus, a runaway slave, not merely as a slave but as a *beloved brother* (οὐκέτι ὡς δοῦλον ἀλλ' ὑπὲρ δοῦλον, ἀδελφὸν ἀγαπητόν, μάλιστα ἐμοί, πόσῳ δὲ μᾶλλον σοὶ καὶ ἐν σαρκὶ καὶ ἐν κυρίῳ. Phlm 1:16). My interpretation goes further, suggesting that Paul's language and the framing of his request carry an implicit condemnation of slavery. This is particularly evident in one of my performances, where the plea for Onesimus's return is juxtaposed with the provocation from the character of Tula, the Curaçaoan revolutionary leader who led a revolt against slavery in 1795.

Tula challenges Philemon (and by extension, the audience) to reconsider the status quo of slavery, suggesting that Paul's diplomatic and seemingly subtle letter contains within it a revolutionary call to view Onesimus not merely as property but as a fully human subject deserving of freedom and dignity. This interpretative layer underscores the letter's potential to provoke critical reflection on issues of freedom, dignity, and the inherent worth of every individual, resonating deeply with themes of liberation and emancipation that are particularly poignant within the Caribbean historical and cultural context.[22]

By framing the letter of Philemon not just as a personal appeal but as a broader call to reconsider the nature of human relationships under the shadow of slavery, my performance elucidates the emancipatory potential of this biblical text. This approach invites the audience to engage with the text not only intellectually but also emotionally and ethically, challenging them to contemplate the implications of Paul's words in their own lives and societies.

---

22. Winedt, "Webcam Video."

But in the other performance, described by Low above, I went back to research the wordplay on Onesimus and made its possible sexual reification of the slave body a deliberate theme in my performance.[23] A key aspect of the Philemon text is where Paul has a play on words on the name Onesimus as being *useful*. The same passage can be performed and thus multimodally translated with different emphases as can be seen in another performance done during a presentation at the SBL conference in 2022.[24] Through the lens of performance criticism and rhetorical analysis, I suggest a diplomatic but subversive handling of the issues surrounding slavery and personal relationships within the early Christian communities by Paul. I emphasize the importance of reconstructing ancient orality and performance as a means to deeply engage with and understand biblical texts. I advocate for a "four-dimensional" analysis that integrates performance to shed light on the text's nuanced meanings. I am referring to an approach that enriches our understanding of the text by incorporating the dimensions of performance criticism, historical context, rhetorical analysis, and translation choices.

So, by employing a "multidimensional" approach, I aim to create a more vivid and comprehensive recreation of the text's analysis through the lens of orality and performance. This involves considering not just the written word but how these words would have been communicated

---

23. Marchal, "Usefulness of an Onesimus." I do not agree with Marchal that Paul was an accomplice of Philemon in the use of the slave's body for sexual pleasure. Paul is exactly condemning Philemon for any possible abuse in the past and maybe just generally referring to the notion that the sexual use (χρῆσις) of slaves in antiquity was a despicable thing. He is employing a sarcastic echo here of the practice which performance can bring out better than writing. Otherwise, Marchal does a good job in showing the evidence for the use of "usefulness" in a sexual sense in ancient times. See also Valentine, *For You Were Bought*, who examines how ancient Greek and Latin views on self-control influence Paul's teachings on celibacy, marriage, and slavery in 1 Cor 7:21–24. She argues that Paul advocated for slave freedom to help them live purer Christian lives, supported by evidence from historical discourses and Corinthian culture.

For an alternative interpretation of Phlm 11 (his characterization of the enslaved Onesimus as ἄχρηστος or εὔχρηστος), see Glancy, "Utility of an Apostle," 72–86. The author explains that recent scholarship on Paul's letter to Philemon delves into Paul's use of the terms ἄχρηστος (useless) and εὔχρηστος (useful) to describe the enslaved Onesimus, focusing on their idiomatic meanings and connections to Stoic philosophy. The author suggests that Paul prompts Philemon to view Onesimus, previously considered expendable, as beneficial, underlining the concept of mutual utility and Onesimus's own agency in leveraging Paul's assistance to better his precarious situation.

24. Winedt, "Performing Philemon: Rhetoric."

orally, the physical and social contexts in which they were performed, and the rhetorical strategies employed by the author. For example, in my presentation, I delve into how performance criticism helps us understand the rhetorical devices used by Paul in his letter to Philemon, particularly in terms of its delivery and reception among its original audience. I explore the historical context of Greco-Roman slavery to provide background on the social and economic underpinnings of the relationships between Paul, Philemon, and Onesimus. Furthermore, I analyze the rhetorical performance within the text, considering how Paul employs various rhetorical techniques to subtly critique the institution of slavery and advocate for Onesimus's new status not merely as a slave but as a beloved brother in Christ. Again, this "four dimensional" perspective is not simply an academic exercise; it serves as a tool to hermeneutically engage with the text, offering a richer, more nuanced understanding of its implications and the transformative power of its message. By considering these three dimensions together, I can enter into the text as an exegete, uncovering layers of meaning that might remain obscured through a more conventional, one-dimensional analysis. This methodology is crucial for deeply engaging with and interpreting biblical texts, allowing us to reconstruct ancient orality and performance practices to better grasp the nuanced communications of the past. And most importantly, to help provide a sound and relevant hermeneutical appropriation. *What does the text say to me now? In other words, who is my Onesimus?*[25]

My argument is that the rhetoric of the letter suggests a complex stance on slavery, exploring various interpretations of Onesimus's situation, including views of him as a fugitive, a brother to Philemon, or part of a patronage system. The characteristics of slavery in the Greco-Roman world, highlighting its non-racial, social fluidity, and the multifaceted dynamics of slave ownership and manumission are discussed. And then we proceed to show how the letter applies some variation of the Aristotelian rhetorical analysis (deliberative, forensic, and epideictic rhetoric), concluding that Paul employs a sophisticated use of rhetoric, characterized by irony and subversion. The debate over Onesimus's *usefulness* connected to a broader discussion on the sexual abuse of slaves in ancient times.

---

25. As part of the one hundred and seventy-fifth anniversary of the abolition of slavery in the Kingdom of the Netherlands, I contributed to a special booklet on the history of slavery by the Dutch Bible Society, accompanied by podcasts led by Prof. Dr. Matthijs de Jong. See Nederlands-Vlaams Bijbelgenootschap, "Called to Be Free." A follow-up article was published (Winedt, "Wie is mijn Onesimus?").

Straightforward, unsophisticated, interpretations of Paul's comments on Onesimus's usefulness have to be challenged. Paul is most probably using irony to critique the institution of slavery. Understanding the letter to Philemon through performance and with attention to its rhetorical complexity reveals a cryptic yet significant critique of slavery. My argument is that Paul's letter, far from being an accommodation to the institution of slavery, seeks to incite real change in the early Christian identity as it relates to personal relationships.

Another Example of Performance Hermeneutics and Identity: Sign Language

In Sign Language Bible translation, we encounter a different modality where it is easy to see how embodiment plays a role.[26] It is not an "isolated" embodiment but an interaction between environment, interlocutor, and the signer. A reference to writing is present even in fingerspelling. The literature on Deaf culture and Sign Language is vast. The importance of visual communication through illustrations and other material alongside Sign Language itself is intrinsic to this multimodal form of communication. By the way, visual thinking and pedagogy are not only good for the Deaf but for different groups of people and for the majority hearing majority world.[27]

Embodiment is central in Sign Language translation; translators do not simply convey words but embody the message, bringing the text to life in visually dynamic form. This involves a profound understanding of the source text and a creative engagement with the target language and culture to ensure that the translation resonates with the deaf community on a deeply personal level. Sign Language shows par excellence why Bible translation cannot only be about the linguistics of the spoken language but in order to be inclusive needs to look at social semiotics resources, which express meaning across communication modes.[28] If we look at the

---

26. We will only touch on the identity aspect of the Sign Language translation. This volume contains an excellent essay on the topic: Trujillo, "Performance in Sign Language Bible Translation," where the link between Sign Language and performance is explained with different examples.

27. Visual thinking strategies for both adults and children are just another proof that any reality is multimodal. See Nolan, "Visual Thinking Strategies."

28. Social semiotic theory, influenced by Michael Halliday, views meaning as arising from social actions and interactions, particularly communication. It highlights three social functions of language: ideational (dealing with states of affairs),

translation of Philemon by the Mexican Sign Language translation team, we can see on the website that there is an introduction first to the text, an explanation of the choices made for the name, and then the video of the text.[29] This is now a Mexican Deaf person who is embodying the text of Philemon. Illustrations play an important role in this form of communication. The Paul that we see here is a Paul who moves from one emotion to the other. The important aspect for us to take in is that for a Deaf community, representation and identity is not just a matter of the signer being deaf (and not a hearing person who can sign), but sociolinguistic matters as gender, age, language variation also play an important role. In a visit with the Peruvian Sign Language teams to Iquitos, a city in the Amazon region, it was clear that the team had to overcome linguistic variation differences and kinetic performance issues which expressed rural identity and not just difference in signing between the urban team and that rural audience.

The challenge of embodiment in Sign Language translation was palpable during COVID when the main translator for a project let his hair grow long. When they were going to finalize the final draft video of the translation, this became an issue, because more conservative groups would not accept the Bible being shared in translation by a long-haired male translator. The solution? The translator had to cut his hair! The uniqueness of Deaf identity lies exactly in the combination of sociolinguistic markers like in the case of the hearing (geographical, racial, or physical characteristics) with the distinctive of belonging to a Deaf world and culture.[30]

Indeed, the visibility of the translator in Sign Language translation, which contrasts with the relative invisibility of translators in spoken or written languages, can impact the translation's credibility and acceptance within the Deaf community. This visibility is influenced not just by the translator's execution of Sign Language but also by performance elements, which are crucial for making the text comprehensible, especially for

---

interpersonal (social relationships), and textual (relations within the text). By expanding Halliday's theory to include all semiotic resources, this framework supports a multimodal approach to meaning-making. Kress, "Transposing Meaning," 28.

29. Biblia LSM, "Filemón."

30. Some Bible translation projects use film animations instead of human signers and there is a question of how AI technology can be leveraged in this case. Truth be told that understandably many a Deaf community and church do not welcome the use of "non-human" signers.

those Deaf community members who are still acquiring Sign Language competency due to language deprivation. Moreover, issues of Caribbean or Creole identity can influence Sign Language translation, with cultural variations in expression and gesture reflecting broader identities, similar to the hearing population. The advancement of multimodality, grounded in a social semiotic approach, affirms the humanity and dignity of the Deaf, validating their communicative strategies and resources as equally expressive of human experience.

Ultimately, the performance of identity significantly affects both the translation process and its outcomes. It encourages the wider community to enter into a deeper exploration of Deaf hermeneutics to enrich and transform the dominant hearing world's engagement with God, Scripture, and biblical information. In the case of Sign Language translation there is also the need for linking the text to the reality of the Deaf community so that the text in its multimodal form truly expresses Deaf identity, instead of being a social semiotic artifact to please the hearing world. Because of the visual language that is used, both in the paratextual material, like vocabulary, introductions, illustrations, the path toward appropriation of the text will be clear and smooth. Moreover, the embodiment of the text in Sign Language has all the potential to cause a Deaf hermeneutics and theology which is not sectarian and will also enrich the hearing community. A new milestone in multimodal translation has been reached as new multimedia translations employ actual biblical characters who use Sign Language in films.[31] This will certainly lead to more theology that arises from their own Deaf reality.

Multimodality as Social Semiotics Discourse

Human communication and certainly translation as embodiment is such a complex subject that there are many valid ways of approaching these topics. No theory has a monopoly on the truth as it tries to describe a very complex phenomenon. The social semiotic theory of van Leeuwen and Kress has the benefit of going back every time to the social context of communication. This method is characterized by an interdisciplinary

---

31. The Deaf Missions Film produced the Gospel of Luke with all the characters using American Sign Language. Iconic Events Now, "JESUS: A Deaf Missions Film." The production team and actors are all Deaf. There are plans to facilitate translations in other Sign Languages. The implications for more profound hermeneutics of the text are huge.

approach, integration of insights from linguistics, sociology, and semiotics, among others, to understand the social functions of language and multimodal communication. Their focus on the material and social aspects of discourse shows a preference for approaches that emphasize social context and power relations over cognitive theories that primarily focus on mental processes and structures. Van Leeuwen's work often explores how language and other semiotic resources are used to construct social identities and power dynamics, indicating a broader interest in the societal implications of discourse rather than individual cognitive processes alone. An approach that from the outset looks at the social setting of every communication event and explores it in terms of multimodality will be more fecund for translation work with hearing and Sign Languages, trans-mediatization (changing the medium of a text), live performance, etc. It is better suited to offer the most relevant tools and insights for the translator, who is not translating in a vacuum, but approximating the text in another modality and for another audience than the original one. The different videos of performances referred to in this chapter have shown us how the performance of Philemon helps to engage the message of the text and its wider implicatures.[32]

Semiotic Resources

Van Leeuwen discusses how semiotic resources are the tools and materials used for communication and meaning making in various contexts. In relation to the performance of Philemon, semiotic resources could include the use of Sign Language, gestures, facial expressions, and body language to convey the narrative and emotions of the characters, particularly reflecting the deep, underlying themes of forgiveness, brotherhood, and social change inherent in the text. For instance, the translator's choice of gestures to represent Paul's plea to Philemon embodies the semiotic resources utilized to bridge the communicative gap between the ancient text and contemporary audiences. Are the gestures soft, rude, effeminate,

---

32. An implicature is thus a piece of information that is suggested or implied by an utterance, rather than being directly stated. It relies on the hearer's ability to infer the speaker's intentions based on the context and the content of the communication. Relevance Theory argues that human cognition is geared toward maximizing relevance through these inferential processes, and that communication is successful when the hearer can infer the speaker's intended meaning with minimal effort and maximum relevance. Sperber and Wilson, *Relevance*; Gutt, *Translation and Relevance*.

manly, irregular, smooth, sparse, abundant, overly dramatized? This all influences the overall meaning and subsequent reception of the text.[33]

Semiotic Change

This aspect explores how meanings and uses of semiotic resources evolve over time. In the context of Philemon's performance, semiotic change can be observed in how modern interpretations and performances adapt and reinterpret the biblical passage to resonate with current societal values and understandings. An example would be how modern performances of Philemon might emphasize themes of equality and justice more strongly, reflecting contemporary social sensibilities, as opposed to historical interpretations that might have overlooked these aspects.[34]

Semiotic Rules

Van Leeuwen examines the rules that govern the use of semiotic resources in different cultural and social contexts. When performing Philemon, the semiotic rules would involve the culturally specific norms and expectations around storytelling and religious discourse within, for example, the Deaf community. Performing Philemon in an academic setting of a conference is different from performing the same text on the street. So, the use of space and signing style in the performance may adhere to the semiotic rules that facilitate clear communication and emotional engagement within the context of Deaf culture and Sign Language aesthetics.[35]

Semiotic Functions

This refers to the roles that semiotic practices play in social and cultural contexts, such as identity formation, social interaction, and power relations. The performance of Philemon through Sign Language not only conveys a biblical story but also functions to affirm the identity and cultural values of the Deaf community. What is the function of Paul's age in the community? Is it a community that respects its elders or is old age seen as a weakness? By choosing certain semiotic practices (like specific

33. Van Leeuwen, *Introducing Social Semiotics*; Kress, *Multimodality*.
34. Kress and van Leeuwen, *Meaning-Making and Transformative Engagement*.
35. Kress and van Leeuwen, *Reading Images*.

signing styles or the inclusion of cultural references), the performance can reinforce the community's shared values and experiences, as well as challenge dominant narratives about disability and communication.[36]

Discourse

Discourse in social semiotics relates to the ways in which texts and communications practices structure knowledge and social relationships. The performance of Philemon engages in a religious discourse that transcends mere storytelling, serving as a dialogue between the ancient text and contemporary moral and ethical questions. This could involve framing Paul's message in a way that sparks discussions on modern issues of justice, redemption, and interpersonal relationships within the audience's cultural context.

Genre

Van Leeuwen's concept of genre refers to the categorization of semiotic practices according to their social purposes and patterns. In performing Philemon, the genre might blend biblical narrative with dramatic monologue or dialogue, adopting conventions from both religious recitation and theatrical performance to engage the audience effectively and convey the scriptural message in an accessible, impactful manner. Can the text be used to oppose injustice? How can it be translated to achieve that goal? Is it valid for a translation to have a different genre than the corresponding source text?[37]

Style

Style pertains to the distinctive ways in which semiotic resources are used, often reflecting individual or group identity. The stylistic choices made in the performance of Philemon—such as the intensity of expressions, the pacing of the narrative, and the incorporation of cultural gestures—can reflect the unique identity of the performer or the cultural background of the audience, personalizing the biblical story and enhancing its relevance.

---

36. Kress and van Leeuwen, *Reading Images*.
37. Bateman, *Multimodality and Genre*.

Modality

Modality in social semiotics deals with the reality conveyed by semiotic practices. In the context of Philemon's performance, modality would concern how the authenticity, credibility, and believability of the biblical characters and their experiences are represented through Sign Language and performance. Effective use of modality would ensure that the spiritual and moral lessons of Philemon are communicated in a manner that feels genuine and relatable to the audience.

Conclusion: Suggestions for Translation Praxis and Future Research

Ultimately, the Bible translation community must begin to apply the more detailed aspects of social semiotic theory in order to develop more specific discourse maps for each modality or rather to apply what social semioticians have already developed. We must be careful not to hop onto another bandwagon that turns into a catchphrase. Performance of biblical text visually, bodily, and in multimedia is nothing else but translation, albeit in a non-traditional fashion. Of course, each modality has its own genius and has its own affordances.[38] Multimodality does not mean that we don't admit that there is social embedding for different kinds of translation outcomes and that there is an expected genre for Bible translation. The socio-semiotic approach, pioneered by van Leeuwen and Kress, has yielded extensive material on the discourse of various modalities, including colors, sound, and the use of illustrations. They delve into the relevant strategies in depth. If translators from all backgrounds were to start with accessible information about multimodality and an understanding of the meaning-making strategies within their contexts, it could significantly advance Bible translation. This approach would prevent the traditional focus on an idealized monomodality, like in the case of the Gutenberg print paradigm. At least one would strive to be as multimodal as possible, not merely because it's currently in vogue. Going multimodal has significant practical and organizational implications for Bible translation,

---

38. Affordances are thus seen as relational—they do not exist in isolation but depend on the capabilities of the individual and the characteristics of the object or environment. We are using it here to indicate what is written, aural, visual, and tactile do each have their own limitations and possibilities as to how or what they can communicate. See Gibson, "Theory of Affordances."

including the need for more interdisciplinary teams, increased oral and visual exegetical support, and bringing technical multimedia strategies closer to translators in the field. As previously mentioned, multimodality reveals power dynamics and shows that Bible translation is not neutral. Rather than a threat, we embrace it as a powerful tool for consciously expressing cultural and social identity through translation.

Suggestions for future research include:

a) A significant need for more research on Sign Language translation.

b) A demand for translation approaches tailored to individuals whose social and cognitive processes differ from the majority.

c) A necessity for Scriptures that resonate with the younger generation in language that not only facilitates understanding, but also rhetorically invites them into their own hermeneutics.

d) An imperative to integrate more visual materials, not merely as supplements but as vital components of the organic communication of translated texts.

e) An imperative to bring to the table different hermeneutical lenses, different perspectives to bear on translation issues. The relevance of the text for the audience can be enhanced by use of multimodal strategies.

f) A need for a more thorough and systematic implementation of voice discourse analysis to Bible recordings or Oral Bible Translation. For example, how do pitch, volume, dialectical differences influence text interpretation?

g) The need for a more interdisciplinary approach[39] and for use of multimodal thinking in translators' training.

The same questions and issues surrounding identity and multimodal translation in the Creole language setting arise, *mutatis mutandis*, for any regional, ethnic, or language group across the globe. Ultimately, it has never been about only one mode of communication, because the human being as *imago Dei* is so complex. Bible translation in all its forms and manifestations is always linked to sociocultural identity. We need to

---

39. "Translation studies' gradual move away from monomodal perspectives increases the need for more genuinely interdisciplinary interactions." Carreres and Noriega-Sánchez, "Beyond Words," 201. This is by implication also true of Sacred Text translation.

continue to explore the implications of how translation as performance and performance as translation is an expression of the validation of all identities as part of Édouard Glissant's *Tout-Monde*. Indeed, Bible translation emerges from a specific social and semiotic context, where its primary aim should be to liberate and humanize. On the one hand, it shows our unique identity as people groups, while on the other hand uncovering the sameness which we share. It serves as a sign pointing toward the One who is both the origin and culmination of the profound process of meaning-making that defines humans. As members of a community, we are *homo significans—"the human who signifies"* or *"the meaning-making human"*—in the truest sense of the word.[40] To express it theologically: Is our Bible translation mission incarnational enough? And can it be truly incarnational without expressing community identity through multimodality?

Bibliography

Barbarick, Cliff. "Philemon." YouTube video, Feb. 19, 2019. https://www.youtube.com/watch?v=RIorVXDVP-4.
Bateman, John A. *Multimodality and Genre: A Foundation for the Systematic Analysis of Multimodal Documents.* London: Palgrave Macmillan, 2008. https://doi.org/10.1057/9780230582323.
Bediako, Kwame. "Africa and Christianity on the Threshold of the Third Millennium: The Religious Dimension." *African Affairs* 99 (2000) 303–23.
———. "African Christian Theology." In *New Dictionary of Theology*, edited by Sinclair Ferguson and David Wright, 8–10. Leicester, UK: InterVarsity, 1988.
Biblia LSM. "Filemón." https://biblialsm.com/filemon-1-25-apodo.html.
Boria, Monica, et al., eds. *Translation and Multimodality: Beyond Words.* London: Taylor & Francis, 2020.
Carreres, Ángeles, and Maria Noriega-Sánchez. "Beyond Words." In *Translation and Multimodality: Beyond Words*, edited by Monica Boria et al., 198–201. London: Taylor & Francis, 2020.
Curaçao History. "Tula, Curaçao's National Hero." n.d. https://www.curacaohistory.com/detail/1795-tula.
Gibson, J. J. "The Theory of Affordances." In *The Ecological Approach to Visual Perception*, 119–37. Boston: Houghton Mifflin, 1979.

---

40. Lukianova and Fell, "Meaning Making in Communication Processes," 614, argue that "those who use . . . quasi-evolutionary terms [to describe human beings like *Homo sociologicus, Homo ludens,* or *Homo totus*] sometimes overlook the fact that the contemporary person does not only consume but also produces new meanings." In Bible translation there is sometimes a tendency to forget that the communities of faith are not just recipients but active agents in the process of meaning making, as *Homo significans*, in interaction with the Sacred text.

Glancy, Jennifer. "The Utility of an Apostle: On Philemon 11." *Journal of Early Christian History* 5 (2015) 72–86. DOI: 10.1080/2222582X.2015.11877317.

Glissant, Édouard. *Traité du Tout-Monde. Poétique IV*. Paris: Gallimard, 1997.

Gutt, Ernst-August. *Translation and Relevance: Cognition and Context*. London: Routledge, 2014.

Halcomb, Michael. "David Rhoads Performing Philemon (English)." YouTube video, Feb. 10, 2014. https://www.youtube.com/watch?v=48YWFNWvzKo.

Halliday, M. A. K. *Language as a Social Semiotic*. London: Arnold, 1978.

Iconic Events Now. "JESUS: A Deaf Missions Film. In Theaters June 20, 2024." YouTube video, May 22, 2024. https://www.youtube.com/watch?v=ag6hvf7KZOQ.

James, C. L. R. *The Black Jacobins*. 2nd ed. New York: Vintage, 1989.

Kress, Gunther. *Multimodality: A Social Semiotic Approach to Communication*. London: Routledge, 2009.

———. "Transposing Meaning: Translation in a Multimodal Semiotic Landscape." In *Translation and Multimodality: Beyond Words*, edited by Monica Boria et al. Kindle. London: Taylor & Francis, 2020.

Kress, Gunther, and Theo van Leeuwen. *Meaning-Making and Transformative Engagement: Notes on Reading Images*. Berlin: de Gruyter, 2022.

———. *Reading Images: The Grammar of Visual Design*. London: Routledge, 1996.

Lukianova, Natalia A., and Elena V. Fell. "Meaning Making in Communication Processes: The Role of a Human Agency." *Procedia: Social and Behavioral Sciences* 200 (2015) 614–17.

Low, U-Wen. "Who Tells the Story: Challenging Audiences Through Performer Embodiment." *Religions* 14 (2023) 1040. https://doi.org/10.3390/rel14081040.

Marchal, Joseph. "The Usefulness of an Onesimus: The Sexual Use of Slaves and Paul's Letter to Philemon." *Journal of Biblical Literature* 130 (2011) 749–70. DOI: 10.2307/23488277.

Maxey, James A. *From Orality to Orality: A New Paradigm for Contextual Translation of the Bible*. Biblical Performance Criticism 2. Eugene, OR: Cascade Books, 2009.

Nederlands-Vlaams Bijbelgenootschap. "Called to Be Free." Webinars. https://www.bijbelgenootschap.nl/lees-de-bijbel/professional-en-bijbel/webinars/webinar-terugkijken-geroepen-om-vrij-te-zijn/.

Nesbitt, Nick. *Caribbean Critique: Antillean Critical Theory from Toussaint to Glissant*. Liverpool University, 2013. DOI: https://doi.org/10.5949/liverpool/9781846318665.001.0001.

Nolan, Shaun. "Visual Thinking Strategies as a Pedagogical Tool: Initial Expectations, Applications, and Perspectives in Denmark." *Journal of Visual Literacy* 42 (2023) 210–27. DOI: 10.1080/1051144X.2023.2261222.

Rhoads, David M. "Performing the Letter to Philemon." *Journal of Biblical Storytelling* 17.1 (2008). https://www.biblicalperformancecriticism.org/index.php/2011-08-26-20-28-44/articles-mainmenu-37/articles/10-rhoads-performing-philemon/file.

Sperber, Dan, and Deirdre Wilson. *Relevance: Communication and Cognition*. 2nd ed. London: Blackwell, 1995.

Valentine, Katy E. *For You Were Bought with a Price: Sex, Slavery, and Self-Control in a Pauline Community*. N.p.: GlossaHouse, 2017.

Van Leeuwen, Theo. *Introducing Social Semiotics*. London: Routledge, 2005.

Wiedorn, Michael. "On the Unfolding of Édouard Glissant's Archipelagic Thought." *Karib: Nordic Journal for Caribbean Studies* 6 (2021) 3. DOI: https://doi.org/10.16993/karib.82.

Winedt, Marlon. "Bible Translation as Incarnation of the Word of God: Transformational Power Through Form and Meaning." *The Bible Translator* 72 (2021) 220-40. https://doi.org/10.1177/20516770211027624.

———. "The Impact of the KJV in Caribbean Bible Translation Work: An Exploratory Introduction." *The Bible Translator* 64 (2013) 185-203. DOI: 10.1177/2051677013491882.

———. "Performing Philemon: A Rhetoric of Accomodation or of Crypot-Revolution?" Vimeo video. https://vimeo.com/796381069.

———. "Performing Philemon—Marlon Winedt 20Nov2023." Vimeo video. https://vimeo.com/889076445?share=copy.

———. "Translation as Performance and Engagement: Performing Philemon from a Modern Caribbean Perspective." *The Bible Translator* 66 (2015) 3-23. https://doi.org/10.1177/2051677015569718.

———. "Webcam Video from January 22, 2015." YouTube video. https://www.youtube.com/watch?v=8lVFbDnadwI.

———. "Wie is mijn Onesimus? Paulus' brief aan Filemon opnieuw gelezen." *Met Andere Woorden* 42 (2023) 36-45.

5

Labyrinths of Meaning
Unstable Signs in Urban Spaces

MATT VALLER

THIS CHAPTER FOREGROUNDS THE PROBLEMATIC of Bible translation in cultural contexts where biblical narratives have a long history. In such contexts, meaning-making processes are inflected—even infected—with biblical resonances such that no new translation is not, at the same time, a re-translation of something already said. The discipline of Biblical Performance Criticism has foregrounded this "repetition," not as a translation problem, per se, but as a meaning-making conundrum in which the "text" is difficult to identify, since it presents in shifting iterations, displaced and deferred by space and time. To consider this conundrum from the perspective of translation, this chapter engages a case study.

Labyrinth is an ongoing project I began in 2015 in which major cities are "hacked" for meaning. This process involves a repeated investigation of urban spaces as "texts," whose complex, multivalent resonances and dissonances can be "read" to "uncover" narratives baked into steel and stone, hiding in the nuances of public art, street design, topography, and historical memory. As part of its storytelling, Labyrinth has sometimes engaged biblical texts as a way of both exploring the traces of biblical meanings in contemporary urban spaces and providing a narrative which is both familiar/unfamiliar against which to read an overfamiliar city space. Two of these labyrinths—at the National Mall, in Washington, DC, and the Alamo, in San Antonio, Texas—are explored as a case study in translation as unstable performance.

The case studies in this chapter are rendered in italics and retain their more colloquial phrasing. At times they are interspersed with commentary. At others, I have quoted them at some length—especially in the case of the labyrinth at the Alamo which is reproduced almost in its entirety. I ask your trust in this journey, dear reader. It is an unusual approach for an academic text, but I have taken it because the conceptual pay-off is made more explicit via the narrative experience of the case studies.

Labyrinth is an experimental project and, as such, this chapter also explores the evolving learnings of a process increasingly theorized in terms of translation. As well as questions that explore the complexities of translating biblical narratives, this chapter highlights the spatial and temporal dynamics that shape translation, place, and performance: an ongoing negotiation between past and present, memory and meaning.

A Quest for Agency

The idea of *translation* in this chapter does not allow for the presence of a stable original. It presupposes that meaning is fluid and, crucially, always on the move. Where it appears stable—in those many moments where we find ourselves able to communicate effectively, to return to the familiar and "make sense" of it once again—powerful forces are arrayed against the default forces of change, halting dissolution and shoring up semiotic ballast in the service of a certain permanence. Some call this God; in the sciences it is known as *negentropy*, or negative entropy.

Negentropy has been a niche but formative term within translation studies over the last two decades. Michael Cronin introduced the term with his reading of Thomas Richards's work on the British imperial archive.[1] As the science of thermodynamics took hold of Victorian intellectual society, the notion of *entropy* struck fear into the collective imagination. Entropy simply indicates that a closed system will always tend toward a state of equilibrium, which in practical terms means that everything will always eventually fall apart. The struggle to maintain

---

1. Cronin, *Identity*, 129–32; cf. *Eco-Translation*, 126–29; 141–45. Cf. Richards, *Imperial*.

archival knowledge in the face of its inevitable dissolution is a feature of imperial dynamics; no matter how much power one has, the threat of its loss drives the continual seizure of more. During the twentieth century, however, Edwin Schrödinger proposed the concept of negentropy as an explanation for how living organisms hold their form.[2] While entropy reigns in closed systems, life on Earth is an open system and the continual supply of new energy from the Sun provides for the conditions in which form can be maintained, and even reproduced, rather than dissolved. Translation is negentropy, argues Cronin, because it continually creates new forms. It cannot be the equivalent reproduction of a stable original, any more than each new organism is an equivalent reproduction of its parents.

Kobus Marais has taken up the science of negentropy in more detail in his biosemiotic theory of translation, arguing that translation is, by definition, "negentropic semiotic work."[3] Though the argument is complex, drawing on evolutionary neurobiology and Peircean semiotics, the concept is straightforward: translation is a fundamental semiotic process that powers permanence. As he writes, "the problem to be explained in semiosis is not change, but stability."[4] The semiotic processes within biology, all the way up to those within human languages, provide the means to conceptualize the continuation, rather than the dissolution, of organisms, cultures, processes: in short, of living systems of all kinds.

The Labyrinth project that provides the case studies in this chapter was motivated by the question of how people find greater agency in the places they find themselves. This is a question about change and permanence. How do people change the systems they find themselves in? Why are some things so difficult to budge? What might be gained by learning to recognize the forces that shape us, often quietly, unnoticed, invisible? When the project was conceived in 2015, I had no reference for thinking these questions in terms of translation. However, over the subsequent years, I have been increasingly provoked to consider this work as a translational phenomenon; indeed, it was this quest for agency that led me to the discipline of translation studies. There has been remarkably little cross-pollination between translation studies and biblical studies, certainly when conceptualizing translation beyond linguistics. This

---

2. Schrödinger, *Life*.
3. Marais, *(Bio)Semiotic*, 136.
4. Marais, *(Bio)Semiotic*, 123.

chapter is thus tentative and exploratory, aimed at a critical reflection on a certain practice that can open possible future lines of inquiry and experimentation.

Dislocation and Foreignization

Labyrinth is a walking experience through a city that reads urban spaces like a text—the architecture, the street design, the public art, the whole effect of the city on our emotions. These are not just silent stones or functional pathways; together they tell a story about what the city means. In fact, they tell many different stories—some of them bolstering each other through symbols and history that resonate, some crashing against each other, creating dissonance in contested spaces. These are stories that shape us, quietly enforcing the rules we live by. A labyrinth seeks to uncover those stories so that together participants cultivate greater agency—perhaps even to rewrite the rules.

The symbolic play of resonance and dissonance can be easily imagined with a prominent national building. To see the US flag atop the White House is to see two symbols that instinctively resonate; both the flag and the building are icons of the US state. To see the flag of another country atop the White House, however, would be immediately dissonant. To view that scenario would be to instinctively, even pre-consciously, respond to this clash of icons. This is a semiotic relationship that is somatic as much as it is cognitive (can those categories be reliably separated anyway?). As bodies move through spaces there are complex relationships of meaning that are continually renegotiated and remade—and they vary dramatically with the myriad of different bodies, whose meaning-making contexts are legion.[5] This is a thoroughly negentropic

---

5. In translation studies, Douglas Robinson has argued persuasively that cognitive processes cannot be separated from the somatic experience of bodies moving through the world, and that the relationship of somatics to the narratives which shape meaning must be thought as an integrated phenomenon. In *The Translator's Turn* he introduced a conceptual division between *ideo*-somatic and *idio*-somatic experience, the former being the effect of cultural ideology on somatic experience, and the latter the effect of the individual's idiosyncratic personal history, which cannot be extricated from the cultural context but can nonetheless be understood as a particular instantiation. In *Translationality*, he brings together subsequent decades of research to argue for a more sophisticated account of the somatic construction of reality and its "neurocultural" character. The relationship of our brains to others is a complex phenomenon, in which we are shaped by external bodies at least as much as our own. Thus, the word "legion" here is used advisedly, and has a productive resonance with the labyrinth at the Alamo

account of meaning, through which collective symbolism is sustained. However, as with the example of a national flag and a national building, this symbolic sustenance sometimes involves dramatic asymmetries of power between symbols and their sustaining bodies.

While some semiotic resonance and dissonance is obvious, much is nuanced and harder to read. No symbol is alone; each carries within it the presence (and absence) of multiple others. This is an entanglement of meaning in which teasing out what resonates, and what is dissonant, requires some careful, attentive work. This example from a labyrinth in Washington, DC, provides an example of this entanglement.

> *All buildings carry symbolism in their design, some very blatant, others very subtle. But it is not just the symbols we are "reading." We also pay attention to the way that spaces make us feel, often for reasons that are beyond our explanation. For me, the National Mall is one of the most sacred spaces I have encountered. I'm drawn to it; arrested by its architecture, entranced by its beauty, silenced by its scale. It is undoubtedly true that America's great ideals have functioned for some as beacons of hope in the world, even as for others they have spelled death; regardless, as we shall see, those ideals are enshrined in this monumental space.*

At this point, as a Brit taking several Americans around their nation's capital, I made a peace offering and handed around a couple of boxes of Thorntons chocolates, a luxury brand popular in the UK at the time.

> *But we also bring our own individual stories to this space and find them caught up with other hidden threads. The family that brought us these chocolates is the same family from the north of England who gave America the most important architect for this Capitol building—a man named William Thornton. Thornton, though a Quaker, used slaves for the construction of the Capitol's foundations. Most of the chocolate produced for European markets—including, most probably, these boxes of Thorntons—is made from cocoa beans farmed in West Africa, often still using forced child labor. In this one simple act of sharing these chocolates together, lines of connections splay out across continents and tangle us up—unexpectedly and uncomfortably—in their stories. We are never just in one place at one time.*

This *dislocation* is a feature of the Labyrinth. Our sense of space is often conditioned by familiarity, ways of being in a place that work to

(see below).

forge familiar pathways. It's a habitual tactic for a species that has learned to settle. We make place through psychological processes that emphasize the familiar and disavow the foreign. Yet the foreign is an inherent part of the familiar. Whether through supply chains, migration, communications technology, or the unconscious fluctuations of the psyche, unknown or poorly understood Others are always part of any familiar present.

Translation studies has reckoned extensively with foreignization. Lawrence Venuti in particular, drawing on Friedrich Schleiermacher, has emphasized the translational value of prioritizing a source language and culture in translated texts as a means of rendering the otherness of a translated world.[6] This finds expression in a different vein through the psychogeographic practices of the Situationists. Performed in Paris in the 1960s, these *avant garde* theorists adopted the *dérive*—the "drift"—as an alternative means of movement that eschewed the "spectacle" of late capitalism and re-opened the city to a playful imagination—making it an unfamiliar, "other" place. While easy to critique with the hindsight of a matured poststructuralism, this insistence on deliberate dislocation provides inspiration for a certain approach to narrative design that, I shall argue, provides for a translational experience.

In reaching for *translational* rather than *translation* I am following Blumczynski, who argues convincingly that translation—at least in English-language uses of the term—cannot (and should not) escape the material etymology of its Latin roots.[7] The *translatio*—the "carrying over"—has been eschewed by translation studies, frustrated with indefensible notions of "equivalence." Yet, as Blumczynski argues, there is no reason to suppose that carrying anything means that it stays the same; that is why transporting something vulnerable or valuable for any great distance requires great care and attention. The default result of movement is change. This experience of change is "translational," in Blumczynski's terms. I shall return to that concept in due course.

Where You Stand Determines What You See

One of the core ideas of the Labyrinth is that where we stand determines what we see. This is an idea familiar to poststructuralism within cultural studies; "objective" knowledge, if by that we mean the knowledge of a

---

6. Venuti, *Invisibility*; cf. Schleiermacher, "Methods."
7. Blumczynski, *Experiencing*.

fully external observer, is a fantasy. In urban spaces this conceptual insight becomes thoroughly practical, and Labyrinth uses it to tease out a relationship between what is seen and what is unseen. To return to the Washington, DC, labyrinth, we are now standing on the gentle slope, about thirty meters west of the Washington Monument.

> *Just take a moment to take in this space. The beautiful cherry trees are in bloom. The fountains dance, the reflecting pool is still. You might notice that from this angle you can't see the pyramid at the top of the Washington Monument, so it looks a bit like a Soviet chimney! So much symbolism is in the eye of the beholder.*
>
> *There's a great quote about monuments by the Austrian novelist Robert Musil. He wrote: "There is nothing in this world as invisible as a monument. They are no doubt erected to be seen—indeed, to attract attention. But at the same time, they are impregnated with something that repels attention. Like a drop of water on an oilskin, attention runs down them without stopping for a moment."[8]*
>
> *I have found that insight particularly true in this space. On the one hand these great monuments grab our attention. At the same time, they only keep it for so long. We already know what they are supposed to mean. They don't have to mean anything more—in fact, to wrestle with their meaning can actually be politically and personally challenging, as if wrestling with a sacred text we feel compelled to accept.*
>
> *So, take a moment. Look around. Look harder. What do these monuments mean?*

This injunction to "look harder" is, of course, open-ended: how does one know when one has looked hard enough? Yet, the unfinished nature of this curiosity finds a parallel in an idea of translation as a continual process. This chapter is making the case that what has generally been termed *exegesis* can be rethought as a form of (re)translation, one that is unfinished and open, and that the material context for this translation is integral to its performance.

A House Divided

To explore this approach further, let us now enter this labyrinth.

---

8. Musil, *Posthumous Papers of a Living Author*, 61.

> We've come to this precise spot, because it is only here that the National Mall reveals itself. This small section of land is the only place where you can see all five of the great monuments that frame it at the same time. Behind us, just visible over the crest of the hill, is the Capitol; to our right, the White House; over to our left is the Jefferson Memorial; and straight ahead is the Lincoln Memorial. And if you look at a map it is impossible to see what the gaps in the trees reveal when you stand here. We are at the intersection of a great Latin cross laid out across the city. This is the nave of a vast open cathedral, the Washington Monument vaulting its frame, its altar facing West to the setting sun. The National Cathedral, out in the north-western suburbs of the city is just a parody. This is the real National Cathedral.
>
> So let's read these monuments that frame this mighty space: stories of America that together tell a sacred national story. America as Liberty [Jefferson], America as Democracy [Capitol and White House], America as Unity [Lincoln], and, at the center of it all, America as Military [Washington]. These are the great symbols of the story of Independence, guaranteed by Washington's military, founded on liberty, secured by democracy, and forged through enduring unity.

At this moment, I would ask participants to look around again and take in this space, to comprehend themselves at the center of a cathedral. I would ask: Do you recognize these stories of America? How do you feel in this great space? The questions of the labyrinth are crucial to the experience, because it is questions that keep the story open and invite the participants to begin to entangle themselves with its complexity.

> It is now time to introduce Mark's Gospel into our experience. There is one very famous quote from Mark's story of Jesus evoked by this space. It's Abraham Lincoln's famous speech that set him on course for the presidency: "A house divided cannot stand," a quote from Jesus in Mark 3:25.
>
> As we stand here at the center of this remarkable Cathedral—the great "house" of America, a space that both echoes and shapes the nation—those words of Lincoln's, of Jesus', ring in our ears.
>
> Lincoln was speaking of slavery, of course. He continued by saying that he does not believe that half the states can persist with slavery and half without. And it is on the fault-line of slavery that this great Cathedral begins to reveal some cracks.
>
> Jefferson, the author of arguably the world's most famous words in celebration of freedom, was a plantation owner with many slaves. And it was under his presidency that slaves were first

> used to work on the construction of both the White House and the Capitol. The symbols of both Liberty and Democracy contain within them the division wrought by slavery.
>
> Washington as well, the symbol of Military that guarantees Independence, owned many slaves. And it was along the fault-line of slavery that the military was divided by the Civil War, with Washington's great federal dream almost torn apart.
>
> And so Lincoln's place here, at the altar of the Cathedral, is important, as the symbol of Unity. A house divided cannot stand.

Once again, through open questions I invite the labyrinth participants to further enmesh themselves in the unfolding story:

> *Look around again, take in this space. It is a truism in American life today that this nation is more divided now than it has been for generations. Where do you stand in relation to this story? Do you gravitate to one of these monuments? What price do you place on unity?*

It is at this point in the labyrinth that I begin to introduce an unorthodox reading of Mark's Gospel in order to further open a different reading of this over-determined physical space. Here I am deliberately playing with the resonances and dissonances between the biblical narrative and the semiotics of the Mall.

> *Jesus' relationship to great monuments in Mark is a major under-reported theme of the Gospel. The New Testament scholar Professor Keith Dyer, from the University of Divinity in Melbourne, has shown how Mark constructs Jesus' whole story by strategically ignoring the major monuments that mark the landscape.*[9] *Jesus comes from Nazareth, an obscure village in the shadow of Sepphoris—the capital city of Galilee in Jesus' youth, on which, as a carpenter, he almost certainly would have labored as a construction worker. Large parts of the story take place around the Sea of Galilee, but Mark never mentions the new impressive capital, Tiberius, established on the Western shore to tax the fishing trade. Jesus visits the villages surrounding Caesarea Philippi farther north, but not the city itself; he passed by Hippos and Scythopolis in the Decapolis without mention; and farther south, at Jericho, he arrives and leaves again in the same verse. It's hard not to read the story as a snub to the Herodian kings and their Roman patrons.*

---

9. These ideas were discussed in a seminar at Whitley College, University of Divinity, Melbourne, 2014.

So perhaps there is a way for us to read the National Mall apart from its monuments? And perhaps we can read Mark's story of Jesus with new eyes.

There are around one hundred statues commemorating historical figures in Washington, DC. However, only five of them are of historical women. Most statues are male, and those of women are mostly nymphs or goddesses, or abstract ideals like justice or virtue. Historical women are almost completely absent.

The most famous statue of an historical woman in the capital is just over the water, hidden in a sprawling memorial to her husband. The first chairperson of the UN Human Rights Commission, responsible for the development of the Universal Declaration on Human Rights, in 1999 a Gallup survey in the US found her to be at number nine in the list of most widely respected people of the twentieth century. Eleanor Roosevelt just about made it into DC with a statue.

In 1939 Eleanor Roosevelt found herself in common cause with another woman, who has no statue in Washington, but whose presence here re-shaped the meaning of this place we are standing perhaps more than any other. Marian Anderson was a world-famous opera singer and had performed in some of Europe's finest concert halls. But when her manager tried to book Washington's Constitution Hall, the Daughters of the American Revolution refused because Marian Anderson was Black. Eleanor Roosevelt (along with thousands of other women) resigned her membership of the DAR in protest, but still nowhere in Washington would provide space for Anderson to perform. So Eleanor Roosevelt quietly arranged for Anderson to perform outdoors, on the steps of the Lincoln Memorial. A huge crowd turned out to hear her sing arias and cantatas. But as her final song, she sang the old spiritual "Nobody Knows the Trouble I've Seen," and the symbolism of the song of the slaves was not lost. It is generally understood that until that moment the Lincoln Memorial symbolized the struggle to preserve the Union. But from the day Marian Anderson performed, it was forever changed into a symbol of the ongoing struggle for emancipation.

And it was for that reason that Martin Luther King Jr. chose the Lincoln Memorial as the site of the Civil Rights protest of 1963 and his iconic speech, "I Have a Dream."

Martin Luther King Jr. is also memorialized with one of Washington's newest monuments, just over the water, near to Eleanor Roosevelt and her husband. Their placement feels symbolic. They stand among the cherry trees, in what is unquestionably the most peaceful part of the city. And yet, as we stand here by the

> Washington Monument, they are on the edge, outside the imagined walls of this great American Cathedral.
>
> This is a space that doesn't know what to do with women. Or people of color. The African-American museum right here in the cathedral is an exception that proves the rule with style. It has forced its way into this landscape in all its glaring difference. That spatial tension, celebrated but removed, included but separate, reflects some of the ongoing struggles of a house still divided.

Once again, I press the questions that open the space for participants to explore their own place here.

> Take another moment now to reflect again on your place in this space. Do you see yourself on the inside or the outside? Are there stories not told by these monuments that you would want to bring to this great Cathedral?

The labyrinth continues through the National Mall and Mark's Gospel, exploring an anti-imperial reading of Jesus' actions in Jerusalem (drawn primarily from the biblical scholarship of Ched Myers).[10] As the journey approaches the Capitol, the story moves to the uncertain ending of Mark's story, with its shorter ending, sudden and vulnerable, and its extended attempt to rescue a victory narrative.

> In the spring of 1968, thousands of people marched right here as part of the Poor People's Campaign, advocating for better labor conditions across all races. Three thousand people stayed for six weeks, in a vast tent encampment, known as "Resurrection City."
>
> And so right here, the question of the ending to Mark's Gospel plays out: at the top of Capitol Hill, the great power of the Establishment; down here on the swampy, rain-soaked Mall, the vulnerability of the encampment; up there, the permanence of pillars; down here, the transience of tents.
>
> So which resurrection story do you choose? Consider the question carefully. It is not an easy choice. The strong pillars offer safety, but only if you can get inside. Order and security is no bad thing, but power corrupts and what good is it to gain the whole world but lose your soul? The tents on the other hand may offer the promise of change, but their vulnerability is real; conditions here in those rain-soaked weeks were poor, and the resurrection community was by no means always safe.

---

10. See Myers, *Binding*.

This uncertain choice leads to an end, which is a beginning. The labyrinth continues toward its conclusion, at which it will attempt to open the largest question of the journey so far.

Having walked this labyrinth we find ourselves back where we started. So we will end at the beginning, in Mark chapter 1. The resurrection story of chapter 16 is an invitation to begin again: with the stone moved from his tomb, Jesus has left the great city of Jerusalem behind and is back in the marginal northern lands of Galilee.

And so we find ourselves with John the Baptist, by the Jordan river, near the wilderness, living as an indigenous person of the land.

The story of the indigenous people of this land is most notable by its almost total absence here. For ten thousand years a complex network of tribes lived in this region of Great Turtle Island. The most conservative estimates put the number dead as a direct result of European colonization at 50 percent. Most estimates are over 90 percent.

This curved building through the trees is the Museum of the American Indian—one of the only signs of indigenous presence in the capital. Its architecture is designed to be a celebration of the landscape in which many indigenous tribes have lived. But the symbolism is a double-edged sword. The long history of forced migration, enslavement, and cultural destruction that has characterized the Native American experience since the fifteenth century was justified because of European ideas about native peoples as "uncivilized." By contrast, the very essence, the most potent symbol, of America's "civilization" is this all-pervasive European, Greek-revivalist architecture that is evidenced in almost every major building surrounding the Mall. The architectural contrast here is a symbol of the question about the value of the center and its great monuments vs. the value of the margins and its wild places.

The great stone has been moved and Jesus is back in the wilderness. John, the indigenous outsider, is standing in the flowing water. Together they will enact the escape from Egypt: Jesus' body plunged under the surface and hauled up again in defiance of Pharaoh's rule. And then back into the wilderness we journey. The indigenous anti-imperial symbol stands as a final choice: with whom does our allegiance lie? With the pillars of power or the transience of tents? With the hewn stone of the citadels or the wind-scarred rock of the caves? With the house divided, or with the land beyond her walls?

[pause]

> One of the great conundrums of history is how the cross of Jesus, a tool of imperial execution, became, in time, the symbol of the very empire that killed him.
>
> For fifteen hundred years after the conversion of the Emperor Constantine, Roman-style Christianity still dominated in Europe as both Protestant and Catholic courts entwined the church around their various empires. And so it was with a vision of a different kind of society, free from religious domination, that America was born. Could the cross be freed from the imperial grasp?
>
> As we finish here, at the foot of this great cross [gestures back up the Mall toward Lincoln], we end our labyrinth and leave with the question: to whom does this cross belong, and what does it mean?

Translating the Marks of the City

I suggest that this labyrinth in Washington, DC, can be described as a translational experience. It does not involve much interlingual translation; even the more unfamiliar interpretation of biblical texts is largely content with established English translations. However, in seeking to embed a certain reading of Mark's Gospel in a certain city space, the journey allows for, and indeed cultivates, translations. Firstly, there is a very literal experience of movement, the physical translation of bodies around an imagined pathway. The transformational power of physical movement in translation should not be underestimated. I have written elsewhere (with Blumczynski) on Latour's concept of translation as a complex negotiation of associations.[11] The movement of bodies into new associations with established monuments creates new meanings, new relationships, and even—in Latour's terms—new "co-existence," a self-consciously philosophical *and* political term.

Secondly, there is a sense in which this space is translated by the labyrinth. Like Musil's oilskin monuments, city spaces can feel both known and unintelligible. That does not mean they are not profoundly somatic; smells, sounds, tastes, and the deep, unnameable sensations of the soul that complicate the body all shape urban experience. However, the process of "reading" the National Mall like a text, albeit an unpredictable one, allows it to make more "sense," in a certain way. Translation studies has historically worked, albeit uncertainly, with a notion

---

11. Valler and Blumczynski, "Reassembling," 334–51.

of "inter-semiotic" translation. Poorly theorized and poorly attended, inter-semiotic translation has, since Marais, been increasingly reconceptualized as semiosis: the ongoing, processual movement of meaning through signs. Following Peirce, Marais provides a compelling account of life as a constant attempt to process meaning and thereby achieve the "negentropic" work that sustains form.[12] There is a certain sense in which the labyrinth both reads and manipulates the semiotics of the National Mall. The reading is undertaken in several registers. There is a semiotics of urban planning, a semiotics of architecture, a semiotics of memory (of Marian Anderson's performance, for example), a semiotics of race and gender, of stone monuments and spoken narratives. There is also an "inter-semiotic" translation, by which these different semiotic layers are pushed into either resonance or dissonance with each other. Again, this is not a translation that functions according to "equivalence," but allows for the novel movement of meaning across porous (or not-so-porous) boundaries. The semiotics of the National Mall find themselves both transferred and transformed (perhaps even transgressed) through the labyrinth.

Thirdly, there is a translation which is undertaken by those who walk the labyrinth, not only in terms of their physical relocation, but also in more complex terms of experience. The concept of the "labyrinth" is drawn from the visual pathways that decorated the floors of various medieval cathedrals. In order to get to the center, one must undertake a series of disorienting twists and turns; yet when one reaches it one finds a dead end! In this moment, there is a moment of reckoning, a choice to quit or retrace one's steps. At city-scale, the labyrinth in Washington, DC, draws participants around an unpredictable pathway which leads to moments of choice. Though no two participants are the same, I suggest there is a translational experience that structures this movement and leads to a renegotiation of change and stability. Translation in this sense is not limited to meaning but understood in the transmutational terms of contested personal and communal transformation.

Conceptualizing Bible translation as a translational experience offers an alternative to the dominant strictures of language translation. There are ethical complications that suggest translation and interpretation should be kept apart; a colonial legacy of exegetical domination has left a sorry history in its wake. Yet the separation of translation and

---

12. Marais, *(Bio)Semiotic*, 136–41.

interpretation is a theoretical distinction that does not hold. To translate is to remake meanings and is therefore to interpret; the labyrinth is a means of making this fact explicit. As biblical scholar Ched Myers suggests, the logic of empire is answers to questions, while the logic of the kingdom of God is questions to answers. Labyrinth insists on questions as an interpretative humility that resists colonial logic. This is why the narrative goal of the labyrinth is not startling insights or even fascinating experience, but better questions. It is the questions which provide the portal to the translational (transformational) experience of the labyrinth.

As a second case study to explore this approach to translation, we journey to the Alamo, in San Antonio, Texas. The physical walk is much shorter—the site is much smaller than the National Mall. However, the translational journey involved arguably travels far further than the physical movement itself.

Remember the Alamo

The structure of this labyrinth is quite different. It takes in five locations, and repeats them, resulting in a walk that circles the old Alamo Mission building twice. The majority of the script is reproduced below. I invite you, as a reader, to allow yourself to experience the imaginative journey, and then I will engage further with the question of the extent to which this can be conceptualized in terms of Bible translation. The immersion in the narrative aids the analysis that follows.

Location 1. Alamo Plaza

> *The story at the Alamo is well-known within Texas, but less so outside. So a quick bit of history . . .*
>
> *Before it was a US state, Texas spent ten years as its own independent republic. Before that, Texas was part of newly independent Mexico. At the beginning of the nineteenth century, the Spanish had withdrawn from Mexico, but by the 1830s US immigrants to Texas were increasingly hostile to the Mexican government. In 1835, the Texas Revolution drove Mexican forces out of Texas, but the army of President General Santa Anna responded and, in late February 1836, a small garrison of around a hundred Texians found themselves under siege by over a thousand Mexican troops. Though a small reinforcement arrived and while the soldiers inside the walled mission inflicted heavy losses on the Mexican army, the mission was eventually taken and all*

the captured Texians were executed. Despite the defeat, the Battle of the Alamo seared its way into the imagination of the Texian revolutionaries, and the wider US, as a symbol of heroic sacrifice. "Remember the Alamo" became the battle-cry of the revolutionaries and lives on as a call to honor the dead.

Location 2: The Cenotaph with the Emily Morgan Hotel behind

So much of what we see is determined by where we stand.

From this view, the cenotaph stands proud, framed dramatically against the Emily Morgan hotel which towers behind it. This V-shaped Gothic-Revivalist hotel building, with a turret that is visible from anywhere around the Alamo, was originally the Medical Arts Building, with several hospital beds inside.

Around the far side of the cenotaph are carved these words: "Erected in memory of the heroes who sacrificed their lives at the Alamo, March 6, 1836, in the defense of Texas. They chose never to surrender nor retreat; these brave hearts, with flag still proudly waving, perished in the flames of immortality that their high sacrifice might lead to the founding of this Texas."

This is the story that made the Alamo famous. It's a story told from the perspective of the White colonial immigrants to Texas, those who ended up in power in the new republic, and then later in the new US state. But even while Texas was joining the Union, there were also many *tejanos* in the region, Mexican Texans who remembered the Alamo as a Catholic mission long before it was the site of a battle.

The shadow of this old medical center reminds us that there is another history to this place. Long before the hotel was built, long even before the famous battle, the Alamo was a hospital facility and a community hub, for a people forgotten by the popular story here.

This labyrinth explores some of the Alamo's forgotten stories. We take a very simple pathway around its walls, to three major hotels. The more we hack this space, the more ghosts we'll encounter.

Location 3. The Emily Morgan Hotel

The legend of Emily Morgan, after whom this hotel was named, is a little historically shaky. But the story goes—and, after all, stories are often more powerful than fact—that Emily Morgan was originally Emily West, a mixed-race indentured servant to a James Morgan of New York, who sent her to work for a year in his new Texas hotel. While there, she was captured by the Mexican army and forced to travel with them across Texas. When the Texian army arrived at Jacinto, for what would be the decisive final battle of the revolution, the Mexican president, Santa Anna, was caught unprepared because he was otherwise engaged . . . in bed, with Emily West.

As a result Emily West became a local legend, associated with the song "The Yellow Rose of Texas." But this story carries some of the complexities of the Alamo and the struggles that surround it.

The Texas Revolution was racially charged, in several different ways. Firstly, the influx of White American colonists changed the population of Texas and fueled its rebellion against Mexico. In the new Republic of Texas, los tejanos did not enjoy the power that Whites achieved. The revolution was also supported by the Southern states of the US because, in Mexico, slavery was illegal. Once the revolution was over, Emily West, a formerly free woman from Connecticut, was automatically regarded as property, her papers having been lost in her capture. The celebrated myth about her role in Texas's independence masks the reality of the profound change that occurred for Texan people of color. Emily West is known here at this hotel as Emily Morgan, her bondsname.

But it's not just Mexican or African-American stories that insist on being heard by this hotel. Finding Emily West in bed with the Mexican president evokes his words on race. He is reported to have said, "We have failed because of our deplorable racial mixture, and the responsibility for this sad state of affairs lies with the Spanish missionaries who saved the Indian from extinction."[13] The Native peoples of the land suffered both from the Spanish—then Mexican—powers, and then later from the insurgent White-American colonists of the new Texan Republic. Now, the story of the ancient peoples of this land is almost entirely erased.

So this first hotel, The Emily Morgan, uncovers the complexity of the Alamo, and the contest over whose stories are told here today.

Location 4. The Crockett Hotel

Hotel number two is the Crockett. Named after Davy Crockett, the famous frontiersman who died at the Battle of the Alamo, the hotel was originally built as a lodge for the Three Link Fraternity, the popular name for the Independent Order of Odd Fellows. If that all seems a little too, well, odd, then it might surprise you to learn that these Odd Fellows overtook the Freemasons in the second half of the nineteenth century as the largest fraternal society in America. Established as a break-away from the original

---

13. Tucker, *Emily D. West*, 176.

Order of Odd Fellows in Britain, the Independent Order was a Whites-only fraternity that practiced, apparently without irony, the "Three Links" of "Friendship," "Love," and "Truth."

Davy Crockett is a symbol of the wild frontier spirit, itself a courageous independence at "odds" with the establishment. It's part of the Texan identity. To be a free place, on the edge of a new world, where governments are suspect and rugged heroes glorified. This is the kind of "odd" that Texas embodies and celebrates. The outlaw spirit lives on.

The Alamo lies between this hotel for Odd Fellows, and the "Odditorium" across the plaza. One is now an homage to Crockett, the odd-man who left Congress for "frontier" San Antonio. The other is an homage to the absurd. When President Johnson was invoking the Alamo in the cause of the Vietnam War, a New York Times article replied, "To dare to retreat from error can be the highest form of courage."[14] The fight to the death against all the odds is absurd. And yet this oddest of myths is the one most celebrated at the Alamo today.

So this second hotel, the Crockett, uncovers the oddity of the Alamo, and the tussle between the establishment and the outside, the sensible and the absurd, that it still embodies.

Location 5. The Menger Hotel

Hotel number three is the Menger. Its name and history are more straightforward than the previous two hotels: The Menger Hotel is one of the most famous—and wealthy—historical hotels west of the Mississippi, and its owners are also responsible for a big chunk of the real estate that runs alongside the Alamo Plaza. But there is one feature that stands out: The Menger has the claim of being the most haunted hotel in Texas!

Who haunts this place? Local legends tell of many varied ghosts, from President Theodore Roosevelt to Sallie White, a hotel chambermaid. But perhaps there are other unnamed ghosts here too?

Apart from the Texan dead remembered by the Cenotaph, there are the several hundred Mexican soldiers who also died at the famous battle. Their collective presence haunts this space; these days the Alamo is in essence a shrine to the fallen. But from centuries past, before the battle, this site was haunted by other ancient graves. It is a very old and sacred Native American burial site.

14. Schoelwer, *Alamo Images*, 168.

> As the US government increasingly forced Native American populations into marginal land over the course of the nineteenth century, the Ghost Dance became a ritual in the resistance against colonial oppression. It was a means to invoke the spirits of the dead to aid the just cause of the living, and this haunted hotel evokes that same memory from this contested site of remembrance. The infamous massacre at Wounded Knee in South Dakota was triggered by the reaction of US forces to the Ghost Dance. The specter of the dead who demand justice can terrorize the living, even—perhaps especially—those with the most power.
>
> So this third hotel, the Menger, uncovers the unpredictability of the Alamo and the questions over justice which still haunt the space today.

Location 6. Alamo Plaza

Participants have now returned to the place where the labyrinth began. There is a sense in which the place could be said to be translated by this simple journey we have taken together. So I ask participants to look around them, and take a moment to contemplate how they feel in this space. Do they experience it differently now, and if so, how?

At this point in the labyrinth I unexpectedly introduce biblical narrative. As with the labyrinth at the National Mall, the resonance and dissonance between the complex semiotics of the space and an unorthodox reading of biblical texts produces new translations of both the place and the biblical narrative as it can be found *here*.

> San Antonio is named after a thirteenth-century Portuguese saint—in English, Saint Anthony. Perhaps appropriately, he is the patron saint of lost things.
>
> San Antonio was a Franciscan, a venerated saint from the same order that established the mission at San Antonio in the early eighteenth century. The Franciscans were famously founded after Saint Francis of Assisi heard a sermon on chapter 10 of Matthew's Gospel, in which Jesus sends his twelve disciples out on a mission to the surrounding villages and tells them not to take any money with them, but to rely on hospitality—and adds that harsh judgment will fall on anyone who doesn't accept their message.
>
> So in this city of lost things, where forgotten stories demand to be told, this labyrinth takes us around the Alamo again, this time with the most unexpected of ghost stories: the one to which the city can trace its foundation.

Location 7: The Emily Morgan Hotel

Have you ever heard ghost stories from the Bible outside hotels? There's a first time for everything! This might seem a bit odd, but then so is the Alamo. Stay with me, it adds a whole other layer to this story.

In Matthew's Gospel, the story from which San Antonio can trace its origins, there's a moment right near the start where John the Baptist appears in the wilderness of Judea, spooking the authorities of his day with his radical preaching. He's proclaiming the Kingdom of Heaven, a phrase we've come to associate with something other-worldly. In a region ruled by Rome, however; preaching an alternative kingdom was enough to get you killed. Sure enough, that's what happens. The ghost in the wilderness is too threatening for the mighty empire.

In one sense, the story of John the Baptist resembles the Franciscan order, preaching in the southwestern wilderness of Texas and establishing their mission by the river. John the Baptist is a figure much like St. Francis, living with just his rough clothes, no money or possessions, and preaching repentance.

But here in San Antonio the similarity is only surface-deep. John the Baptist preached in the shadow of an aggressive, antagonistic empire. The Spanish Franciscans who founded the mission at San Antonio, on the other hand, preached on behalf of an empire. Though both preached in a wilderness, away from the center of power, the Franciscan baptism offered people a chance to align themselves to imperial rule. John's baptism, by contrast, was a symbolic defection from the Roman Empire, recalling the Israelites' escape from Egypt through the Red Sea. This difference asks questions about where the power lies in the stories surrounding the Alamo.

Here at the Emily Morgan hotel we're reminded that the story of the Alamo doesn't begin with the Texas Revolution. And that it is a story that cannot avoid the complexities of race, or of conquest, war, and slavery.

The story goes back to the imperial Spanish conquest and its Franciscan religious arm, providing local medical care on the one hand and lending legitimacy to the subjugation of Native American peoples on the other. There's the long and brutal history of African-American enslavement, the opposition it faced from Mexico, and the support it received from the new Republic of Texas. And there's the complexity of the tejano *identity, where Mexicans in Texas were at the margins of Mexican power way* before White European immigrants headed west from the US to start a new republic.

As you stand in the shadow of the Emily Morgan hotel, where do you fit in this story? Do you see yourself nearer to the center or the margins of an Empire?

Location 8: The Crockett Hotel

Further into Matthew's Gospel, Jesus heads to Gadara, a town way off the page from the rest of the story. As he's approaching, two people emerge from the tombs, riddled with demons, and aggressively block the road. They're screaming at Jesus, and then pleading with him to send them into the nearby herd of pigs. Jesus tells the demons to leave and the two people are released, but the herd of pigs get overtaken and charges down the steep hill into the sea. When the people of Gadara find out what happened they beg Jesus to leave. An odd story for an odd hotel!

This is a story that needs some background. Pigs were considered ritually unclean in ancient Jewish society. But by Jesus' day they had come to symbolize more than that. Their unclean presence was a way of symbolizing the foreign occupation of the Promised Land. The Romans were the "pigs" who weren't supposed to be there.

Gadara was a town in the region of Gerasa, a major Roman military center. The symbol for this garrison was . . . a boar.

The "possession" of the two people from the tombs turns out to be the effect of the imperial possession of the land which takes over every aspect of life: economy, culture, civil freedom—and that affects mental health in a deep, spiritual way. The symbol of the foreign occupying power drowning in the sea evokes the seminal moment in Israel's history: the drowning of the imperial Egyptian armies in the Red Sea—the same moment recalled by John's antiimperial baptism. So it turns out this ghost story of the tombdemons and the pigs is a powerful symbolic exorcism of Rome from the land. No wonder the people of Gadara beg Jesus to leave! That's also enough to get you killed.

There is a kind of madness brought on by empire. The Crockett Hotel—the Oddfellows' house then named for an odd fellow—asks, what makes us odd? The Odditorium over on the Plaza turns oddity into entertainment, but before all else being odd is something political. "Normal" is decided by those with the power. Oddness gets assigned by default: if you can't fit in, play by the rules, you're odd.

Davy Crockett, hero of the Alamo, finds himself at the between-place of two empires, one waxing, the other waning—committing to the madness of fighting and dying for the new Texas. But it's lesser-known that he only came to the western frontier because his career in Congress was finished when he voted against the forced removal of Native Americans from the Southeastern states. For his Tennessee voters that stance was just too odd.

Back in the 1830s, Texians and tejanos found common cause in the revolutionary fight against the centralizing Mexican administration. Now, as a powerful US state, the relationship between Texas and Mexico is very different. Here, among the tombs, perhaps Matthew's story of Jesus asks us to imagine how things might be different if the empire was exorcised.

Location 9: The Menger Hotel

I hate spoilers, but I'm gonna gamble with this one: at the end of Matthew's Gospel Jesus gets killed. It's dramatic! The sky goes dark, Jesus cries out, the massive curtain in the Temple is torn from top to bottom, there's an earthquake, rocks split apart, tombs break open and the bodies of dead people wander into Jerusalem.

Turns out Matthew's Gospel includes a zombie apocalypse.

This passage gets read out publicly each year, but most preachers skip over the bit where dead people wander into Jerusalem. But what if it was the main event?

We've made zombies into comedy figures. But that's what we often do with the things we fear the most. The ever-advancing, un-killable terror taps into a primal fear that the dead will return to haunt us. That there is some demand we have not yet met; some justice not yet fulfilled. Zombies are ghosts with bodies.

In Matthew's story the zombie drama happens at Jerusalem. It's a complex city; a religious center at the edge of the Roman Empire. Do the zombies head to the Temple to menace the corrupt establishment who put a price on Jesus' head? Or to Pontius Pilate's palace to haunt the imperial executioners?

Outside this haunted hotel, ask yourself—if you dare—which ghosts haunt this place, and what do they want? From whom do we still hear an unmet demand for justice?

This may surprise you, but by some measures the Alamo City is the most unequal place in America. There are other places with richer people and poorer people. But inequality between zip codes is starkest here—and that inequality is structured almost entirely along racial lines. The city is set up so that rich White people live just a block or two away from poor Black or Hispanic people, but they never need to meet. That is a level of economic segregation that takes a long time to build.

It's a story that, with its own twists and turns, can trace its way back to the Alamo. The iconic battle in the war through which Whites took control.

Location 10: The Alamo Plaza

Matthew's Gospel ends with an empty tomb—a cenotaph. Jesus and his followers are back in Galilee, in the marginal northern lands, near Nazareth, far away from Jerusalem, where he was buried.

They are up a mountain, echoing the moment straight after Jesus is baptized by John the Baptist—when he returns north to Galilee, goes up a mountain, and delivers his famous Sermon on the Mount. It begins with famous words: "Blessed are the poor in spirit; blessed are the meek," and so on. They are called the Beatitudes, celebrated as a sublime moral code. But this ignores the haunting.

That word "blessed" is the English translation of the ancient Greek word makarios. *It does mean "blessed," but those translations ignore the freight of the word* makarios, *which is associated through its use in Greek mythology with the "blessed" life of the gods. The things that Jesus associates with* makarios *run up against the power, wealth, and glory that counted as "blessed" in the Greek-speaking world. So there's an alternative way of translating* makarios *which reads these Beatitudes as an invocation, one that threatens the gods and their power.*

Here at the Alamo, after the zombie invasion and with the undead-Jesus back in the Galilean mountains, it reads like an invocation for ghosts.

Here come the depressed; they own the future

Here come the grieving; they will be comforted

Here come the enslaved; they will have the whole earth

Here come the ones who are starved of justice; they will be filled

Here come the gracious; they will be shown grace

Here come the uncorrupted; they will see God

Here come the peacemakers; they will be protected

Here come the oppressed; they own the future

Here you come, you wrongly accused; take heart! They did this to your heroes whose ghosts will not die.

> For residents of San Antonio the contest over the stories in this space has immediate relevance. But for those of us who live elsewhere, they may be closer to home than we think.
>
> The ghosts that walk among these tombs ask tough questions about what justice looks like for San Antonio today. The tussle over the location of the cenotaph can mask the much more pressing tussle over who has access to resources in San Antonio, whether education, finance, housing, employment, citizenship, healthcare, and so on.
>
> These questions are not limited to San Antonio, but are being asked in cities all over the world. How will they be answered? One thing we know: the ghosts are coming . . .

Translating the Haunting

What is getting translated through this labyrinth journey? As with the labyrinth in Washington, DC, the physical movement, and the engagement with the semiotics of the space, translates the Alamo and the people who participate through what I described above as a translational experience. However, the nature of that experience, at this particular site, introduces some additional translational dynamics. There is obviously the specific interlingual translation of the biblical use of *makarios*, which proves pivotal in the narrative journey. But I suggest this must be set in a much broader context in which the translation of the biblical narrative reveals a haunting, through which the past and present are caught in a translational tussle.

Once again, this is not an unfamiliar notion to interlingual translation, and especially to Bible translation. Translating a text involves engaging something already written—a past moment—and remaking it in the present. Working with ancient texts requires that pasts are acknowledged and respected. The pasts of a text are many, however, as biblical performance studies has insisted. Biblical texts mask the oral performance history to which they are themselves translations, and new translations and their ongoing performances become new pasts in complex trajectories of meaning.

However, in this labyrinth at the Alamo, the invocation of a haunting problematizes any straightforward notion of a past. The *presence* and *absence* of the past—as both *here and not here*—remakes time within the borders of the Alamo and opens the possibility of a new encounter.

Constraints of space preclude a full discussion of time, and the ways we might credibly, or otherwise, imagine pasts as present. Let me simply suggest that translation must also be conceived as a temporal negotiation, in which the past lays a claim to our present, an idea with which Bible translators are deeply familiar, but which the concept of the labyrinth problematizes as a phenomenon mediated by the material semiotics of a place and the specific play of its resonances and dissonances. In contexts where biblical texts are already familiar, or overdetermined, this translational negotiation with past meanings is many layered and requires a different sensibility to tease out new possibilities for an old story to live.

The Translation Zone

In their special edition of the journal *Translation Studies*, Michael Cronin and Sherry Simon introduced the concept of "The City as Translation Zone."[15] The notion of a translation zone situates translation; it suggests that translational activity is in some way rooted, earthed, embedded. For Bible translation this is a common concept; translators often devote lifetimes to the cultures and language communities into which they translate. However, while linguistic and cultural commitments may be real, conceptions of translation—even among biblical scholars—still often imagines translation as (a) a fundamentally linguistic activity, and (b) a movement through which some essential stability is maintained. To situate translation in a "zone" is to designate a bounded context in which meaning must reckon with the added complexities of multiple layers of semiotic insistence. It is not enough to find new words to express ancient ones; these new words must run a gauntlet through which their claims to pertinence must be proved. Through this process, a translation proves itself worthy of the time and place in which it emerges.

I am not in a position to claim that these labyrinths are translations that meet this challenging criteria. What the Labyrinth does suggest, however, is that translation *could* be imagined as something that emerges through a more thorough entanglement with the material semiotics of a place. Performance studies has long understood that the work of performers cannot be separated from the work of stagehands, set design, lighting, acoustics, and the physical arrangement of audience bodies. (Within translation studies, Robinson has conceptualized this as the

---

15. Cronin and Simon, "Translation Zone."

"translationality" that makes translation possible.[16]) What Labyrinth as an approach to Bible translation suggests is that the performance of translation can find itself in an alternative zone—in this case a city space—and find new semiotic constraints that deepen the context for performance.

Cronin and Simon raise an additional question which has provoked substantial re-evaluation of the Labyrinth project on my part. It is the question of the ecological dimensions of a place, which form the vital lines of any translation zone. They argue that "the need for a post-anthropocentric view of the relationality between human beings and all the other inhabitants of the planet demands in our cities the emergence of a translation ecology which mobilizes thinking around perhaps the least understood or theorized part of translation—namely, intersemiotic translation."[17]

Marais's[18] biosemiotic approach to translation takes this context far more seriously, as does Cronin's *Eco-Translation*.[19] How can the ecological dynamics of a place be "read" alongside and through the semiotics of steel and stone? I have found this to be a profoundly difficult question to answer. Jakob von Uexküll's notion of *Umwelt* offers some resources to this challenge; every place contains multiple worlds as various species negotiate the need for habitat. In this conception, human place-making can be reconceived as one habitat-forming activity among many other more-than-human worlds. Indeed, vast disparities between members of our own species suggest that the multiple worlds of one place are in need of translation between each other in the ecological task of negotiating viable futures.[20]

This conundrum relates to one other, more prosaic, challenge to the labyrinth as an approach to translation. As many different bodies tread similar pathways, these different worlds are brought into co-existence, but not with equitable power. Differently coded bodies experience different invisible border zones that may prove hostile or welcoming, familiar or foreign. Labyrinth has always aimed at making space for a plurality of experience, and facilitating dialogue among participants. In this ideal, translation is communal, plural, unfinished, and contested. However, in

16. Robinson, *Translationality*, ix–x; 66.
17. Cronin and Simon, "Translation Zone," 127.
18. Marais, *(Bio)Semiotic*.
19. Cronin, *Eco-Translation*.
20. This ecological question of this paragraph forms the context for my PhD thesis: see Valler, "Taking the Measure."

practice this has not been straightforward. The "hacking" of cities is a slow, time-consuming process; the labyrinths explored in this chapter are my own readings, worked into narrative designs. While the pathways arguably succeed in opening critical questions for participants, they are nonetheless constrained by a myriad of choices I have made. The potential of communal readings persists. It is a familiar conundrum of translation, where the work of a lone creative tends to prevail over the aspirations of a more communal, democratic approach to the emergence of new meaning in new places. Biblical Performance Criticism has highlighted the communal norms through which audience participation is integral to meaning making, and the dialogue between this sub-discipline and translation studies, explored by this volume, is generative for the development of my own practice.

Conclusion

The reader of a book on Bible translation would be forgiven for thinking this chapter has largely focused elsewhere. That is deliberate. There is an assumption about Bible translation that is so ingrained, even across otherwise incommensurate traditions, that to question it feels absurd: namely, that to translate the Bible one must focus on the Bible. Yet in certain contemporary contexts—especially in Europe and North America—the Bible is so ubiquitous that its meaning functions like Musil's monuments. Retranslations abound, with new phrasing and new literary sensitivity, but deeply ingrained meanings swallow new creations in their pervasive norms. One of Labyrinth's aims is to design a journey that helps people who are familiar with a place to experience it, at least in a certain way, as if for the first time. In relation to Bible translation, my motivation is similar: how to break open these pathways to allow the Bible to be experienced, if not for the first time, then at least as something unfamiliar with the capacity to remake new meanings?

This chapter has made the assertion that translation need not be limited to linguistic processes, but instead can be conceptualized as a complex experience of semiotic negotiations between people, place, and text. In this translational experience, the movement of bodies, and the somatic negotiation of meanings, is central. The narrative journey is fragile; it does not reproduce an original, whether biblical text or urban. Instead, it continually negotiates the resonances and dissonances produced by the play of people, place, and past. The Bible is translated not as a separate text that it is possible to easily pick up and set down at will, but as an entangled text whose meanings are uncertain and generative in equal measure.

Bibliography

Blumczynski, Piotr. *Experiencing Translationality: Material and Metaphorical Journeys.* London: Routledge, 2023.
Cronin, Michael. *Eco-Translation: Translation and Ecology in the Age of the Anthropocene.* New Perspectives in Translation and Interpreting Studies. New York: Routledge, 2017.
———. *Translation and Identity.* New York: Routledge, 2006.
Cronin, Michael, and Sherry Simon. "Introduction: The City as Translation Zone." *Translation Studies* 7 (2014) 119–32.
Marais, Kobus. *A (Bio)Semiotic Theory of Translation: The Emergence of Social-Cultural Reality.* Routledge Advances in Translation and Interpreting Studies. New York: Routledge, 2019.
Musil, Robert. *Posthumous Papers of a Living Author.* Translated by Peter Worstman. Hygiene, CO: Eridanos, 1987.
Myers, Ched. *Binding the Strong Man: A Political Reading of Mark's Story of Jesus.* Maryknoll, NY: Orbis, 2008.
Richards, Thomas. *The Imperial Archive: Knowledge and the Fantasy of Empire.* London: Verso, 1993.
Robinson, Douglas. *Translationality: Essays in the Translational-Medical Humanities.* New York: Routledge, 2017.
———. *The Translator's Turn.* Baltimore: Johns Hopkins University Press, 1991.
Schleiermacher, Friedrich. "On the Different Methods of Translating." Translated by Waltraud Bartscht. In *Theories of Translation: An Anthology of Essays from Dryden to Derrida*, edited by Rainer Schulte and John Biguenet, 36–54. Chicago: Chicago University Press, 1992.
Schrödinger, Erwin. *What Is Life? The Physical Aspect of the Living Cell.* Cambridge: Cambridge University Press, 1945.
Schoelwer, Susan Prendergast. *Alamo Images: Changing Perceptions of a Texas Experience.* Dallas: DeGlolyer Library and Southern Methodist University Press, 1985.
Tucker, Phillip Thomas. *Emily D. West and the "Yellow Rose of Texas" Myth.* Jefferson, NC: McFarland, 2014.
Valler, Matt. "Taking the Measure of High Cross: Translating the Many Worlds of Truro at the Time of the Anthropocene." PhD diss., Queen's University Belfast, 2024.
Valler, Matt, and Piotr Blumczynski. "Reassembling the Ruins: Revisiting Latour's Concept of Translation in Modernity's Growing Aftermath." *The Translator* 30 (2024) 334–51.
Venuti, Lawrence. *The Translator's Invisibility: A History of Translation.* Routledge Translation Classics. New York: Routledge, 2017.

6

Increasing Communication Bandwidth

From Multimodal Translation Process to Four Revised Qualities of Bible Translation

SEBASTIAN FLOOR

Introduction: Limitations of the Qualities of Accuracy, Clarity, and Naturalness?

For decades, three qualities of a good translation have been standard in the Bible translation (BT) movement. These include accuracy, clarity, and naturalness (ACN). These qualities have served the translation movement well, and still do, but more recently concerns have been raised whether they can continue to promote translation quality going forward. Like most ideas and standards, evaluative qualities evolve, develop, get enriched, or get replaced.

One concern with the ACN qualities relates to terminology. What do these terms really mean? What associations and connotations and desirable and undesirable applications may they imply? A second concern stems from recent developments in translation studies (TS). The ACN qualities have remained unchanged for fifty years and there are doubts that these terms, and the concepts surrounding them, have kept pace with new developments in linguistics and TS. Do these terms still serve the Bible translation movement well? A third concern relates to the origin of the qualities. They originated with the international BT agencies who implemented a form of "outside gatekeeping" with this quality framework. To quote Dr. Simon Crisp, International Translation Officer of the United Bible Societies at the time:

> The practice of Bible translation was understood as being governed by theories and assumptions about the interpretation of the Bible which were elaborated far away from almost all the communities in which translation was actually carried out. This meant that standards of accuracy and faithfulness, also, were defined externally and understood as universally applicable, and this in turn meant that some degree of outside gate-keeping was essential if such universal consistent standards were to be maintained.[1]

This has been a fairly significant indictment of the system of quality assurance (hereafter QA). Are the ACN qualities enduring universal qualities, as they are currently still promoted, or are they only terms arising from a certain academic tradition in a certain part of the world, which now need to be reconsidered? One issue in particular this chapter explores relates to whether the ACN framework overemphasizes the role of the written text. Separating the quality of a text from its context, especially its communal and cognitive context, is problematic. There is a collective experience of quality, a community assessing and assigning of quality. A translation has to be collectively perceived to be of good quality. It does not only have an intrinsic objective quality of trustworthiness that can conveniently be separated from the end users. These concerns and their significance are discussed throughout the chapter.

In this chapter I provide a brief literature review of BT qualities and a critique of the ACN quality framework. I then provide a background on recent efforts to recalibrate the approach to evaluative criteria for BT quality assessment. Finally, I describe in more detail the revised translation quality standards from a multimodal and multimedia perspective. This perspective represents wider communication bandwidth which will highlight the significance of the recalibrated qualities.

---

1. Crisp, "Translation Consultancy," 3.

Literature Review of the Bible Translation Qualities

Early Bible Translation Theory on Qualities of a Good Translation

The accuracy, clarity, and naturalness qualities for BT have a long history. Maxey gives a good overview:

> Nida did open the door to meaning equivalence when he stated: "meaning must be given priority, for it is the content of the message which is of prime importance for Bible translating" (Nida and Taber 1969:13). In addition, this type of equivalence was supported by Nida's componential analysis and the so-called conduit model of communication, following generative linguistics' notion of the kernel (Nida 1975). Other Bible translators latched on to the notion of equivalent meaning and, once they did, the criteria for assessing translations became entrenched as accuracy, naturalness, and clarity (see for example Beekman and Callow [1974] 1984; Barnwell 2002; Larson [1984] 1997).[2]

Barnwell defined these three translation qualities in the following way (emphasis in original):

> A good translation should be:
> **ACCURATE** The translator must re-express the meaning of the original message **as exactly as possible** in the language into which he is translating.
> **CLEAR** The translation should be **clear and understandable**. The translator aims to communicate the message in a way that people can readily understand.
> **NATURAL** A translation should not sound "foreign." It should not sound like a translation at all, but like someone speaking in the natural, everyday way.[3]

In the fourth edition (2020) of her manual she added **ACCEPTABILITY**.[4] Here she includes under acceptability if church leaders are happy with the style of a translation, with the dialect chosen, with the choice of key terms, and issues surrounding the translators and the denominations they represent. We will be looking at this again later in this chapter.

---

2. Maxey, "Alternative Evaluative Concepts," 6.
3. Barnwell, *Bible Translation*, 29–30.
4. Barnwell, *Bible Translation*, 30.

The Turns in Translation Studies

In TS, new perspectives on translation and cognition developed that challenged the ACN categories. Relevance Theory, and the theory of pragmatics underlying it, represented a significant turn away from linguistic theory which takes language to be essentially a structure of forms and meanings. Relevance Theory's application to Bible translation was developed by Ernst-August Gutt.[5] His approach to translation calls for a pragmatics-based inference model of communication and not a code equivalence model. Meaning making is much more than only decoding a code. The focus shifted to how language is used and the cognitive processes in speakers' and hearers' minds. Now communication means more than decoding a code. Meaning is inferred from both the linguistic signs and the contextual assumptions, which together yield meaning as contextual implications. This has opened the door for the quality of translations to be measured by more than the language systems used, but also by cognition. This in turn led to the adoption of different but equally valid translation types and styles. The original meaning can be expressed in more than one way. I will use this concept later to challenge the concept of "accuracy."

Skopos theory and the function of a translation has been another significant development in TS that has impacted standards around translation quality.[6] According to Nord, a functional translation is a good translation. In other words, a good translation is loyal to the goal and requirements set out for it, rather than possessing an ideal of accuracy that is good across the board. Translation purposes can vary, and so can the translations themselves.

The First Challenges to ACN

Despite the fact that TS has cast doubt on ACN, there has been little critique of them from within Bible translation theory and practitioners. At the 2008 Bible translation conference in Horsleys Green, UK, I presented an unpublished paper titled "What Do We Mean by a *Clear* Translation? The Access to Meaning and the Limits of Clarity."[7] In it, I questioned the scope of one quality, namely clarity. The main point was that the contents

---

5. Gutt, *Translation and Cognition*; Gutt, *Relevance Theory*.
6. Nord, *Translation as Purposeful Activity*.
7. Floor, "Limits of Clarity."

and subject matter of Scripture are so vast in grandeur, our knowledge of the original languages so far from complete, and the historical and cultural gap between the original compositions and now so wide, that instant and complete understanding and clarity for individual readers is not realistic to expect. The rich contents of Scripture can only be retrieved by the individual in fellowship with an interpreting community, the church, and over time.

James Maxey wrote probably the first significant challenge mounted against the ACN framework. He discusses translation evaluation with a critique of equivalence, the influence of modernism, and the print bias.[8] I will discuss all three. The concept of equivalence underlies the translation quality of accuracy. On equivalence as seen as code symmetry, Maxey commented that TS questioned the validity and value of equivalence as a goal and measure of translation for several decades.[9] He quotes Mary Snell-Hornby, who jettisoned equivalence as presenting "an illusion of symmetry between languages which hardly exists beyond the level of vague approximations and which distorts the basic problems of translation."[10]

On modernism as claiming that one clear author intent can be identified in the text, Maxey questioned the assertion that there is only one intended author meaning and that it can be discovered in exact terms.[11] He critiques the practice that translations are evaluated by comparing them to the source text to determine what is lost, what is not there. To determine what is gained is seldom discussed, and often critiqued as "adding" something. He (and TS) also critiques the approach to translation as a neutral process, fully objective, finding equivalences with the translators and the context not influencing the translation process. This view of equivalence is a modernist view. This relates to maintaining ambiguities in the translation. On avoiding ambiguities to achieve accurate and clear translation, Maxey has this to say: "In addition, the assumption that translations were to be clear—disambiguating the options for readers—demonstrated a modern view of monovalent meaning. As for clarity, a singular authorial intention and readers' capacities to decipher

---

8. Maxey, "Alternative Evaluative Concepts."
9. Maxey, *From Orality to Orality*, xx.
10. Maxey, "Alternative Evaluative Concepts," 58.
11. Maxey, "Alternative Evaluative Concepts," 61.

this text-bound meaning was assumed."[12] Related to the concern of clear, unambiguous translation, I offered a critique of autonomous individual interpretation:

> Among other influences from modernism, the 18th Century philosophy of Common Sense Realism[13] contributed to this presupposition, as argued by Osborne (1991:9–10): "... the application of Common Sense Realism to Scripture has led many to assume that everyone can understand the Bible for themselves, that the surface of the text is sufficient to produce meaning in and of itself."[14]

Gutt touched on the same issue when addressing the problem of the code model of comprehension and mentioned the fact that such a model assumes that "if the meaning is expressed correctly, it will be understood correctly."[15]

The third point that Maxey raises in his critique of ACN is that of print bias:

> Despite its historical roots in orality, the Bible in the modern era is often synonymous with the printed book. Theories, principles, and methods of translation were developed with the assumption of the print medium. This assumption reinforced the criteria for the evaluation of translations. Non-print translations of the Bible (into song, [theater], and film, for example) were designated "adaptations" and not considered "faithful translations."[16]

Beyond their relationship to equivalence, these assessment criteria reflect a bias toward print translation that is inadequate for translation beyond print. Initially BT was restricted to the print medium. However, over the past decades, various types of non-print translations of the Bible have been produced, but they continue to be evaluated according to the same concepts as those of print translation that follow from a paradigm of equivalence.[17]

---

12. Maxey, "Alternative Evaluative Concepts," 59.
13. As a modernist epistemology, the Common Sense Realism is associated with eighteenth-century Scottish philosopher Thomas Reid.
14. Floor, "Limits of Clarity," quoting Thompson, *Clear and Present Word*, 34.
15. Gutt, *Translation and Cognition*, 51.
16. Maxey, "Alternative Evaluative Concepts," 62.
17. Maxey, "Alternative Evaluative Concepts," 57–58.

As an alternative set of terms for translation qualities, Maxey preferred carefulness for accuracy, transparency for clarity, and authentic language for naturalness, based on the metaphor of hospitality.

Two more recent areas in translation merit our attention too, as we consider translation quality: aesthetics and emotion in translation.[18] There is no space to develop these two new dimensions here, but what they communicate is that translations also need to have the right appeal. We will return to the concept of appealing translations later in this paper.

Another significant paper on translation qualities was that by Tim Jore in which he argues for translations to be trusted and trustworthy, a move away from ACN toward community attitudes.[19] Other important BT voices, like Ernst Wendland, started to argue for *acceptability* in addition to ACN, but acceptability, as appropriate a quality as it is to Bible translation, was the odd one out, dealing with community concerns and attitudes about a text, whereas ACN is text-based.[20]

In summary from the above literature overview, the considerations concerning the limitations of the concept of equivalence, the inadequate view of singular author intent and singular meaning, the avoidance of ambiguity, the print bias not accounting for non-print, the lack of attention to community attitudes toward the text, and more recent dimensions of aesthetics and emotion in translation all call for a critique of ACN.

A Critique of ACN

In the light of the issues raised above, the next step is to scrutinize accuracy, clarity, and naturalness a bit more carefully to determine if the concerns are justifiable. We will start with accuracy.

The Problem with Accuracy

The challenge that Maxey raised against the term "accuracy" is based (1) on the understanding of the concept of equivalence, and (2) on the notion of a modernist approach to singular meaning and access to author intention based on text alone, as set out above. He also argues that accuracy is (3) harder to apply with non-print media: "Foley's premise is

---

18. Morrison, "Euphony as Crucial Component"; and Frost, "Method for Exegeting Emotions."

19. Jore, "Trustworthy and Trusted."

20. Chemoreon, "Considerations for Acceptability in Bible Translation."

that one should take into consideration the medium when defining accuracy: in regard to media, then, there are no perfect and complete—no universally accurate—representations. There is only a selection of lenses, each of which offers a particular kind of accuracy, an idiosyncratic take on reality."[21] The actual term "accurate" does not work either. Accuracy as a word has associations of precision, of binary: accurate versus inaccurate.[22] In practice, nobody wants an inaccurate translation. How can an absolutely accurate translation be guaranteed? In similar terms, accuracy cannot mean that it is bi-polar, right or wrong, accurate or inaccurate. There is a range of what can be more or less approximate and equivalent, and therefore more or less acceptable and trustworthy. There can be degrees of faithfulness to the source text, but one cannot really have degrees of accuracy. Furthermore, in translation practice, accuracy is sometimes unwittingly used to infer that there is only one correct option to translate something into a particular language, that there is only one possible rendering that is best. Cognition, language, and translation are more complex than that. Meaning making is more than only a linguistic process, let alone a literary linguistic one. The impact of cognitive linguistics, pragmatics, and especially Relevance Theory on TS and BT suggest that accuracy does not easily account for spectrum and the possibility of range of interpretive resemblance.

If accuracy is to be used as an evaluative term, it is best suited to evaluate a very literal translation. But even in the case of a very literal translation like the Brazilian Portuguese NAA and ARC versions, these have tended to veer away to more dynamic renderings more than once. Does that make them "inaccurate"? For example: in the Nyaneka Ps 99:6, the Hebrew has been translated as "answered" but both the Brazilian Almeida Corrigida e Actualizada versions have "heard." Is this an inaccurate translation? The Almeida versions are literal, corresponding translations. From a scientific and literal point of view it is inaccurate, but it may still be a trustworthy translation. The Portuguese idiom preferred to use "heard"; for them it communicated the meaning better.

To come back to the point about equivalence, the difficulty with accuracy is knowing which equivalence it is measuring. There are syntactic equivalence, semantic equivalence, pragmatic equivalence, and cognitive

21. Maxey, "Alternative Evaluative Concepts," 64.
22. This is why people say the Qur'an cannot be translated. Precision and exact equivalence cannot be achieved in translation, it is argued, hence all "translation" of the Qur'an is called interpretation.

equivalence. Syntactic equivalence across different language families is a real challenge. Finding semantic equivalence in the environment of different semantic mappings of biblical key concepts, for instance the attributes of God, is complex as it is. Pragmatic and cognitive equivalences are even more complex. Maxey wrote that accuracy can be measured differently, that textual accuracy has different features and values than that of oral or electronic accuracy.[23]

Language interfacing with communication modalities, culture, use, society, and cognition is complex. This raises the question if any quality assessment of a translation can still be done. It can, however the evaluation and measuring need to be done in a more comprehensive way. And for that, we need a new set of evaluation vocabulary.

Lastly is the issue of the original source text to be translated accurately. According to Esala's helpful discussion in this volume,[24] there is not a fixed, standard, original text of the Bible anywhere available. There is a range of manuscripts, and they sometimes vary. Exactness here is a too high a standard.

In summary, the translation quality of accuracy is too language-based and text-based, not taking into account artistic and social dynamics, pragmatics, cognition, and multimodality. Oral "accuracy" is more difficult to measure. Other factors over and above language make a translation good. Other terms have been suggested, like faithfulness, loyalty, and carefulness. A translation can be measured in terms of approximate similarity of thought and form. There can be a range of rendering that is still reliable and trustworthy.

The Problem with Clarity

Barnwell noted that a "translation should be clear and understandable. The translator aims to communicate the message in a way that people can readily understand."[25] But she also states clearly the limits of clarity, and that it should be recognized that some parts of the Bible are harder to understand. Spiritual insight by the Holy Spirit, further teaching, and further background knowledge are also needed.[26]

---

23. Maxey, "Alternative Evaluative Concepts," 66.
24. Esala, "Re-Translating a Contested Performance Tradition," 153–84.
25. Barnwell, *Bible Translation*, 23.
26. Barnwell, *Bible Translation*, 24.

Floor argued that to keep the term "clarity" as a translation quality, it is necessary to state what clarity is not: clarity does not necessarily entail easy syntax and limited vocabulary.[27] Clarity does not necessarily mean transparent language, meaning language that minimizes figures of speech and that has a high degree of literal reference. Clarity is not the same as immediate semantic transparency through information made explicit. Clarity also does not mean, in Relevance Theory terms, that all implicatures as well as all explicatures are to be made explicit. This is an unrealistic goal. Clarity does not mean that there are no more ambiguities in the text. Often translators fear that an ambiguous text will be misused, while in fact there is ambiguity even in the original text of the Bible. Clarity also does not mean under-translating metaphorically rich terms, known as weak communications. Weak communication is less specific communication that leaves most of the interpretation of its meaning to the audience, in contrast to strong or more specific communication that leaves less room for audience interpretation. In the case of metaphors, for instance, translating only a select few of the contextual implications leads in turn to a translation poorer in meaning. An example of such under-translating is "The Lord is my Protector" in Ps 23:1, instead of "The Lord is my Shepherd." By under-translating the metaphor, selecting only one aspect of "shepherd," the audience is denied access to other implications. And lastly, clarity does not mean that it is necessary to translate poetry into prose, translating away literary poetic features like parallelisms, for instance.

Two further examples will illustrate what clarity is not. The walking metaphor in the command in Gen 17:1 *"walk before my face."* A translation team in Mozambique at first drafted "be obedient to me." But on closer scrutiny the translators discovered that a slightly more literary rendering *"walk in my presence"*—a fully natural turn of phrase—would communicate equally well, if not better. Or take for instance *"The Lord is near"* in Phil 4:7, which could mean near in time or near in space or both. In such cases it is better to maintain the ambiguity if the language allows for it, allowing the readers/hearers to infer relevant meaning.

Clarity or intelligibility in Bible translation is only achieved when the meaning is retrievable or accessible by individuals-in-community, but it also holds that clarity is a process and a continuum and that suggesting

---

27. Floor, "Limits of Clarity."

instant clarity as a desirable translation quality may lead to unwanted consequences.[28]

A further complication is that if a translation is only text-based, it is difficult to achieve real, authentic, natural language as it is spoken. Texts have of course their own authentic literary quality in languages with a writing tradition, but that is not the same as conversational language. Texts tend to have less redundancy, and the correct oral discourse marking is less likely to be successfully achieved in translation when only working in text. Oral and multimodal translation methods stand a better chance of achieving clarity and intelligibility.

Clarity is not far off the mark in terms of intelligibility and comprehensibility, but it remains misleading in that it communicates full transparency and instantaneous accessibility, and even ease of understanding, which cannot be the case for everything in Scripture. Understanding is a wider concept, more suited as a translation quality. Maxey's transparency is better here, but even transparency can be an issue. Parts of Scripture are not immediately transparent. This is even more the case with clarity, which can infer the capacity of an individual. It makes the unrealistic assumption that the individual reader has sufficient capacity to basically understand the text with first reading. What is needed is a term that embraces message difficulty as well, oral or written or signed, where the correct meaning is accessible and retrievable, even if it takes time and community to retrieve the information. Understanding is aided by increased communication bandwidth that different modes of communication open up.

The Problem with Naturalness

What do we mean by natural? Is it limited to conversational language? Does it include only certain registers of speech, or all of them? How can naturalness be measured in different genres? Several of the genres of Scripture do not use natural spoken language or conversational language. Some genres are not generally conversational language, like very formal language for legal documents, or poetic language. Furthermore, if natural language is defined as conversational language, even the written is immediately unnatural. It is basically impossible to have full conversational language in a translation, especially a written one. There are additional

---

28. Floor, "Limits of Clarity," 11–12.

complications with naturalness: the Biblical message has a double foreign character, not only the fact that it is an ancient message from a different time, with at least two thousand years separating us, but also, according to general conservative belief, it is a supernatural revelation over a long time. It is a sacred message calling to be respected as such. To fully domesticate such a sacred message to the point that it is so natural that no foreign element can be traced in it, is basically impossible without compromising the message. Alterity is a translation feature that ACN maybe cannot easily handle.

Translations frequently have less than conversational language. A term that may be helpful is defamiliarization. Defamiliarization is a concept introduced by Heimerdinger, and it refers to linguistic constructions, like marked constructions, that are not unfamiliar but contain unexpected shifts in word-order for pragmatic effect.[29] That is still authentic language, using Maxey's term.

The term "naturalness" is too restrictive for a translation quality. What is required is a wider term that includes multimodality (both writing and speaking and other signs like white space on printed text, the formatting, the pitch and speed of voice, and many more), as well as marked, defamiliar language. Economy of words fall in this category too: too many words, all completely natural, may not make for a good translation.

In summary, I want to suggest that accuracy and clarity are too misleading and naturalness too limited in scope to be effective evaluative terms for multimodal communications. The ACN qualities, as they stand, do not really measure all what needs to be measured. At best, they can point to a goal in written translation, but even that can be questioned as noted above.

A range of issues need to be addressed by translation quality assurance. The following list, though not exhaustive, is a start:

1. The meaning of a translation is not limited to a written text only. Translations can also be in other modes and media, with meaning making equally expanded to more modes. Additional modes of communication have now come into view in BT and in TS, moving away from a text-based theory only. Orality and especially multimodality are important considerations in evaluating translation.

29. Heimerdinger, *Topic, Focus and Foreground in Ancient Hebrew Narratives*; Lunn, *Word-Order Variation in Biblical Poetry*.

2. The meaning of a communication is not limited to the actual words of a text or an utterance. There is meaning making in the minds of the speaker/author as well as the audience/reader. A translation quality cannot be limited to only the actual words used, but also by what is implied and assumed. Add to this non-linguistic signs like font, illustrations, voice quality and pitch in the case of oral and audio, and so forth.

3. The range of fidelity needs to be accounted for. It may be more accurate to view quality being on a spectrum rather than a specific point on a line—as a matter of degree, with many factors influencing it. It is less about precision and exactness, because something that is not exact and precise can still be close enough to be trustworthy.

4. Community dynamics must be included in any theory of translation quality. We need a new set of qualities that touch on more than only the text and linguistics.

5. The wider context of a translation also plays a role in translation quality: a translation should fit its purpose. *Skopos* theory emerged with a new approach to translation function.

6. Paralinguistic and non-linguistic semiotic systems need to be accounted for, like typography and illustrations, and emotion, pitch, motion, and even music.

7. Aesthetics in translation also plays a role. This is a more recent perspective. Appropriate and attractive publications in multimedia or monomedia form part of translation quality.

8. Multiple genres and language styles need to be reflected in translation qualities. Conversational language is not the complete picture.

Recently, within the BT movement, in the quest to find new ways to define quality assurance and the translation qualities the QA is based on, there has been a conscious attempt to re-evaluate ACN and to search for alternative terminology that may capture translation qualities better.

The Background to Recalibrating the Bible Translation Qualities

The Shift to Multimodal Translation: Increasing Communication Bandwidth

Since the coming of focus on orality and oral BT, other modes of communication have been introduced to BT.[30] Sign Language BT is an earlier development, with performances of Sign Language gestures another genre of communication. Until very recently, the modes of sight (reading and writing) and sound (hearing and speaking) have been kept apart as parallel tracks in BT, but the reality of multimodality has now increasingly been recognized in BT. Several have called for bringing orality and the written together.[31] TS preceded this turn to multimodality in translation.[32] In addition to simply combining oral and print, inter-semiotic translation is needed, wherein multiple modes and semiotic systems interact with each other.

Carol O'Sullivan wrote that traditionally translation is about the "printed word, but in today's multimodal environment translators must take account of other signifying elements too. Words may interact with still and moving images, diagrams, music, typography or page layout."[33]

There are two general views of the different modalities in multimodal communication. One is based on the five senses, and for our interest in Bible translation, sight, sound, and touch are the pertinent.[34] The other view is multimodality combining more than one semiotic system. According to Calvin Chong, these systems, and what they comprise, are the following:[35]

1. Linguistic: vocabulary, generic structure, and the grammar of oral and written language.

2. Visual: color, vectors, and viewpoint in still and moving images.

---

30. Maxey, *From Orality to Orality*; and Floor, "Oral-Based Bible Translation."

31. Maxey, *From Orality to Orality*, 82–84; De Vries, "Local Oral-Written Interfaces," 69, 94–96; Gravelle, "Orality and Literacy Revisited," 20; and Floor, "Seamless Integration of Orality and Literacy," 10–11.

32. Kaindl, "Multimodal Conception of Translation."

33. O'Sullivan, "Introduction: Multimodality."

34. Qian and Chuanmao, "Research on Multimodal Translation," 872.

35. Chong, "Text as Multimodal Experience," 23–24.

3. Audio: volume, pitch, and rhythm of music and sound effects.
4. Gestural: movement, speed, and stillness in facial expression and body language.
5. Oral-spatial: proximity, direction, position of layout, and organization of objects in space.

These two definitions of multimodality overlap. In both sound and sight modes, for instance, there are linguistic and non-linguistic semiotic systems. The linguistic system is also visual, gestural, and audio. The senses-based model is more desirable because the semiotic systems fit well into the sense modes as more generic categories.

In BT, there is exclusively a written source text. Information of the context can be inferred from the text and what is known about the history and culture of the time, but the non-linguistic semiotic systems of sound, like music as in the case of the Psalms, is unknown to the Bible translator. The original text gives a very limited window into the original communication situation.

Some of the semiotic signs are translatable, but some are not. Illustrations are a mode that communicate very effectively; they are more than only supplementary, they contribute vitally to meaning making. Certain emotions can also be inferred from the original text, but many cannot. So, in multimodal translation making use of performance of a translated scripture, new sets of signs are introduced. For instance, using certain electronic print fonts or font sizes: this was unknown technology when the original sacred message was composed, maybe first orally and later written down for verbatim preservation. Measuring exactness of equivalence is essentially impossible.

Communication takes place in several modes, be it with oral, written, digital, live performance, still and moving pictures, verbal and non-verbal signs. Opening more communication channels, now with more bandwidth, brings additional meaning-making opportunities, and the overall communication is enriched. The communication bandwidth has been increased. The elements of such an expansion of communication bandwidth are laid out in the table below:[36]

---

36. Floor and Harmelink, "Multimodality in Bible Translation," 14.

Table 1

	Scripture translation process by communication genre	Scripture products by communication media (incl. digital media)
Intra-modal translation	written text to written text	intra-medial printed Scripture (books, etc.)
	spoken text to spoken text	intra-medial audio Scripture (recordings)
Multimodal translation	written text to combined written text and images	multimedia Scripture comics
	written text simultaneous with spoken sound	1) multimedia performance of public reading of Scriptures 2) multimedia Scripture 3) audio-visual Scripture (live performance, film), for example, the Scripture Builder App
Inter-modal translation	written text (and images) to spoken text	transmedia Scripture - audio recordings of Scripture readings - oral Bible translation - printed text with oral-aural prompts (for example, cantillation marks)
	spoken to written text	transmedia transcription and adaptation
	written text and images to Sign Language gestures	transmedia Sign Language Scripture (live performance, film)
	written and/or spoken text to braille	transmedia braille Scripture

Even in intra-modal translation for written and print, multimodal aspects can be included. Study Bibles are attractive examples of this: color, maps, photos, illustrations, lists, and notes are presented attractively. This is not new either: the initial printed copies of the Bible in the sixteenth century feature fonts, supplementary notes and illustrations not seen in modern publications of the Bible. Accuracy and naturalness do not cover these multimodal aspects. These features are enhancements to the translation, and although a linguistic text can be made more understandable with these additions, it is not because of any increased clarity in the text itself.[37]

Likewise, for intra-modal oral translation, the non-linguistic audio modes of pitch, speed, and emotion are not easily derived from the original manuscripts, but they serve as enhancements to communication and can make a translation more appealing and appropriate for its context. Again, the ACN qualities seem inadequate.

Multimodal performance of the biblical text in a public reading of Scripture, an ancient practice in antiquity, enhances the communication experience by opening up simultaneous bandwidth with a range of modes and semiotic systems. With digitalization, even more can be added. The multimedia Scripture Builder App,[38] with simultaneous sound and sight, brings together several modes into a single communication. Add to that video, something planned for the performance of psalms in the Psalms That Sing project, where the user will have a scripture experience that includes a video performance of the psalm with sound and with a separate window where the text is displayed and progress scrolled.[39] For such a complex communication, translation quality needs to be evaluated with appropriate measurements different from ACN.

The embodiment of meaning in performance, preceded by multimodal meaning-making processes, has become an exciting new possibility in BT, integrating different communication modes and so increasing communication bandwidth:

> Just as our recognition of multilingualism requires a recalibration of our methods for BT, so too will our recognition of Multimodal Translation (MMT). It is not enough to overlay old print-based methods or even limited oral-based methods on MMT projects. Likewise, the ways we conceive of quality are being challenged by MMT. This is becoming evident as old print-based quality assurance views are insufficient for MMT. Accuracy, naturalness, and clarity have served their print-based model well. But they are insufficient to address quality issues in MMT. One of the organic side effects of OBT was the

---

37. In a sense, the current practice of domesticating the message by making a text more natural is an enhancement to the text. The natural language of the translation is not necessarily similar to the original form. The original Greek and Hebrew in many instances do not exhibit conversational language; it cannot be assumed that the original is conversational language in every case.

38. https://software.sil.org/scriptureappbuilder/.

39. A prototype of this application is in development, March 2024.

reunification of translation and engagement. This is equally if not more true with MMT. MMT processes integrate engagement into translation.[40]

The rise of multimodality in translation as a concept is new and still unproven, but it reflects the latest insights from TS and theoretically and practically makes sense. The following is an overview of recent efforts to experiment with these new concepts in various places around the globe.

The Discovery Process of the Recalibrated Qualities: The ETEN Innovation Lab

In early 2021, Every Tribe Every Nation (ETEN), a collaboration of the major BT agencies in the USA, established the Innovation Lab. The Innovation Lab consists of three different labs, one on quality assurance, one on technology, and one on publishing and copyright. The Innovation Lab on QA started to meet online in September 2021 on a weekly basis. Initially they considered ways to address the need for more consultants but within months it became clear that an altogether different approach is needed to broaden the involvement of the church in the QA processes for the remaining BT task.

The QA Innovation Lab was invited to get involved with a church-based Bible translation movement in the Madang and Milne Bay provinces of Papua New Guinea, a movement led by BATTLE, a national Bible translation agency, in association with Global Partnerships. As the ideas around multimodality were developing, so was the need for different processes, rhythms, and translation agents, and together with that, the need for a curriculum designed for these unique circumstances.[41]

By early 2022 it was decided to reconsider the translation qualities current at the time, namely accuracy, clarity, and naturalness, and the Lab started to explore different terms. The Lab wanted to base the new curriculum on a set of translation qualities reflecting multimodal values and processes, as in *Skopos* theory, Relevance Theory, cognitive approaches, and so on. During 2022 the first training workshops implementing an early draft of the curriculum took place. By the end of the year, the core contents of the curriculum, now called the Church-Based

---

40. Maxey, "Mono to Multimodal Translation," 11.

41. For more information, see etenlab.substack.com; ETEN Lab, "Innovation Lab Recommendations V4."

Bible Translation (CBBT) curriculum was agreed upon. During 2023 the curriculum was developed, training provided, and the initial results evaluated.

Next to the development of the CBBT curriculum, the Innovation Lab for QA has collaborated with SRV Partners to develop oral materials for translators, materials designed to end up in the Bible Well of the Aquifer.[42] The first book completed was the Gospel of Mark. This process led to the rise of the so-called FIA process. FIA stands for familiarization, internalization, and articulation. These concepts were elaborated and proven in the orality movement and especially oral Bible translation. FIA is the engine of multimodal translation or MMT. FIA is essentially an oral-first approach, with transcription only added later. The FIA process does not fit well with ACN. The difference is that with FIA there now emerged a need for translation qualities that have more flexibility in terms of QA and better reflect the wider multimodal bandwidth and other issues related to cognition, pragmatics, and community attitudes, all key to quality in BT.

The QA Lab started experimenting with different terms for quality, and came up with five: trustworthy, consistent, intelligible, appropriate, and appealing. The qualities were constantly revisited until the Lab settled on the current four translation qualities. Consistent was later brought under trustworthy. The actual terms underwent changes too, replacing intelligible with understandable, and adding to trustworthiness the quality of being true. Finally, the Lab wrote checklists based on the CBBT curriculum.

The Recalibrated Translation Qualities

The recalibrated translation qualities terms are trustworthy, understandable, appropriate, and appealing (TUAA). The qualities of appropriateness and appeal are largely influenced by the wider bandwidth introduced by multimodality, but not exclusively.

---

42. https://app.well.bible/.

Trustworthy Translations

Faithful, loyal, close, tight, and careful have all been suggested as good alternatives to accuracy.[43] The ETEN Innovation Lab found Tim Jore's suggestion of trustworthy translation closest to the evaluative quality required for a multimodal translation experience and product.[44] A trustworthy translation is a true translation; it is true to the original in the sense that it is as close a representation of the original that is possible in the context of multimodal, cognitive, and pragmatic considerations. The term also includes an acceptability dimension. A translation is trustworthy to a person or group(s), and therefore trusted by them. What makes this term even more useful is the analogy with the Hebrew term *'emet*, a key concept with its meaning covering concepts like truth, faithfulness, but also reliability and trustworthiness. Reality and reliability coming together. This is exactly what a true and trustworthy translation hopes to be. When something is true, it is true to the reality it reflects, it is genuine, it is representative and can therefore be trusted.

Trustworthy translation is the first and primary quality of a good translation. It is at the heart of the qualities. A good quality translation is a genuine translation, a translation true to its originally intended meaning. It can be relied upon. As discussed earlier, the quality of true and trustworthy translation is preferred to accurate translation since accuracy infers precision, something not always achieved in the multi-semiotic context in which translation is done.

There is a spectrum, a continuum of true-ness, and hence trustworthiness. The target language within its target culture is multimodal; communication context is more than only a local textual context or a literary context. It is wider, further back in history, in the framework of both the oral and the written. In that context the communication was received. Translation quality assessment needs to evaluate that implied context too, not only the text.

Trustworthy translations are faithful and loyal to the original text and intention. The users' interpretation of the translation resembles that of the original readers: the users infer the same information, same emotion, and same impact. Trustworthy translations:

---

43. Maxey, "Alternative Evaluative Concepts."
44. Jore, "Trustworthy and Trusted."

1. Have **nothing** that has been **left out**.[45]

    It is not uncommon for a word, phrase, sentence, or even a verse to be left out. Questions to ask are is there a verse missing? Or a sentence? Maybe a clause, a part of a sentence? Or maybe even an important word?

2. Have **nothing** that has been **added**.

    No additional ideas or concepts should be introduced into the translation. This does not mean that translators may not make more explicit some of the implicit meanings that can be inferred from the context. The problem arises when totally new ideas are added. Is the translation saying anything extra that the original source language is not saying? What makes a translation not faithful to the original, and therefore not trustworthy, is when some new meaning is added that does not reflect anything in the source version (for example, Bartimaeus the blind man crying out: "Jesus Christ, son of David." *Christ* is not in the original, and it would not be a trustworthy translation if it is added).

3. Have **nothing** that has been **changed**.

    Unfaithful and untrustworthy translation is when some original meaning gets changed (for example, when the original says, "Jesus said . . ." and the translation has "Jesus shouted . . . ," or, in the case of Bartimaeus the blind man crying out, "Jesus, Son of *God*" instead of "Jesus, Son of *Man*").

4. Have **implicit information** in the form of assumptions and implications.

    It is not necessary to make every aspect of the meaning explicit. Indeed, it is not possible for the whole meaning of the passage to be expressed in words. But it is translated in such a way that the users will infer the same things that the original users did. Part of the meaning is always implicit, which is unavoidable (for example, in Mark 1:6, John seems to be a weird person: *camel's hair, leather belt*, with a strange diet: *locusts and wild honey*. What is the meaning of all of this? And do all the different things here

---

45. This has been clearly argued before in ACN as well in Barnwell, *Bible Translation*.

have any specific meaning? How will the local audience react to such a person? Are such eccentric prophets known in rural areas?).

Key biblical information is another way to track the quality of trustworthy translations. Good translations effectively provide access to key biblical information. This is essential for a translation to be trustworthy. Translating key biblical concepts like salvation, holiness, glory, righteousness, and so on needs to be faithful to the original meaning. Having these wrong will greatly undermine the trustworthiness of the translation. Key biblical concepts must be faithful, intelligible, authentic, and as close as possible to the meanings of the concepts in the original–exactly equivalent, no, but approximately so. Are the key terms in line with the key concepts underlying them? Does the word or phrase used provide a window to the complete concept it refers to?

Translator-friendly guiding principles for the trustworthiness of the translation of key biblical concepts and key terms are the following:

- Key concepts between languages do not exactly map.
- Key concepts are not always translated exactly the same way in every instance.
- Key terms with exactly the same meaning are translated consistently.
- Key terms may be borrowed from another language if it is necessary and appropriate.

In short, trustworthy translation is translation that is true, faithful, and loyal to the original communication, in that nothing is intentionally added, left out, or changed that could not be accounted for in the implicit information. At the same time, it is understood that trustworthiness includes a spectrum on the range of equivalence. Exact equivalence is not possible.

Understandable Translations

The Innovation Lab also suggested a theoretical movement from clear translation to intelligible or understandable translation. A translation in which everything is immediately clear to everyone at first reading or hearing is suspect. The supernatural message of the Scriptures, written in a context far removed from our own, cannot easily be reduced to a few clear propositions. Intelligible or understandable translation means that the biblical information is somehow transparent (Maxey's term) and retrievable, even if it takes multiple hearings or readings, or even a deep study, or only after an improved level of biblical literacy has been achieved, or even only after a communal understanding process, to make the information relevant and accessible. Understandable translations:

1. Use **accessible language**.

    Wherever possible, translations should use familiar and accessible language. Of course this can be interpreted in different ways. Questions to ask are the following: Is everyday, conversational language acceptable, or should something be said in a more formal and unfamiliar way while still accessible? Not all renderings are easy to understand, however. Always ask if the translation of this passage is accessible language. Does it make sense? Will the people understand it? Are the words more or less familiar? What about loan words? Will people understand them? What about heavy, authoritative, and archaic words that only the elderly people still know and use? Be mindful of the generation or age-group being targeted.

2. Have a clear **discourse flow**, a **discourse progression, cohesion, and coherence**.

    The transitions between sentences and verses are correct and flow nicely, the reference to the different participants is clear, everything makes a cohesive unit. Does the story flow nicely and easily? Does the passage form a cohering unit, or does it feel disconnected and jolted? Are the correct verbs used for narratives, for instance (for example, in Mark 1:6, there is a shift from the foreground storyline to important background information to help hearers and readers understand the story better. Background information is now provided following the "*Now*." How is that best handled, so that the audience does not think this is on the main storyline)?

3. Have effectively dealt with **unknown concepts** by providing access to the original context and background.

    There are many concepts in the Bible that may be unknown to the local situation. Identify those in the passage. They are real translation challenges, potential problem points. Have they been translated correctly? There are different ways to handle them, like footnotes, more descriptive phrases, pictures, and glossaries, but not everything difficult can be explained in one translation. In the end, the church needs to teach about these difficult concepts over an extended period (for example, in Mark 1:3 *"the wilderness"*— what is it? A dry and uninhabited place? A place with only rocks and sand? What about a "wilderness" in the Papua New Guinea context? Maybe using a picture or photo here will illustrate it).

4. Have effectively dealt with **figures of speech and idioms**.

   Languages differ and the Bible may have unfamiliar idioms and figures of speech in a passage. Identify the idioms and check if they have been translated in a proper way in your language. Such figures of speech can be metaphors, metonyms, similes, personification, hyperbole, merism, and so on (for example, in Mark 1:5, the "*all*" in "*all of Judea and all of Jerusalem*" is a hyperbole. It does not mean that absolutely everybody came. The idiom used here in the names of the cities is called a metonym. A metonym is when part of something represents everything; in this case the "*all*" with the name of the city refers to a large cross-section of the population of that city).

Appropriate Translations

The quality of appropriateness in translation accounts for the wider socio-semiotic context of the translation—including the perceptions we have of what translation of a sacred text should be—and is inspired by increased communication bandwidth and multimodality. This is more than just clear and natural; it should be authentic.[46] Functionality is in focus here. It includes community acceptability, but it also is fit for purpose, using the most effective mode and medium, or combination of modes and media, for successful communication. The appropriate quality of a good translation also includes the community-preferred translation type and register, as well as the right variant in relation to neighboring variants within the linguistic, cultural, and ecclesiastical ecosystems a community

---

46. Maxey, "Alternative Evaluative Concepts," 66–67.

finds itself.[47] There are several translation types: literal/corresponding translations (like the KJV, ESV); resembling translations (like NIV), clarifying translations (like the NLT, TEV), and simplifying translations (like the CEV). It is normally agreed upon at the start of the project what type of translation the church wants. Most churches settle for a style that is either resembling (type 2) or clarifying (type 3) or something in between, which is quite hard to do. Once a decision has been made, it is necessary to be consistent. A question to ask is this: Is this passage consistent with the translation type as agreed upon at the beginning of the project? Not everything needs to be rendered in one specific type; that is basically impossible to achieve. But a translation should try to generally reflect one type. The principle behind the types is that it is possible to say the same thing in more than one way. It is not wrong to use a freer or a more formal way. It just needs to be agreed by all. (For example, to become more aware of such translation type differences, take a very literal translation like the KJV and translate it word for word in a language of wider communication. Then try to make it a little bit clearer while staying very close to the KJV. Then try to say it in an even clearer way, using the language of the young people maybe. Then compare the three versions you developed and notice the differences. Then ask yourselves which one you prefer.) Appropriate translations:

1. Appear in all the **acceptable media**. Questions to ask are the following: Is it an oral or written translation? If it is oral, are all the right oral features of the language properly employed? Or are you aiming to have both an oral and written translation eventually? It is desirable to do both simultaneously. Normally the process starts with the oral translation. This oral translation gets transcribed and then edited to make it more acceptable for reading. All of this is normally agreed upon at the beginning of a project, but in the reviewer and church leaders' review, it needs to be checked if the appropriate speech form is used. (For example, oral translations are often wordier. For transcription, it may be necessary to consider deleting some of the oral words like exclamations and ideophones and redundant pronouns.)

2. Have considered the preferred **dialect or variant issues**. This is decided on at the start of the project. The language of the translation can be mixed with a Language of Wider Communication or

---

47. Floor, "Four Translation Types."

English, or even with words from a neighboring language, unless it is agreed that variants and dialects can be mixed in the translation. For instance, there are differences between the language spoken in rural villages and cities. Which one is preferable? Can both be used in a mixed way?

3. Use appropriate **language register** for Scripture and **religious expression**. Some language registers may be inappropriate for the Bible. At the same time, carefully consider religious-sounding, archaic words that may no longer communicate anything, or may communicate the wrong information, or just may not be understood well or at all. A question to ask is if the language used in this passage is in the right register—formal, or informal, or casual language for instance—for this translation? For instance, a question to ask here is if there is anything offensive in the translation of a passage.

Appealing Translations

Of the four qualities, the appealing quality is new. It includes naturalness but goes further. While monomodal translations, print or audio, can contain appealing language, increasing communication bandwidth by using more modes and different configurations of mode in translation processing and in media products can theoretically achieve higher degrees of appeal.

Maxey's authentic language comes close to appealing language. Authentic language has appeal, but not all authentic language has equal appeal. Appeal is something more: it is the verbal art dimension.

With only one or two text translators, it will be much harder to achieve an appealing translation, unless they are verbal artists with literary gifting, translators like Martin Luther or William Tyndale and their like. Most translators are not there. A larger group of translators multimodally interacting with each other and with the meaning stand a better chance to reach an appealing translation.

It is not only linguistic appeal that makes a translation good. For printed translations, the cover, page formatting, font size and color, and use of illustrations, maps, and other supplementary materials will also contribute. This makes the appealing quality immediately multimodal. Likewise, with live oral performances and audio recordings, voice quality, voice melody specific to the language and the genre, rhythm, intonation, adequate use of pauses, and music where appropriate, will all contribute to a multimodal experience of the appealing quality of a translation.

As already mentioned above, not all authentic language is necessarily natural language—the common way a community speaks a language. It is therefore preferable to use natural language as only one of several characteristics of appealing language, which includes authentic, artistic, beautiful, and economical language, that is, using the minimal amount of words for the maximum meaning. By themselves, beautiful written language or appealing spoken language do not capture all the richness of appealing communication in its widest, multimodal sense. Appealing translations:

1. Are **natural** translations. Conversational language is the minimum standard. So always ask: Is the passage translated into conversational language, the normal, authentic way the language is being spoken? Does it sound right? This is the great advantage of oral translations: one can quickly hear if it sounds right, and it is virtually impossible to speak something that is not natural and authentic language. For instance, are there expressions and renderings that will be jolting or even hard to say? Reading or reciting a translation will quickly reveal if the language is unnatural. We will find it hard to pronounce, we will stumble over the words, it will not roll well off the tongue.

2. Are **discourse-appropriate** translations. They employ appealing discourse features that boost the translation. Leaving them out is not wrong, but the translation will be impoverished. Over and above the translation flowing nicely, appealing translations make use of some aspects of the language that boost communication and make it more effective: for instance, clever word-order variation, smart use of small particles, the right verb tenses for narration, and more. Questions to ask: Does the translation make use of other nice discourse features like appropriate sentence length, varied speech introductions, the signaling of emphasis, and typical oral words like exclamations, and ideophones? For example, in Mark 1:2, the particle "*behold!*" is an attention grabber, but also a word that indicates that what follows was not expected. It is a surprise. Some translations leave them out altogether, but in oral translation, such a marker of unexpectedness and surprise will be

very meaningful. And in Mark 1:4, for instance, does the language prefer events to be in a chronological order? If yes, would it be possible to switch the clauses around in such a way that the events talked about strictly follow each other?

3. Are **economical** translations. Economy of language means that no unnecessary long wording is used. The rendering is just right for what needs to be communicated. Something can be implied, and the translators and reviewers will know that intuitively. For instance, no phrases, clauses, or sentences that are unnecessarily long or otherwise too short. Ask if the translation has been done as economically as possible in terms of its wording. For example, in Mark 1:4, the phrase *preach baptism of repentance and forgiveness of sins* is very complicated to translate. The Greek is very economical in terms of wording; it says a lot of things in a few words. Translations can easily make it into a very long verse.

4. Are **beautiful** translations. They employ beautiful and artistic expression wherever possible. Always ask: Is the translation beautiful? Does it sound nice? Does it have appeal? Will people be excited when they hear it? Would even unbelievers be impressed when they hear it? What would a good storyteller say about it? Would they approve? For example, in Mark 10:50, Bartimaeus threw off his cloak and sprang up. Very drastic, vigorous language. How will you translate to bring the feeling out, for beauty and the effect here?

Conclusion: Significance of TUAA to Account for Acknowledging Increasing Communication Bandwidth

How significant are the recalibrated qualities of translation for increasing communication bandwidth? Why is this recalibration relevant? The expanded requirements for translation qualities do not fit under ACN. The terminology is too limiting, too restrictive. They need to be recalibrated to account for the requirements laid out earlier for translation qualities:

1. Trustworthy: The meaning of a communication is not limited to the actual words of a text or an utterance.

2. Trustworthy: The range of fidelity needs to be accounted for. Is the translation close enough to the original?

3. Appropriate: *Skopos* theory: Community dynamics need to be included in any theory of translation quality.

4. Multimodal Translation: Additional modes of communication have now come into view in BT and TS, moving away from a text-based theory only.

5. Trustworthy and Appropriate: Paralinguistic and non-linguistic semiotic systems need to be accounted for, like typography and illustrations in the case of print, and emotion, pitch, motion, and even music in the case of oral and signed translations.

6. Trustworthy and Appealing: Aesthetics in translation needs to be accounted for.

7. Understandable and Appealing: Multiple genres and language styles need to be reflected in translation qualities.

TUAA meets the above requirements for quality categories in a more satisfactory way. It accounts for multimodality, cognitive context, community, and the directions of translation theory in general. And lastly, TUAA will impact day-to-day translation. TUAA terms lend themselves well to the practice of translation. The CBBT curriculum has been successfully built around these qualities. Effective checklists have been derived from these four qualities, and the qualities are easy to teach and are popular with users. The ACN qualities are not wrong as such, they are just inadequate for a translation theory that includes not only language and the written text, but also other modalities, cognition, pragmatics, *Skopos*, social dynamics, aesthetics, emotion, and genres. This all called for a recalibration.

Bibliography

Andersen, T. D. "Perceived Authenticity: The Fourth Criterion of Good Translation." *Notes on Translation* 12 (1998) 1–13.

Barnwell, Katharine. *Bible Translation: An Introductory Course in Translation Principles*. Dallas: SIL International, 2020.

Blumczynski, Piotr, and John Gillespie, eds. *Translating Values*. Palgrave Studies in Translating and Interpreting. London: Palgrave Macmillan, 2016.

Chemoreon, Diphus Chosefu. "Considerations for Acceptability in Bible Translation." *Verbum et Ecclesia* 30.2 (2009) 1–5.

Chong, C. "Encountering Text as Multimodal Experience." In *Oralities and Literacies: Implications for Communication and Education*, edited by C. Madinger, 23–36. International Orality Network, 2016.

Crisp, Simon. "Translation Consultancy: Set in Stone or Historically Conditioned?" Paper presented at the 2011 Bible Translation Conference, Dallas, TX.

De Vries, Lourens. "Local Oral-Written Interfaces and the Nature, Transmission, Performance, and Translation of Biblical Texts." In *Translating Scripture for Sound and Performance*, edited by James A. Maxey and Ernst R. Wendland, 68–98. Biblical Performance Criticism 6. Eugene, OR: Cascade Books, 2012.

Dressman, Mark. "Multimodality and Language Learning." *The Handbook of Informal Language Learning*, edited by Mark Dressman and Randall William Sadler, 39–55. Malden, MA: Wiley Blackwell, 2020.

ETEN Lab. "Innovation Lab Recommendations V4." 2024. https://etenlab.notion.site/Innovation-Lab-Recommendations-v4-083548c20fad40a2bc98dc85f364054c.

Floor, Karen J. "Oral-Based Bible Translation: A Contextualised Model for the Nomadic Himba People of Southern Africa." *In Die Skriflig/In Luce Verbi* 55 (2021) 6. https://doi.org/10.4102/ids.v55i3.2752.

Floor, Sebastian J. "A Reflective Overview of Oral Bible Translation in Southern Africa, with Special Focus on the Need for an Oral Translation Brief." Paper presented at the 2018 OBT Conference, Richmond, VA.

———. "The Search for a Seamless Integration of Orality and Literacy in Bible Translation: Some Perspectives from Southern Africa." Unpublished paper presented at the 2011 Bible Translation Conference, Dallas, TX.

———. "What Do We Mean by a *Clear* Translation? Some Thoughts on the Limits of Clarity." Unpublished paper presented at the 2008 Bible Translation Conference, Horsleys Green, UK.

Floor, Sebastian, and Bryan Harmelink. "Multimodality in Bible Translation: Could It Contribute to Quality Assurance?" In *Quality in Translation: A Multi-Threaded Fabric*, edited by Stephen Watters and Reinier de Blois, 166–95. Dallas: Pike Center for Integrative Scholarship, 2023.

Frost, Joshua C. "A Method for Exegeting Emotions in the Bible for Higher Quality Translation." In *Quality in Translation: A Multi-Threaded Fabric*, edited by Stephen Watters and Reinier de Blois, 171–215. Dallas: Pike Center for Integrative Scholarship, 2023.

Gravelle, Gilles. "Orality and Literacy Revisited." *Oralities and Literacies*, edited by Charles Madinger, 23–36. Roswell, GA: International Orality Network, 2016.

Gutt, Ernst-August. *Relevance Theory: A Guide to Successful Communication in Translation*. Dallas: SIL, 1992.

———. *Translation and Cognition*. Manchester: St Jerome, 2000.

Harmelink, Bryan. "Oral Bible Translation." Paper Presented at the 2019 Annual Meeting of the Forum of Bible Agencies International, Albuquerque, NM.

Heimerdinger, Jean-Marc. *Topic, Focus and Foreground in Ancient Hebrew Narratives*. Journal for the Study of the Old Testament Supplements 295. Sheffield: Sheffield Academic, 1999.

Jore, Tim. "Trustworthy and Trusted: Equipping the Global Church for Excellence in Bible Translation." *Unfolding Word*, Nov. 2024. DOI: 10.6084/m9.figshare.27794577.

Kaindl, Klaus. "A Theoretical Framework for a Multimodal Conception of Translation." *Translation and Multimodality: Beyond Words*, edited by Monica Boria et al., 49–78. London: Routledge, 2019.

Lunn, Nicolas P. *Word-Order Variation in Biblical Poetry*. Paternoster Biblical Monographs. Milton Keynes, UK: Pater-noster, 2006.

Maxey, James A. "Alternative Evaluative Concepts to the Trinity of Bible Translation." In *Translating Values*, edited by Piotr Blumczynski and John Gillespie, 57–80. Palgrave Studies in Translating and Interpreting. London: Palgrave Macmillan, 2016.

———. "From Mono to Multimodal Translation: Beyond OBT to MMT." Unpublished paper presented at 2023 Bible Translation Conference, Dallas, TX.

———. *From Orality to Orality: A New Paradigm for Contextual Translation of the Bible*. Biblical Performance Criticism 2. Eugene, OR: Cascade Books, 2009.

Maxey, James A., and Ernst R. Wendland, eds. *Translating Scripture for Sound and Performance: New Directions in Biblical Studies*. Biblical Performance Criticism 6. Eugene, OR: Cascade Books, 2012.

Merz, Johannes. "Bible Transmediation in Theory and Practice." *The Bible Translator* (2023) 1–18.

Merz, Johannes, et al. "Rethinking Anthropology for Quality in Bible Translation." In *Quality in Translation: A Multi-Threaded Fabric*, edited by Stephen Watters and Reinier de Blois, 171–215. Dallas: Pike Center for Integrative Scholarship, 2023.

Morrison, James E. "Euphony as a Crucial Component of Quality." In *Quality in Translation: A Multi-Threaded Fabric*, edited by Stephen Watters and Reinier de Blois, 216–42. Dallas: Pike Center for Integrative Scholarship, 2023.

Nida, Eugene A. "Intelligibility and Acceptability in Bible Translating." *The Bible Translator* 39 (1988) 301–8.

Nord, Christiane. *Translating as a Purposeful Activity: Functionalist Approaches Explained*. London: Routledge, 2006.

O'Sullivan, Carol. "Introduction: Multimodality as Challenge and Resource for Translation." *Journal of Specialised Translation* 20 (2013) 1–13.

Qian, Yan, and Tian Chuanmao. "A Review of Research on Multimodal Translation." *International Journal of English Literature and Social Sciences* 5.4 (2020) 872–81. DOI: 10.22161/ijels.54.7.

Sperber, Dan, and Dierdre Wilson. *Relevance: Communication and Cognition*. Oxford: Blackwell, 1986.

Thompson, Mark D. *A Clear and Present Word: The Clarity of Scripture*. Nottingham: Apollos, 2006.

Wendland, Ernst R. *Orality and the Scriptures: Composition, Translation, and Transmission*. Dallas: SIL, 2013.

7

Re-Translating a Contested Performance Tradition

NATHAN A. ESALA

Introduction

The question this chapter addresses is how communities can translate/perform a contested[1] and diverse biblical tradition in life-enhancing[2] ways in changing contexts where different sectors or groups struggle to survive and live with dignity. How can a community explore an ideo-theological[3] variety of translational and interpretive options[4] as they translate/perform[5] a biblical tradition?

---

1. The concept of contestation is related to the theological concept of "struggle" developed in South African Black theology in resistance to apartheid and racial capitalism. Race, culture, and the Bible are all contested sites of struggle. West, *Stolen Bible*, 319, 342, 336–37.

2. Ngwa, *Let My People Live*, 2–3, 27.

3. Draper, "African Contextual Hermeneutics"; West, "Accountable African Biblical Scholarship"; West, "African Biblical Scholarship as Post-Colonial."

4. Drexler-Dreis, "Option for the Poor as a Decolonial Option."

5. Kobus Marais uses the terms "meaning-makers" and "meaning-takers" to heuristically distinguish meaning producers from meaning receivers in the meaning-making process. *(Bio)Semiotic Theory of Translation*, 130. John Miles Foley argues that "composition and reception are two sides of the same coin." *How to Read an Oral Poem*, 138–39. On the one hand, translators and scribes are meaning-takers who read/interpret a received tradition. On the other hand, translators/scribes are meaning-making performers as they make texts for future performance events.

I have been thinking and writing about this question for some time.[6] During the course of this book project, I met with the other contributors online, read their chapters, and responded to their questions. These interactions drove me to read and think more deeply about translation, performance, and semiotics. One insight that has risen to prominence in the writing of this chapter is a focus on "constraints" in the meaning-making process.[7] When ancient translators and scribes produced their manuscript versions of the tradition, they did so with certain constraints, which affected how the versions emerged within the tradition's broader set of possibilities. Similarly, constraints affect contemporary translators/performers as they extend a meaning-making tradition.[8]

The chapter has three parts. Part 1 analyzes the different narrative possibilities in the extant manuscript traditions of Ruth 2:7. Part 2 describes how contemporary groups explore narrative possibilities using a method called Contextual Bible Study. Part 3 asks how translating communities should ethically navigate the reality of different constraints resulting in contrasting interpretations of the same narrative.

Part 1 demonstrates that the biblical manuscript tradition (re)produced by scribes and translators in relation to one verse, Ruth 2:7, is not singular; it is diverse and contested. While the manuscript tradition is linguistically and semiotically diverse, individual manuscripts limit the possibilities for their audience. One manuscript translates what David Jobling calls a "hesitation" in the tradition one way, while another manuscript deals with the hesitation another way. What constraints might account for the choices that ancient scribes and translators made as they performed instantiations of the manuscript tradition? What constraints might motivate a (re)producer of biblical tradition to present it as contested or uncontested? How do the audience's knowledge and expectations of the tradition constrain meaning making?

---

6. Esala, "Translation as Invasion," 358.

7. "How does it happen that, from the universal stream of meaning and information in humanity, this particular text has materialized in this particular way? What were the constraints that distilled the chaotic soup of meaning into this form? What is the nature of form, and how does it constrain the meaning, and to what effect?" Marais, *(Bio)Semiotic Theory of Translation*, 125.

8. From a semiotic and poststructuralist viewpoint, the possibilities are infinite. However, from the point of view of a performer in a performance event, there are constraints.

Part 2 approaches the issues of contestation from the contemporary side of what Brian Blount has called "the meaning line."[9] Part 2 explores how different sectors of a contemporary community approach translating/interpreting Ruth from their "lived reality" in front of the text.[10] Using the Contextual Bible Study method[11] to help people translate from their lived reality, I describe the process of male translators translating with young women struggling with economic scarcity in a context where age-disparate sex is common. I describe a series of Contextual Bible Studies on the book of Ruth and what I am calling multisectoral translational dialogue for decolonial liberation. I focus my comments on the re-translations that Contextual Bible Study participants articulate in relation to Ruth 2:7, concluding that participants identify similar hesitations in the tradition as I discerned in the ancient manuscripts on the other side of the meaning line.

Part 3 returns to the question of constraints, recognizing that different constraints may lead to alternative translation choices that affect the interpretation of the characters and the plot. Care is offered as an ethical constraint to guide translating communities as they consider how to prioritize and integrate these contrastive options in multimodal Bible translation.

My Social Location as a Presenting and Publishing Scholar

My explorations into the tradition of Ruth are motivated by my life experience coming from towns and suburbs in the midwestern United States and being "translated"[12] into a subsistence agrarian African community

---

9. Blount, "Souls of Biblical Folks," 9.

10. Ricoeur and Thompson, *Hermeneutics and the Human Sciences*, 77–80.

11. The Ujamaa Centre for Community Development and Research, "Doing Contextual Bible Study."

12. Salman Rushdie's famous quotation, "We are translated men," draws upon the Latin meaning of *translatio* meaning "to bear or carry across." Rushdie, *Imaginary Homelands*, 117. Drawing on the Greek and Latin roots of the English word "translation," Piotr Blumczynski undertakes a semasiological study of the word, arguing that translation initially referred to "someone carrying something—prototypically using their hands . . . from one place to another." Blumczynski, *Experiencing Translationality*, 11. Blumczynski demonstrates that translation involves the material and corporeal transfer of bodies and relics. Translation later developed into a metaphor for linguistic transfer. The implications of Blumczynski's argument are massive for translation studies.

in northern Ghana. My vocation was to help produce and circulate biblical texts in Komba-speaking northern Ghanaian churches and communities. The rural agrarian context offered unique resources for biblical studies and Bible translation, linking contemporary and ancient contexts.

In my PhD studies at the University of KwaZulu-Natal in South Africa, I learned how my ideo-theological commitments structure how I connect a contemporary context and an ancient text.[13] At the University's Ujamaa Centre for Biblical and Theological Community Development, alongside scholar-activists, I learned to practice the Contextual Bible Study (CBS) method.[14] The CBS method helps scholar-activists be methodologically accountable[15] to concrete communities and partially constituted by the life interests[16] of marginalized groups in those communities. I am indebted to colleagues at the Ujamaa Centre and to the people I lived among in northern Ghana. They have modeled for me how to be humane in relation to human and more-than-human agents in the world. I seek to emulate their dispositions as I present in academic circles and publish articles and books for academic readers, theologians, and (Bible) translation practitioners.

Three Assumptions

Writing is difficult when I do not know what assumptions I share with my readers. I hope the following three assumptions help make sense of the argument I am trying to build.

My first assumption is that a biblical text such as the book of Ruth is part of a performance tradition that has been circulated[17] by various performance events in different spaces and times.

Biblical Performance Criticism (BPC) helps biblical scholars think with scholars of folklore and performance studies about how people make meaning using cultural forms like texts, stories, and physical objects like ancient manuscripts or a book called the Bible. BPC understands that making meaning involves performers (storytellers, scribes, lectors, preachers, scholars, etc.), traditions (a physical text or an internalized

13. Draper, "African Contextual Hermeneutics"; West, "African Biblical Scholarship as Post-Colonial."
14. Esala, "Translation as Invasion," 273.
15. West, "Accountable African Biblical Scholarship."
16. West, "Interrogating the Comparative Paradigm," 38.
17. Briggs, "Contested Mobilities."

"text"), audience(s), situations, and media.[18] These five constituents are all a part of what Performance Studies describes as a "performance event." Perry defines performance "as a communication event re-expressing traditions before an audience."[19] Perry describes a manuscript as a remnant of a past performance event, whereas a text or a script is a potential constituent in a future performance event.

My second assumption is that the tradition of Ruth was/is contested at its sites of production[20] and at its sites of reception.[21] Ruth has been circulated for centuries. In its earliest circulations, the Naomi–Ruth–Boaz story was performed orally.[22] Each time the story is performed, a performer (a storyteller, a scribe, a translator, or a lector) employs "practices, ideologies, and technologies" as part of the performance event in that location and situation.[23] The practices, ideologies, and technologies employed in the performance are linked as "assemblages"[24] to the Naomi–Ruth–Boaz tradition. When the story is performed at another time or in another location, features of previous performance events are brought into the next performance event. However, in each performance event, "some actors, interests, languages, conflicts, technologies, and the

18. Perry, "Embodiment and Cognition."

19. Perry, "Biblical Performance Criticism," 5; Schechner, *Performance Studies*, 29.

20. Redaction criticism argues that texts embody their prior sites of production. Itumeleng Mosala emphasizes an ideological dimension to redaction criticism. *Biblical Hermeneutics and Black Theology*, 32, 101. See West's discussion, *Stolen Bible*, 328–40. For an application of "contestation" to the canonical arrangement of the book of Ruth, see West, "Scripture as a Site of Struggle."

21. Esala, "Translation as Invasion," 243–45.

22. Giles and Doan argue that the earliest circulations of this narrative tradition were performed by women storytellers or women singers for audiences of women. *Story of Naomi—Book of Ruth*, 15–26. With a distinct ideo-theological agenda, elite male scribes took the oral tradition, which Giles and Doan call "the Naomi story," and produced a written scribal text known as "the book of Ruth." *Story of Naomi—Book of Ruth*, 42–3; 75. Giles and Doan use a series of methods "to propose a reconstruction of the oral tradition upon which the literate version was based." *Story of Naomi—Book of Ruth*, 42. See also Campbell, *Ruth*, 23–8. Without disputing a Naomi-focused story, there is an invitation in the biblical tradition to explore the perspectives of Ruth and Boaz and even non-central characters like the young men and women working in the fields. Chapman and Collins, *House of the Mother*, 28; Leeb, *Away from the Father's House*.

23. Briggs, "Contested Mobilities," 287.

24. Briggs, "Contested Mobilities," 287.

like must disappear."[25] As cultural forms move across time and space, just as features from previous performance events get linked to the cultural form, there are simultaneous processes erasing features from previous performance events.[26] In other words, when viewed as a tradition, Ruth is not a single story.[27]

When I say Ruth is not a single story, I mean two things corresponding to this chapter's first two parts. First, the manuscript tradition of Ruth, produced by translators and scribes, is contested, as different agents, interests, languages, conflicts, and technologies are employed to perform the story in written form. In the snapshot of the manuscripts we will explore in part 1 of this chapter, we will notice that some of the contested or dialogical elements in the tradition get erased or weakened. Some manuscripts contain more disagreement[28] or dialogism in their discourse than others. When the manuscripts are taken together and viewed as remnants of a shared performance tradition, the tradition appears polyphonic[29] and contested. I contend that the tradition is energized by the gritty interactions between Naomi, Ruth, Boaz, and the other characters as they navigate economic practices and their influences on the fertility of the land and people.

The second thing I mean when I say Ruth is not a single story focuses on the word "story." I am not interested in reconstructing an original story. I am interested in the conflict and the interactions between the characters. In part 2 of this chapter, I explore the interactions between the characters by observing how contemporary people translate the story, making leaps into the story world from their own experiences.[30] Transla-

---

25. Briggs, "Contested Mobilities," 287.

26. Bowker and Star, *Sorting Things Out*.

27. Adichie, "Danger of a Single Story." The inflections of the characters in the book of Ruth are entangled with the perspectives of young men, young women, older men, and older women in contemporary contexts.

28. Sergey Dolgopolski, drawing on fifteenth-century Spanish Talmudic scholar Isaac Canpanton, argues that Talmud is not as a text or set of books, but an "event" that at its heart is about "the art of disagreement." Septimus, Review of *What Is Talmud?*

29. "The written narrative is the product of both the biblical historian . . . and of the folk, imprinting on the text their polyphony." Aschkenasy, "Reading Ruth Through a Bakhtinian Lens," 443.

30. Kwame Bediako writes, it is "possible to think of the Scriptures also as a context, a context that the reader (or hearer) may enter and so actually participate in their world of meaning and experience." "Biblical Exegesis in the African Context," 18; Hartman, *Kwame Bediako*, 85.

tions are enriched when people in contemporary contexts compare their experiences and consider whether they inhabit analogous positions as the characters do. My experiences facilitating the Contextual Bible Study method with young women, mature women, young men, and more mature men have yielded rich translational and interpretative results.

This leads to my third assumption: contexts matter. Ancient contexts are reconstructed in contemporary contexts. Acknowledging and excavating the detail and multiplicity of contemporary contexts enriches the engagement with ancient (con)texts.

For example, the story of Ruth is set in a peasant agrarian context.[31] The story engages complex, contested, and evolving ideo-theological relationships between social groups in cities and agrarian areas. My experience confirms that ordinary people living in analogous contemporary circumstances have experiential knowledge that can help them make meaning out of biblical stories relevant to their lives and the critical study of the Bible. Briggs observes that even when processes of erasure seem to have eliminated important indices in a tradition's prior reception history, there may be audiences or audience members who "get interpellated down the line" who can "infer elements that have been erased while others are unable even to decode foregrounded elements."[32]

Richard W. Swanson's chapter in this book cites an analogy that I think illustrates what Briggs is arguing. Swanson cites Elisabeth Lenk's metaphor of nested wooden dolls that stack inside one another, describing the relationship between performances and audiences of the play *Medea*, who are separated by time and space. Each era in which the *Medea* is performed is like a nested wooden doll. Subsequent versions in future eras are like slightly larger dolls, such that the performances and audiences of the *Medea* nest inside one another across time and space. Lenk writes, "the walls around time-periods are extremely close to one another."[33] Contemporary audiences can hear the performances of earlier eras, and earlier eras can hear "the phonographs blaring" from later eras. Lenk's description of time as "achronistic" is similarly described by Achille Mbembe's philosophical concept of African time as "entangled."[34]

---

31. Davis, *Scripture, Culture, and Agriculture*; Boer, *Sacred Economy of Ancient Israel*.
32. Briggs, "Contested Mobilities," 287.
33. Lenk, Epigraph to *Medea*, by Christa Wolf.
34. Mbembe, *On the Postcolony*, 14, 16–17; Esala, "Translation as Invasion," 32–33.

Neither Mbembe nor Lenk conceptualize time in a strictly linear fashion. Periods of time interpenetrate one another. This philosophical conception of time as entangled or nested supports Briggs's argument that groups in contemporary time and space may be able to perceive truncated signs, or even erased indices, from earlier performances that intervening groups might not have been able to perceive.

Drawing on this philosophical understanding of time and space, in part 2 of this chapter, I show that "reading with"[35] ordinary people from northern Ghana who share an analogous cultural environment with the ancient world where the story was circulated and who share analogous social experiences with characters in the story world can "experience translationality"[36] through Ruth's narrative across time and space, with social sectors in ancient audiences.

But first, in part 1, I explore ancient manuscripts produced by scribes and translators in relation to one verse, Ruth 2:7. I chose this verse because of its syntactic and interpretative difficulty.[37] Verses that commentators describe with phrases like "the Hebrew is difficult" can be read as a signal that the tradition is especially contested at this point.

Part 1: Exploring a Tradition's Expansions, Erasures, and Hesitations Using Evidence from the Manuscripts of Ruth 2:7

Hebrew Bible scholar David Jobling argues, "The versions we receive are possible tellings of the story. Disagreements within a version or between versions are to be read as points of hesitation over the meaning of the past."[38] In this section, I explore the ancient versions of Ruth 2:7, including the Greek translation known as the Septuagint or LXX, the Aramaic Targums, the Syriac Peshitta, the Latin Vulgate, and the Masoretic Text

---

35. Ordinary people interpret the Bible using an epistemological toolbox shaped by their lived experience within their homes and religious communities. West and Dube, "Reading With," 7.

36. Blumczynski, *Experiencing Translationality*, 35.

37. Todd Linafelt avers that Ruth 2:7 contains "the most difficult Hebrew in the whole book." *Ruth*, 31.

38. Jobling, *1 Samuel*, 19.

Leningradis (MT^L), which is the manuscript[39] of the Hebrew Bible, known as Biblia Hebraica Quinta (BHQ).[40]

Hesitations in Ruth 2:7 stem from ambiguity around the nature of Ruth's request to gather grain "among" the sheaves and ambiguity around the young man and Boaz's interactions with Ruth. The hesitations could be useful or threatening to a translator in relation to the religious and cultural discourses taking place within a translator's audience between young men, older men, and vulnerable women.

Drawing on folklore studies theorization of how texts circulate, I observe that when a text is translated into a new context, the audience may or may not know much about the circulation history of the story. Some translators pass on a story in a context where their audience knows a lot about the narrative's multimodal[41] circulation history. Some translators (and their reception community or audience) are more or less ignorant about the narrative's prior circulation history.

So, a significant constraint on what form an instantiation of the Ruth tradition takes depends upon how much knowledge of the circulation history performers and audiences share.

The Masoretic Text Leningradis (MT^L) is the youngest manuscript of all the versions I list below. But it makes interesting decisions in the way it navigates the hesitations in the tradition of Ruth 2:7. If a translator compares different translations of Ruth 2:7 without access to the Hebrew version, it is clear that there are hesitations in the tradition of Ruth 2:7. However, if a translator has access to only one translation, in some cases, the translator might not recognize the hesitations in the tradition of this verse. The MT^L version is distinctive in that it makes the hesitations obvious in its own version, especially to a translator/performer living in a community with active gleaning practices.

The MT^L tradition has influenced my experience with different English translations of this verse. Even so, I did not perceive any hesitation or discontinuity at first. It was only as I started making meaning out of this narrative while living in a rural agrarian community in northern Ghana that practices gleaning that I perceived a hesitation in Ruth 2:7. How can one request to "gather among the sheaves?" as the MT^L translated

---

39. A manuscript refers to a written remnant of a past performance event, including ancient codexes, scrolls, and fragments.
40. Waard et al., *Biblia Hebraica Quinta*.
41. Kress, *Multimodality*.

into English puts it? This seems like a strange request.⁴² On the surface, one would think that Ruth is requesting to gather grain from the already harvested sheaves of grain. If translators/performers communicate this request as it appears on the surface of the MT^L, what will their audiences think? It does not matter much in communities with no communal harvesting and gleaning practices, which is why I passed over the odd wording in English without a second thought. But in subsistence farming communities where gleaning is practiced, what do translators do with this request, reportedly from Ruth? Most translators imagine that they are lifting up Ruth as a model for the young women in their churches and communities to emulate. How will farmers and male landowners in their churches and communities respond if young women enter their fields and request something like Ruth purportedly requested? The ancient translations show evidence of sensitivity to this problem.

The preceding paragraph identifies two more constraints that inform how the tradition of Ruth 2:7 is articulated. First, what is the audience's knowledge of subsistence practices of gleaning? More to the point, how will an audience familiar with gleaning understand a request like Ruth's to glean among the sheaves in their own culture? Second, what expectations do performers and audiences have that constrain how the character of Ruth is supposed to behave? Is Ruth being characterized as an example for young women to emulate in the contemporary context? If so, how does this request sound? How do performers shape the tradition given these constraints?

A second point of hesitation occurs in the second half of v. 7. See lines 7cd in table 2 below. Most of the translations are somewhat choppy. When read together, the translations differ significantly from each other. Again, the youngest manuscript, the MT^L version, which reaches back to earlier Hebrew scribal tradition, is the most difficult to understand. The Hebrew syntax of v. 7, line cd, is so difficult that a reader/translator/performer must slow down and think and try to interpret the written

---

42. Eskenazi and Frymer-Kensky perceive the difficulty of this request, asking, "Does gleaning 'among the sheaves' mean gleaning among the grain that has already been bundled, thus going beyond law or custom? This is the conclusion of a number of interpreters." Eskenazi and Frymer-Kensky, *Ruth*, 33. Eskenazi and Frymer-Kensky list the following: Hubbard, *Book of Ruth*, 148–50; Campbell, *Ruth*, 94–95; Bush, *Ruth, Esther*, 113–19; Melzer, "Ruth," 15.

signs in a way that makes sense. Contemporary Hebrew scholars all do something slightly different in their English translations of this verse.[43]

In tables 1 and 2 below, I offer five close English translations of five ancient versions of Ruth 2:7: Rahlfs's edition of the Septuagint (Greek LXX),[44] the Aramaic Targum,[45] the Syriac Peshitta,[46] the Latin Vulgate, and the Hebrew Masoretic Text Leningradis (MT^L). I also include two empty sets for the oral tradition[47] and the ancient scribal tradition.[48] Following Marjo Korpel's analysis, I have divided the verse into two lines: 7ab and 7cd. Each line is composed of two cola.[49]

Table 1. Ancient versions of Ruth 2:7 line a-b[50] translated closely into English

Oral Tradition	(characterized by variation within limits)
Hebrew Scribal Tradition	(preceding the Masoretes)
Greek LXX	And she said, I will collect *therefore*, and I will gather in the sheaves/*handfuls*[51] after the harvesters.
Aramaic Targum	She said, I will gather *now* and glean *ears* among the sheaves *which are left* [*on the ground*][52] after the reapers.

43. Waard et al., *Biblia Hebraica Quinta*, 54.

44. The letters LXX refer to the Roman number 70. The ancient letter of Aristeas indicates that there were seventy translators for the Greek Septuagint. The term Septuagint is from the Latin word *septuaginta*, or seventy.

45. Beattie and McIvor, *Targum of Ruth*.

46. Tully, "Character of the Peshitta Version of Ruth."

47. A key feature of oral poetry is variation within limits and flexibility within rules. Foley, *How to Read an Oral Poem*, 18.

48. There appears to have been a major change in the hermeneutics of text transmission after 70 CE. Sanders, "Text and Canon," 20–21.

49. Korpel's delimitation of cola is based on the ancient manuscript evidence of MT^L and the LXX. The analysis begins with delimiting "feet" (one stress mark), which build into a cola. If the scribes could afford to waste space, they put the cola on separate lines or used a wide space. Masoretic accents may help determine the delimitation of cola. The analysis of colan builds into the analysis of lines, strophes, and paragraphs. Lines can be mono-cola, bicolan, tricolan, or more. The analysis of lines depends only on the MT^L witness. Korpel, *Structure of the Book of Ruth*, 2:33–41.

50. Korpel, *Structure of the Book of Ruth*, 2:104–5.

51. Sheaves of cut corn stalks. Liddell et al., *Greek-English Lexicon*, 447. There is a variant, δράχμασιν, which may indicate a handful or a pinch.

52. Two Targum manuscripts include "on the ground." See Beattie and McIvor, *Targum of Ruth*, 23.

Syriac Peshitta	She said: "Let me gather gleanings after the workers."[53]
Latin Vulgate	And she *desired* to glean the ears of corn that remain, following *the steps of* the reapers.[54]
Hebrew MT[L]	And she said, let me glean, *please*, and I will gather *among*[55] [into][56] the sheaves behind the harvesters.

Table 2. English back-translations of the ancient version of Ruth 2:7 line c-d[57]	
Oral Tradition	
Hebrew Scribal Tradition	
Greek LXX	She came and stood from morning until *evening*,[58] and did not[59] rest, [even] a little, *in the field*.
Aramaic Targum	She came and stood, *and has remained here* from *early* morning until just now. *It is but a short time that* she has sat in the house for a little.
Syriac Peshitta	And she *has gleaned* from the *early* morning until *the time of rest*.[60]
Latin Vulgate	and she hath been *in the field* from morning till now, *and hath not returned*[61] home *for one moment*.
Hebrew MT[L]	And so she came and has stood from *then*, this morning until now—this. . . . *her sitting*[62] . . . the house. . . . a little.

53. The phrase "among/into the sheaves" is omitted in this version.

54. The phrase "among/into the sheaves" is omitted in this version.

55. While "among" the sheaves is clear enough grammatically, it is difficult to understand what the grammar signifies culturally. Boaz appears to fix the difficulty by using "between" the sheaves in v. 15.

56. The Hebrew Old Testament Text Project (HOTTP) suggests Ruth's work is to make bundles. See also the LXX translation. Schipper suggests that the object of glean is implied to be "the ears of grain," and thus, the preposition indicates the result of the verb "gather" and not its object, which is why he translates "into." Compare Isa 17:5. Schipper, *Ruth*, 119.

57. Korpel, *Structure of the Book of Ruth*, 2:114–15.

58. The Old Greek manuscripts (G) have καὶ ἕως ἑσπέρας, "and until evening." Rahlfs's R recension reads ἕως νῦν τοῦτο, "until now this" with the MT[L].

59. The Greek may be taking the Hebrew particle *zeh* as a negative.

60. Peshitta removes the verb and an adverb, shifting a lexeme (from "sit" to "rest"), and reducing a clause to a single noun. Tully, "Character of the Peshitta Version of Ruth," 192.

61. The Latin is taking the Hebrew *shivtah*, "sitting," to be *sh-w-v*, "return."

62. Qal infinitive construct third person feminine singular.

How Ancient Manuscripts Handle Hesitations in the Performance Tradition

I have already articulated three constraints that likely influence how translators and scribes compose their versions of the larger tradition. How much knowledge do performers and audiences share about the circulation history of the tradition? What knowledge do performers and audiences share about gleaning practices and the social implications of Ruth's request? Also, is Ruth's character expected to be a role model in the contemporary context?

What else can we extrapolate about the constraints that may have influenced these translators' decisions? It is clear to me that the overall performance tradition, which these ancient manuscripts are all a part of, involves a gap or a hesitation regarding what Ruth reportedly asked to do and what she did in the field. It is not too strong to say there is some anxiety in the tradition about what she may have said and about what she may have done.

Some of the translated manuscripts try to clarify this uncertainty with specific detail. This is apparent in the translations of line 7cd in table 2.

The cleanest solution is to erase potentially disruptive or confusing details, but that strategy is only possible when an audience is not aware of the gap or hesitation in the tradition, or if they are aware, they prefer to keep potentially distracting details out of the tradition.[63]

For example, line 7ab of the Syriac Peshitta, when read alongside the other versions, cuts off potentially confusing or disruptive details that exist in the LXX and MT^L. The translators of the Peshitta had access to the Greek and probably had access to manuscripts from the Hebrew scribal tradition. Whatever sources the Peshitta translators had available to them, it appears that the audience of the Peshitta did not know about the hesitation in the Hebrew tradition. The Peshitta translators may have been concerned about how their version of Ruth in Syriac would be understood in relation to gleaning practices in their own communities. The translators may have felt that passing on the ambiguity in the tradition would create unnecessary confusion for their audience as they tried to make meaning from the translated narrative. It is likely that the Peshitta translators and their associated community wanted to characterize Ruth

---

63. Storytellers use this strategy when their story refers to names, places, and details that are unfamiliar and overwhelming to their audience.

as an example and chose to present the tradition in a way that made Ruth into what they imagined was a good exemplar of faith and social life. In other words, she would not have asked to glean among the sheaves, and even if she did, it was certainly not intended to be disruptive to the social order.

By contrast, the Greek LXX translation presents a hesitation or a gap[64] in its two versions of v. 7, line ab, which I have translated as "in the sheaves/handfuls." The LXX variant that describes Ruth gathering into handfuls clarifies she is gleaning and not touching the harvested sheaves.

The MT[L] manuscript tradition is similar to the LXX, only there is no "handful" variant. The MT[L] version of v. 7, line ab, pairs the preposition ב with its object, "sheaves." This preposition can be translated as "among" or "into."

What are the implications of this gap or hesitation in the tradition? Is Ruth asking to go beyond what is usually allowed in gleaning, to gather among the sheaves? Or is she simply asking to make small bundles of grain as a part of gleaning? Is Ruth misunderstanding the gleaning process in Hebrew culture? Or are we, as readers, ignorant of the intricacies of these ancient gleaning practices? Or is Boaz's worker mischaracterizing what Ruth actually said? This phrase to gather "among the sheaves" is even more interesting when compared to what Boaz says in v. 15. In the MT[L] manuscript, Boaz uses a different preposition than Ruth when he tells his servants that Ruth will glean "between" the sheaves. Then he goes on to instruct them to "pull out" or "plunder" grain from the heaps for her, seemingly capitulating to what the foreman reported that Ruth requested in v. 7.

As already stated, the implications of opening up uncertainty about what Ruth said and did are most acutely perceived in subsistence agrarian communities. The scribes who produced the MT[L] were part of a scribal community that was careful about passing on details of the tradition, including some uncertainty or variation within the tradition. Furthermore, it is likely that the audiences for MT[L] knew about the hesitation in the tradition and judged the inclusion of the hesitation more valuable than its deletion. Perhaps scribes refrained from adding extra explanatory detail into the tradition, leaving room for the community to fill in that implicit detail rather than making one interpretation explicit.

64. Wolfgang Iser has theorized the concept of syntagmatic and paradigmatic gaps in texts that invite readers/interpreters/translators to make meaning. Lategan, "Current Issues in the Hermeneutical Debate," 12.

We know those who composed and later wrote down the Aramaic Targums were aware of the Hebrew scribal tradition, of which the MT^L manuscript was a tenth- or eleventh-century instantiation. The Hebrew tradition was read and heard in worshiping communities alongside the Aramaic Targums. Compared to the MT^L, the Aramaic version offers more information to its audience, closing the gap in the LXX and MT^L with clarifying details. The audiences of the Targums would have known about the gleaning traditions in Lev 19 and Deut 24. They may still have been practicing gleaning or at least retained communal memories of gleaning practices.

English translations of this verse follow the grammar of the MT^L in English. However, most audiences of English translations do not practice gleaning or gathering grain for vulnerable populations. The gap in the narrative is lost on most audiences of English translations. They simply read past it. By contrast, Today's English Version (TEV), also known as the Good News Bible, with its preference for clear English, does not replicate the language of the MT^L, closing the possibility of a gap for its audience. The TEV translators made decisions similar to those of the Peshitta's translators.

Looking at line cd in v. 7, the versions describe the young man explaining something about the young woman Ruth before the landowner Boaz. The versions appear to be more interested in how Ruth is portrayed to their audience than in how the young man portrays Ruth. The LXX characterizes Ruth as a hard worker. The Peshitta characterizes her neutrally. Other versions explain aspects of her behavior. The Targum says, "She is sitting down," and the Vulgate explains, "She has not gone home." Frequently, the explanations open up new gaps for audiences to explore. The fact that all the translations do something different to clarify by expansion or deletion suggests that they all recognize the hesitation, the gap, and the ambiguity in line cd of Ruth 2:7.

Line cd in the MT^L is the most difficult to understand syntactically. Schipper's translation of 7cd of the MT^L suggests that the supervising young man is stumbling as he speaks: "This ... her sitting ... the house ... a little."[65] The insertion of the ellipsis points is intended to convey stumbling speech. They serve as a cue for the reader that there are performative and interpretative options. Jonathan Grossman perceives the

---

65. Schipper, *Ruth*, 27.

young man's stumbling speech and suggests it could signal disingenuousness in his characterization of Ruth.[66]

Based on the discussions about this verse that I have been a part of in northern Ghana with young men, older men, younger women, and older women in a subsistence agricultural community, the hesitation signals ambiguity and complexity. Unpacking the ambiguity can be an opportunity for what I call multisectoral translational dialogue. Unpacking the ambiguity from different perspectives is a valuable practice, which will be addressed in section 2.

The ancient versions made different choices about how they expected their audiences to deal with ambiguity or hesitations in the tradition. In Ruth 2:7, the MT^L manuscript invites the audience to unpack the ambiguity it is signaling. The scribes of the MT^L must have expected that their audiences would have the resources to unpack or at least manage the ambiguity.[67]

Other ancient translators may have perceived that passing on the ambiguity or hesitation in the tradition would cause confusion or even conflict in their audiences. Hence, they either tried to clarify some confusing details to make it more understandable or, in some cases, deleted or altered the material to eliminate the potential for questions, confusion, and controversy. This is a normal part of being a communicative translator.

In part 1 of this chapter, I have shown that the tradition of Ruth 2:7 is complex. Ruth 2:7 is a part of a tradition that is not a single story. Translators and scribes turn the tradition into an instantiation of the tradition, a story for their audiences. They anticipate what their audiences know and what resources their audiences have to unpack the signs the scribes or translators have made. They try to anticipate what effect the translated story will have on their context, shaping it more or less toward a positive effect based on their ideo-theological assumptions. In one way or another, all of the manuscripts refract or rewrite[68] the traditions they translate.

---

66. Grossman, "'Gleaning Among the Ears.'"

67. Relevance Theory argues that communicators will only expend extra effort to understand something if they expect an interpretative benefit. Sperber and Wilson, *Relevance*.

68. Lefevere, *Translation, Rewriting, and the Manipulation*. Tymoczko prefers Lefevere's use of the term "refraction." *Enlarging Translation*, 81.

In part 2 of the chapter, I move from investigating meaning making on the ancient side of the meaning line to investigating meaning-making on the contemporary side of the meaning line. Using the Contextual Bible Study (CBS) method as "translational and interpretative praxis,"[69] I explore how ordinary people in northern Ghana use their lived experience in a rural agrarian context to enter into the narrative conflict of the Ruth–Boaz–Naomi story world.

Part 2: Foregrounding Social Contestation, Multisectoral Translational Dialogue, and Liberation

On the contemporary side of the meaning line, translating/interpreting begins with people's lived reality[70] as people translate the dynamics of a story from inside their bodies, experiences, and imaginations. I remind the reader that I am more interested in recreating story dynamics than I am in authorizing a single version of the story.

I adopt the Contextual Bible Study (CBS) method because it starts with a contested theme or social issue in a contemporary context as a pathway into dialogically (re-)translating/(re-)interpreting a biblical text, making meaning for social change. CBS does not start with context alone. CBS starts with a contested social issue or theme in a context. This distinction is crucial because it shifts the tendency from translating in an idealized manner to translating/interpreting/performing for the purpose of meaning making that leads to life-giving, liberating action in the real world.[71]

I remind the reader that what I am describing here is not substantially different from how meaning making occurs for interpreters interested in the ancient side of the meaning line. All interpretation happens on the contemporary side of the meaning line, implicitly or explicitly. I argue that explicitly focusing translational dialogue on social contestation on the contemporary side of the meaning line helps people unpack

---

69. Mojola, "Bible Translation in Africa," 162; Esala, "Translation as Invasion," 272.

70. Carlos Mesters defines the term "lived reality" as "the real problems of people," including economic, political, and social problems. "Use of the Bible in Christian Communities," 121.

71. "In theory, the sign process never ends, but for pragmatic reasons, to be able to act on knowledge constructed through the sign process, the process is stopped at a particular point in time in order to act." Marais, *(Bio)Semiotic Theory of Translation*, 94.

ambiguous or confusing details that they find in the tradition they have received. In other words, people's lived experiences can help them unpack hesitations in the ancient text/tradition.

CBS uses multisectoral translational dialogue for liberation to help different community sectors unpack knots in the narrative or hesitations in the manuscript tradition. Put differently, contestations in a contemporary context are entangled[72] with contestations in ancient contexts, such that multisectoral translational dialogue can (re)connect the social contestation in a contemporary context to analogous social contestation embedded in a tradition. The Contextual Bible Study method facilitates this kind of multisectoral (and multimodal) translational dialogue motivated by life-enhancing liberation.[73]

The CBS Method, Age-Disparate Sex, and Ruth

The CBS method has been honed over thirty years in post-colonial South Africa to draw lines of connection between various contested social issues and selected biblical texts for social liberation. Gerald West and Beverly Haddad developed a CBS for the narrative of Ruth around the issue of age-disparate sex, connecting Ruth and Boaz's relationship to a spectrum of age-disparate sexual relationships that exist in South Africa and across much of the continent.[74]

I adapted the CBS developed by West and Haddad for use in northern Ghana as part of a Bible translation program, a program in which I have been an active member for more than a decade. In my dissertation and forthcoming book, I describe several CBS engagements re-translating Ruth 2–3 with young women in school, younger and mature women and men in sewing and tailoring apprenticeships, and younger and mature women in churches.[75] Before I describe how those engagements relate to the ancient manuscript tradition, I describe what I mean by multisectoral translational dialogue for liberation.

---

72. Mbembe, *On the Postcolony*, 14, 16–17.

73. Ngwa, *Let My People Live*, 27, 44.

74. West and Haddad, "Boaz as 'Sugar-Daddy'"; Haddad, "'Taking the Wanting Out of the Waiting.'"

75. Esala, "Translation as Invasion," 333–59.

CBS as Multisectoral (and Multimodal) Translational Dialogue for Liberation

CBS is a method of interpreting the Bible for liberation that emerged in apartheid South Africa, developed after South African liberation, and has been adapted in contexts worldwide.[76] I describe CBS as a practice of (re-)translation. My description of CBS as a form of translation is rooted in my socio-historic analysis of translation in pre-colonial, colonial, and post-colonial time[77] in northern Ghana.

There were pre-colonial concepts and practices of translation. Yet colonization was a watershed that influenced how translation is popularly conceived and practiced in northern Ghana. Similarly, the Bible was introduced as part of the colonial agenda of invasion and conquest in many contexts around the world.[78] Furthermore, biblical tradition is entangled with ancient imperialism.[79] Nevertheless, at the same time, the Bible has been stolen, interpreted, and translated for liberation from colonizing influences.[80]

Because of this complex history, contemporary Bible translation practices in post-colonial time are entangled with liberating practices and those that serve a neo-colonial paradigm.[81] Therefore, for churches and Bible agencies concerned about the damaging and ongoing influences of imperial and colonial systems, agents of Bible translation must develop an intentionally decolonial[82] practice of Bible translation in contested post-colonial time and space. To the extent that colonial systems, practices, and logic contribute to the motivations and practices of translation, then there is a need to "turn over"[83] translation practices away from agendas of invasion and conquest toward social healing for African

---

76. West, "Contextual Bible Study in South Africa."
77. Esala, "Translation as Invasion," 32–34, 241.
78. Esala, "Translation as Invasion," 20–21.
79. Mosala, "Use of the Bible in Black Theology."
80. West, *Stolen Bible*.
81. Esala, "Translation as Invasion," 232–33.
82. Decolonial theory urges delinking from (neo-)colonial cultural and economic influences in translation and biblical interpretation.
83. Some African languages use verbs that mean "to turn (something) over" or "to flip (something)" to metaphorically refer to linguistic translation. Compare Blumczynski, *Experiencing Translationality*, 11.

communities, reworking the Bible from a document that justifies social invasion into a source of social healing in a shared environment.

Drawing on the work of Sharon Deane-Cox[84] and Deborah Shadd[85] on retranslation, I describe CBS as a form of re-translation.[86] CBS is a decolonial form of (re-)translation because it reintroduces aspects of pre-colonial translation practice into translation practice in post-colonial time and space.[87] For example, in oral tradition, different community sectors perform different poetic genres at specified times in community life, expressing their embodied and sectoral perspectives as part of the ongoing social dialogue. Because of what has happened under colonization, it is difficult, if not impossible, to return to a pristine pre-colonial practice; instead, CBS facilitates a method of reintroducing sectoral dialogism into spaces struggling with the ongoing entanglements of colonization related to interpreting the Bible. CBS initiates community dialogue about the translation and interpretation of the Bible by privileging marginalized sectors of a community that colonial systems have ignored. Through the CBS method, marginalized sectors of a community engage in dialogue with the other sectors of their community, making meaning with the Bible. CBS does not attempt to return to a pristine pre-colonial oral-only method of translation. Instead, CBS moves between visual, oral, and written modes of discourse as part of its multimodal decolonial practice of re-translating the Bible for life.

Contextual Bible Study comprises a structured set of questions. These questions take study participants on a hermeneutical journey where they (re-)translate and (re-)interpret a biblical text from their own embodied and sectoral points of view. The theological driver of CBS assumes that God is on the side of those who suffer from ideo-theologies that participate in colonial systems that erase, alienate, and extol singular exceptions to the rule of collective oppression.[88] While colonial

---

84. Deane-Cox, *Retranslation*, 2–3.

85. Shadd, "Retranslation and Revision."

86. I insert the hyphen to signal struggle. Re-translations struggle with established translations for (ideological) survival. For example, see Marais, *(Bio)Semiotic Theory of Translation*, 16.

87. Esala, "Translation as Invasion," 96–101.

88. Kenneth Ngwa describes a triple consciousness embedded in colonial systems, which drives experiences of erasure, alienation, and singularity. Ngwa's triple analysis is countered by life-enhancing practices that foreground survival, return/restoration, and community. *Let My People Live*, 2–3.

oppression has many facets,[89] CBS begins its meaning-making dialogue for community liberation with groups that are "pain-bearers" for a social problem, issue, or theme, as described above.[90]

Multisectoral Translational Dialogue for Life in Ruth

Returning to the contested issue of age-disparate sex in northern Ghana as a path for re-translating Ruth in a dialogical and life-giving manner, the CBS method encourages communities to start the process of multisectoral translational dialogue with people who are suffering social and physical pain in relation to the contested issue.[91] In the context of northern Ghana, women experiencing economic vulnerability are systemically caught up in a "sugar daddy" system, referenced above. Rejecting individualist explanations that would morally fault young women for being open to an older man who exchanges gifts for sex, the Komba Bible translation team's social analysis of their context concluded that vulnerable women engage in age-disparate sex for economic survival. Their situation is not so different from Ruth's when she came to Bethlehem without land, without a male patron so they could access land and the agricultural mode of food and economic production.[92]

The CBS questions we developed to encourage participants to translate from their social perspective were as follows:

1. What is this story about? Or what are some of the themes of this book?

Read Ruth 1:22 and 2:1–3.

2. What was Ruth's plan upon arriving in Bethlehem?

Read 2:4–7. Dramatize the scene for them, acting it out in space.

---

89. V. Y. Mudimbe's alternative triple analysis of colonialism observes that colonial powers sought to dominate native space, native minds, and native economic histories. *Invention of Africa*, 4.

90. Drawing on Walter Brueggemann's notion of the embrace of pain, June Dickie writes, "'Pain-bearers' is a general term including those who bear physical or emotional pain, and those caught in situations of political, social, and economic distress." "African Youth Lament," 7.

91. Esala, "Translation as Invasion," 336–41.

92. However, Ruth was a childless widow. See Esala, "Translation as Invasion," 353. But what about Naomi owning land in 4:3–4?

3. Re-read 2:7.
    a. In your culture, can someone ask to glean among the sheaves?
    b. Based on Ruth's request to glean among the sheaves, what might Ruth's dream be for economic survival for herself and her mother-in-law? (Optional: Read 4:3–4. Did this land somehow belong to Naomi?)

Read 2:8–16.

4. What does Boaz say to Ruth? Re-read 2:8–9, 14–16. What is his intention?
5. What does Ruth do or say that shows her intention? 2:10, 2:13.

Read Ruth 2:17—3:18.

6. What was Naomi's role in what happened? What was Naomi's intention?
7. What were Ruth's hopes and fears as she approached the threshing floor?
8. Is this a sugar daddy relationship?
9. What is a sugar daddy in your context?
10. What are the benefits and risks of a sugar daddy relationship?
11. From your perspective, what systems need to change in your churches, mosques, communities, schools, and families to help young women?

Dialogically and Sectorally Re-Translating Ruth 2:7 for Life

When the Komba Bible translation team facilitated a CBS on Ruth with young women in school, the energy in the room was cautious until one of the facilitators, Elijah Matibin, spontaneously began to perform the gleaning process as if he was a woman gleaning in a landowner's field.[93] It was entertaining for the women to see a successful farmer performing the role of a vulnerable woman gleaning in a field.[94]

---

93. Oelbaum writes, "Standard notions of private property do considerable violence to traditional tenure arrangements." *Spatial Poverty Traps and Ethnic Conflict Traps*, 22.

94. Esala, "I Will Gather Among the Sheaves!," 92; Esala, "Translation as Invasion," 349.

Matibin's performance of gleaning, described in Ruth 2:7, prompted young women to recognize the sexual and flirtatious dynamics of Boaz's interactions with Ruth in 2:8–9 and 2:13–14. Some participants answered question five as follows:

- He asked the reapers to pull out some grain from the bundles for her.
- Boaz showed love to Ruth.
- Boaz intended to take care of her.
- Boaz intended to marry her.

When they saw Matibin's performance, it was as if a switch was flipped, and the young women began to use their own experiences to translate and interpret Ruth's story. At that moment, they became active translators, which continued throughout most of the study.[95]

In a subsequent CBS engagement with young women and men in sewing and tailoring apprenticeships, some men became attuned to the dynamic of competition between older and younger men over young women in their context. Their awareness of this contextual dynamic was prompted by what they perceived as an analogous dynamic in the text. They observed that Boaz instructed Ruth in 2:8, "Do not go to glean in another field or leave this one." One group of men observed that "Boaz wanted to keep Ruth's attention on him."[96] Many young men who are not wealthy cannot attract a woman to marry them. They feel marginalized by the economic realities that contribute to the sugar daddy system.

This dynamic of male competition also surfaced in the CBS we facilitated with younger and mature women in churches. The mature women revealed that in some communities, when a young woman first comes to town, perhaps to attend school, sometimes young men immediately rape that young woman before the wealthy older men in the community can entice her.[97] Gender violence appears to be part of the dynamic in

---

95. At one point, some of the male facilitators became uncomfortable with how freely some of the young women were speaking. See Esala, "Translation as Invasion," 352, 357.

96. Esala, "Translation as Invasion," 351, 360. This competitive dynamic surfaces again in 3:10 in Boaz's speech to Ruth on the threshing floor when he says, "You have not gone after young men, whether poor or rich."

97. Esala, "Translation as Invasion," 353.

Ruth 2:5–7.[98] That dynamic may explain why the young man's speech is difficult to decipher in the Hebrew (MT[L]) version of 2:7cd.[99]

There is one other sectoral interpretation of male competition that is worth mentioning. When answering question seven about Naomi's role in what happened with Ruth and Boaz on the threshing floor, a group of older male tailors suggested that Naomi and Boaz most likely made a plan about Ruth, even though such a plan is not mentioned in the story. This plan would reflect the kind of entrapment that young women experience when their mothers conspire with older, wealthier men so that their daughters enter into a sugar daddy relationship that benefits the older woman economically.

The contested and multisectoral translations/interpretations I shared in this section were from young women, young men, older women, and older men, who energetically and dialogically made meaning through this story. Upon reflection, the reason that participants can jump into ambiguities and gaps in the story world in such a rich and dialogical way is that CBS is willing to engage the lived experiences of young women on their terms, including their sexual and economic realities. The constraint of engaging the lived experiences of marginalized sectors of a community may produce translations and characterizations of Ruth, Boaz, and Naomi that do not assume they are ideals to emulate. They are characters who must navigate complicated economic and social realities like people in analogous circumstances today.[100]

Part 2 illustrates what translation and interpretation can look like when they are produced under the constraints of CBS. CBS is intentionally constructed as a process of decolonial liberation that privileges members of a community who are often marginalized. They enter into the narrative knots or hesitations and consider narrative options through multisectoral dialogue. This results in characterizations and details in the plot that are underrepresented in contemporary translations, commentaries, sermons, and songs.

Part 3 returns to the constraints that Bible meaning-makers face in churches, communities, and the broader Bible industry. How can translators and translating communities allow for different constraints in

---

98. Shepherd, "Violence in the Fields?"

99. Schipper, *Ruth*, 27; Rulmu, "Stumbling Words for a Determined Young Lady."

100. The difference here has been described as decent theology compared to improper or indecent theology. Esala, "Translation as Invasion," 351–52; Althaus-Reid, *Indecent Theology*.

translation? Or do they have to choose some and not others? What ethics should guide their choices?

Part 3: An Ethic of Care in Bible Translation

CBS is intentionally decolonial and emancipatory in constraining its meaning-making activities. Meaning making in Bible translation programs is usually constrained to serve church members and reach out to people beyond the church with the stories of the Bible. These differing constraints usually result in different ideo-theological portrayals of the main characters in the narrative. How can these differing constraints be reconciled? Or must one choose between them?

Practicing an ethic of *care* can guide communities and individuals as they consider whether and how[101] to translate/interpret biblical texts as constituents in meaning-making performance events.

An ethic of care is not simply a practical concern that exists only on the contemporary side of the meaning line. Care informs how translators/interpreters/performers approach the ancient manuscripts and the communities that passed them on to us as remnants of meaning-making cycles.[102] The concept of alterity has been raised as an ethical concern in Bible translation, encouraging translators to be concerned about the alterity or otherness of biblical texts and the cultures, languages, and communities that produced them. More expansively, alterity focuses on translation as a process of ongoing human connection and movement through time and space.[103] An important component of human care includes caring for the sacredness of all human and more-than-human life, past and present, and cultivating living interconnections through time and space.

In section 1 of this chapter, I model practicing care as I cross the ancient side of the meaning line by translating Ruth 2:7 from ancient manuscripts and languages, focusing on the semantic variety in the biblical tradition. I translate carefully[104] because biblical narratives have

---

101. Cronin, *Translation and Globalization*, 167.

102. Holly Hearon's multimodal social semiotic approach, described in this book, would help contemporary translators better understand the complex meaning-making cycles that have gone on before them and help them better understand the affordances of each modality they use as they communicate.

103. Towner, "Translation from the Other Side."

104. Maxey, "Alternative Evaluative Concepts," 66.

been shaped by communities struggling for life, even if that struggle is expressed differently. I attend to the careful use of language, recognizing that minoritized communities who have experienced imperial trauma, like the Judean community after the Babylonian invasion, use language as "a mode of liberating care for those traumatized by imperial violence."[105] That said, an ethic of care recognizes that communities that have experienced violence and trauma often use language in a way that reenacts or mimics aspects of the violence they have experienced, even across generations.

An ethic of care is comfortable with groups recognizing and articulating disagreement, pain, anger, and grief. Being comfortable with so-called negative emotions is necessary for social healing, developing empathy, and practicing solidarity.

In section 2 of this chapter, I apply an ethic of care in translation, focusing the translational journey on the contemporary side of the meaning line. An ethic of care is not always easy to apply to translation because different community sectors, which are differently constrained, may produce interpretations/performances that clash. But rather than fostering misunderstanding and violence, an ethic of care facilitates multisectoral analysis and articulation, listening, and an insistence on highlighting what is liberating and life-giving from different points of view while gently moving groups toward practices of solidarity. Applying an ethic of care encourages groups to make meaning with "pain-bearers" in their community and to dialogue about translation options in pursuit of a better life together. Applying an ethic of care to translation requires living inside the story from the perspective of contemporary and ancient "others"[106] to consider how to navigate the complexity of the situation.

An ethic of care focuses group dialogue on what is life-giving, recognizing that what is life-giving might look different depending on one's experience and perspective. Ultimately, applying an ethic of care to translation dares to dream by foregrounding the pursuit of co-liberation,[107]

---

105. Cuéllar, "Ironic Contestations," 182.

106. Draper, "African Contextual Hermeneutics," 10.

107. The term "co-liberation" is attributed to Skeena Rathor, co-founder of Extinction Rebellion. It is a principle that links any human individual or group's liberation with the liberation of all human and non-human beings. Cochrane, "Cosmopolitan Christ," 32–33.

social[108] and environmental healing, and solidarity without collapsing the degrees that separate social groups.[109]

Even though a straightforward story is easier to tell, and some audiences express that as their preference, applying an ethic of care to translation requires translators to tell a story that can go more than one way. Applying an ethic of care to translation encourages translators to attend to the points of view of various groups of pain-bearers in their audience and community as they produce signs for their audiences to dialogue about as they translate/interpret.

A Concluding Example

As this chapter has asserted, translators are constrained to varying degrees by the expectations of their constituent communities.[110] Practically speaking, many groups involved in Bible translation programs want their translated version to follow another established version. Respecting this as a productive constraint and being guided by an ethic of care and a commitment to the lived experiences of all the sectors of their community, including pain-bearers, how can Bible translators in the guild of Bible translation creatively signal more narrative options than their model translation does?

Using Ruth 2:7 as an example, translators can carefully look at the history of the manuscript tradition and appreciate the variety found there. This knowledge can motivate translators to suggestively[111] select signs that engage the embodied experiences of Ruths, Naomis, and Boazes in their communities, encouraging multisectoral interpretation.

Even if the versions that Bible translators produce only minimally open up decolonizing and liberating options,[112] they can encourage sectors of their audience to enter into the story from their experience and their lived reality in an emancipatory and decolonial manner. Once inside

---

108. Dube Shomanah, *Postcolonial Feminist Interpretation*, 192.

109. Haddad, "South African Women's Theological Project."

110. A community's expectations are not static. Translators should be in dialogue with their community's constituents.

111. Esala, "I Will Gather Among the Sheaves!," 96.

112. Julius Nyerere's translation of the Gospels and Acts exemplifies an overtly decolonial approach to translation, using the indigenous poetic form of tenzi to ideo-theologically re-translate the Swahili Union Version. West, "Moffat's seTlhaping Translation," 5–6; Noss and Renju, "Mwalimu Nyerere Engages His People."

the story of the Bible, translators can prompt different sectors of the audience to re-translate portions of the story in ways that are life-giving for them, using multiple modalities, such as visual art, poetry, and song.

Some versions of the Bible's transmission history have been lost to scholars, as I illustrated with the empty set for oral tradition in tables 1 and 2 above. But the voices behind those versions are a "real presence" upon which the translations we have today depend.[113] Perhaps the presence of voices from the past will encourage groups to get inside the narrative's knots and hesitations so they can re-translate the story in life-giving ways. In so doing, such groups have the opportunity to reconnect to discourses flowing through time and space that must not be forgotten, that must be re-membered. Caring for these voices, past and present, is essential for discerning what social healing and co-liberation look like today.

Bibliography

Adichie, Chimamanda Ngozi. "The Danger of a Single Story." TED: Ideas Worth Spreading, July 2009. https://www.ted.com/talks/chimamanda_ngozi_adichie_the_danger_of_a_single_story.

Althaus-Reid, Marcella. *Indecent Theology: Theological Perversions in Sex, Gender and Politics*. London: Routledge, 2000.

Aschkenasy, Nehama. "Reading Ruth Through a Bakhtinian Lens: The Carnivalesque in a Biblical Tale." *Journal of Biblical Literature* 126 (2007) 437–53. https://doi.org/10.2307/27638447.

Barthélemy, Dominique, Adrian Schenker, and Alliance biblique universelle Comité pour l'analyse textuelle de l'Ancien Testament hébreu. *Preliminary and Interim Report on the Hebrew Old Testament Text Project [Compte Rendu Préliminaire et Provisoire Sur le Travail d'Analyse Textuelle de l'Ancien Testament Hébreu]*. New York: United Bible Societies, 1980.

Beattie, D. R. G., and J. Stanley McIvor. *The Targum of Ruth/ Translated, with Introduction, Apparatus and Notes by D. R. G. Beattie. And, The Targum of Chronicles/ Translated, with Introduction, Apparatus and Notes by J. Stanley McIvor*. Aramaic Bible 19. Collegeville, MN: Liturgical, 1994.

Bediako, Kwame. "Biblical Exegesis in the African Context—The Factor and Impact of the Translated Scriptures." *Journal of African Christian Thought* 6 (June 2003) 15–23.

Blount, Brian K. "The Souls of Biblical Folks and the Potential for Meaning." *Journal of Biblical Literature* 138 (2019) 6–21. https://doi.org/10.15699/jbl.1381.2019.1382.

Blumczynski, Piotr. *Experiencing Translationality: Material and Metaphorical Journeys*. New York: Routledge, 2023.

---

113. West, "Redaction Criticism as a Resource," 530, 535.

Boer, Roland. *The Sacred Economy of Ancient Israel*. Library of Ancient Israel. Louisville: Westminster John Knox, 2015. http://www.netread.com/jcusers/1389/ 2910033/image/lgcover.5177907.jpg.

Bowker, Geoffrey C., and Susan Leigh Star. *Sorting Things Out: Classification and Its Consequences*. Cambridge: MIT Press, 1999.

Briggs, Charles L. "Contested Mobilities: On the Politics and Ethnopoetics of Circulation." *Journal of Folklore Research* 50 (2013) 285–99.

Bush, Frederic William. *Ruth, Esther*. Word Biblical Commentary 9. Waco, TX: Word Books, 1996.

Campbell, Edward F., ed. *Ruth: A New Translation with Introduction, Notes, and Commentary*. Anchor Bible 7. Garden City, NY: Doubleday, 1975.

Chapman, Cynthia R., and John J. Collins, eds. *The House of the Mother: The Social Roles of Maternal Kin in Biblical Hebrew Narrative and Poetry*. New Haven: Yale University Press, 2016. https://doi.org/10.12987/yale/9780300197945.001.0001.

Cochrane, James R. "The Cosmopolitan Christ: A Contemporary Agenda?" *Journal of Theology for Southern Africa* 177 (2023) 21–40.

Cronin, Michael. *Translation and Globalization*. New York: Routledge, 2003.

Cuéllar, Gregory Lee. "Ironic Contestations as a Care Strategy in Lamentations." In *Irony in the Bible: Between Subversion and Innovation*, edited by Tobias Häner, Virginia Miller, and Carolyn J. Sharp, 181–93. Biblical Interpretation Series 209. Leiden: Brill, 2023. https://doi.org/10.1163/9789004536333_013.

Davis, Ellen F. *Scripture, Culture, and Agriculture: An Agrarian Reading of the Bible*. New York: Cambridge University Press, 2009. http://catdir.loc.gov/catdir/toc/ecip0822/2008027119.html.

Deane-Cox, Sharon. *Retranslation: Translation, Literature and Reinterpretation*. Bloomsbury Advances in Translation Series. London: Bloomsbury Academic, 2014.

Dickie, June. "African Youth Engage with Psalms of Lament to Find Their Own Voice of Lament." *Journal of Theology for Southern Africa* 160 (Mar. 2018) 4–20.

Draper, Jonathan A. "African Contextual Hermeneutics: Readers, Readings, and Their Options Between Text and Context." *Religion and Theology* 22.1–2 (2015) 3–22.

Drexler-Dreis, Joseph. "The Option for the Poor as a Decolonial Option: Latin American Liberation Theology in Conversation with Teología India and Womanist Theology." *Political Theology* 18 (2017) 269–86.

Dube Shomanah, Musa W. *Postcolonial Feminist Interpretation of the Bible*. St. Louis: Chalice, 2000.

Esala, Nathan A. *Biblical Translation as Invasion in Postcolonial Northern Ghana*. International Voices in Biblical Studies 18. Atlanta: SBL Press, 2024. https://www.sbl-site.org/assets/pdfs/pubs/9781628376333_OA.pdf.

———. "I Will Gather Among the Sheaves! Facilitating Embodied and Emancipatory Translation of the Book of Ruth for Translational Dialogue." *Journal of Theology for Southern Africa* 160 (2018) 75–101.

———. "Translation as Invasion in Post-Colonial Northern Ghana." PhD diss., University of KwaZulu-Natal, 2021. https://researchspace.ukzn.ac.za/handle/10413/19690.

Eskenazi, Tamara Cohn, and Tikva Simone Frymer-Kensky, eds. *Ruth: The Traditional Hebrew Text with the New JPS Translation*. JPS Bible Commentary. Philadelphia: Jewish Publication Society, 2011.

Foley, John Miles. *How to Read an Oral Poem*. Urbana: University of Illinois Press, 2002.

Giles, Terry, and William Doan. *The Story of Naomi—The Book of Ruth: From Gender to Politics*. Biblical Performance Criticism 13. Eugene, OR: Cascade Books, 2016.

Grossman, Jonathan. "'Gleaning Among the Ears'—'Gathering Among the Sheaves': Characterizing the Image of the Supervising Boy (Ruth 2)." *Journal of Biblical Literature* 126 (2007) 703–16.

Haddad, Beverley G. "The South African Women's Theological Project: Practices of Solidarity and Degrees of Separation in the Context of the HIV Epidemic." *Religion and Theology* 20 (2013) 2–18. https://doi.org/10.1163/15743012-12341248.

———. "'Taking the Wanting Out of the Waiting': HIV, Transactional Sex, and #Blessed, in the Context of Neo-Liberal Christianity." *Journal of Theology for Southern Africa* 161 (June 2018) 5–17.

Hartman, Tim. *Kwame Bediako: African Theology for a World Christianity*. Minneapolis: Fortress, 2022.

Hubbard, Robert L. *The Book of Ruth*. New International Commentary on the Old Testament. Grand Rapids: Eerdmans, 1988.

Jobling, David. *1 Samuel*. Berit Olam. Collegeville, MN: Liturgical, 1998.

Korpel, Marjo. *The Structure of the Book of Ruth*. Vol. 2, *Pericope: Scripture as Written and Read in Antiquity*. Assen: Van Gorcum, 2001.

Kress, Gunther R. *Multimodality: A Social Semiotic Approach to Contemporary Communication*. London: Routledge, 2010.

Lategan, Bernard C. "Current Issues in the Hermeneutical Debate." *Neotestamentica* 18 (1984) 1–17.

Leeb, Carolyn S. *Away from the Father's House: The Social Location of Naʿar and Naʿarah in Ancient Israel*. Journal for the Study of the Old Testament Supplement Series 301. Sheffield: Sheffield Academic, 2000.

Lefevere, André. *Translation, Rewriting, and the Manipulation of Literary Fame*. Translation Studies. London: Routledge, 1992.

Lenk, Elisabeth. Epigraph to *Medea: A Modern Retelling*, by Christa Wolf. New York: Doubleday, 1998.

Liddell, Henry George, et al., eds. *A Greek-English Lexicon*. Rev. ed. Oxford: Clarendon, 1996.

Linafelt, Tod. *Ruth*. Berit Olam. Collegeville, MN: Liturgical, 1999.

Marais, Kobus. *A (Bio)Semiotic Theory of Translation: The Emergence of Social-Cultural Reality*. Routledge Advances in Translation Studies. New York: Routledge, 2019.

Marais, Kobus, and Ilse Feinauer, eds. *Translation Studies Beyond the Postcolony*. Newcastle: Cambridge Scholars, 2017.

Maxey, James A. "Alternative Evaluative Concepts to the Trinity of Bible Translation." In *Translating Values: Evaluative Concepts in Translation*, edited by Piotr Blumczynski and John Gillespie, 57–80. Palgrave Studies in Translating and Interpreting. London: Palgrave Macmillan, 2016.

Mbembe, Achille. *On the Postcolony*. Berkeley: University of California Press, 2001.

Melzer, Feivel. "Ruth." In *Five Scrolls*, edited by Pivel Malzor. Daʾath Miqra Commentary. Jerusalem: Mosad Ha-Rav Kook, 1973.

Mesters, Carlos. "The Use of the Bible in Christian Communities of the Common People." In *The Bible and Liberation: Political and Social Hermeneutics*, edited by Norman K. Gottwald, 119–33. Maryknoll, NY: Orbis, 1983.

Mojola, Aloo Osotsi. "Bible Translation in Africa." In *A History of Bible Translation*, edited by Philip A. Noss, 141–62. History of Bible Translation 1. Rome: Edizioni di storia e letteratura, 2007.

Mosala, Itumeleng J. *Biblical Hermeneutics and Black Theology in South Africa*. Grand Rapids: Eerdmans, 1989.

———. "The Use of the Bible in Black Theology." In *The Unquestionable Right to Be Free: Black Theology from South Africa*, edited by Itumeleng J. Mosala and Buti Tlhagale, 175–99. Maryknoll, NY: Orbis, 1986.

Mudimbe, V. Y. *The Invention of Africa: Gnosis, Philosophy, and the Order of Knowledge*. African Systems of Thought. Bloomington: Indiana University Press, 1988.

Ngwa, Kenneth Numfor. *Let My People Live: An Africana Reading of Exodus*. Louisville: Westminster John Knox, 2022.

Noss, Phil, and Peter Renju. "Mwalimu Nyerere Engages His People: Scripture Translation in Swahili Verse." *Journal of Translation* 3 (2007) 41–53. https://doi.org/10.54395/jot-28r5t.

Oelbaum, Jay. *Spatial Poverty Traps and Ethnic Conflict Traps: Lessons from Northern Ghana's "Blood Yams."* London: Overseas Development Institute (ODI), 2010. http://www.odi.org.uk/resources/download/4530.pdf.

Perry, Peter S. "Biblical Performance Criticism: Survey and Prospects." *Religions* 10 (2019) 1–15. https://doi.org/10.3390/rel10020117.

———. "Embodiment and Cognition from a Performance Criticism Point of View." San Antonio, SBL 2023. https://vimeo.com/937723903?share=copy.

Ricoeur, Paul, and John B. Thompson. *Hermeneutics and the Human Sciences*. Cambridge: Cambridge University Press, 1981.

Rulmu, Callia. "Stumbling Words for a Determined Young Lady: Notes on Ruth 2:7b." *Biblical Theology Bulletin* 42 (2012) 115–18.

Rushdie, Salman. *Imaginary Homelands: Essays and Criticism, 1981–1991*. London: Granta, 1991.

Sanders, James A. "Text and Canon: Concepts and Method." *Journal of Biblical Literature* 98 (1979) 5–29. https://doi.org/10.2307/3265909.

Schechner, Richard. *Performance Studies: An Introduction*. Edited by Sara Brady. 3rd ed. London: Routledge, 2013.

Schipper, Jeremy, ed. *Ruth: A New Translation with Introduction and Commentary*. Anchor Yale Bible 7D. New Haven: Yale University Press, 2016.

Septimus, Zvi. Review of *What Is Talmud? The Art of Disagreement*, by Sergey Dolgopolski. *AJS Review* 34 (2010) 124–27.

Shadd, Deborah. "Retranslation and Revision in a Rapidly Changing World." paper Presented at the 2017 Bible Translation Conference, Duncanville, TX.

Shepherd, David. "Violence in the Fields? Translating, Reading, and Revising in Ruth 2." *Catholic Biblical Quarterly* 63 (July 2001) 444–63.

Sperber, Dan, and Deirdre Wilson. *Relevance: Communication and Cognition*. 2nd ed. Oxford: Blackwell, 1995.

Towner, Philip H. "Translation from the Other Side: Process Before Product or 'In Defense of Lost Causes.'" *The Bible Translator* 69 (Aug. 2018) 150–65. https://doi.org/10.1177/2051677018785420.

Tully, Eric J. "The Character of the Peshitta Version of Ruth." *The Bible Translator* 70 (Aug. 2019) 184–206. https://doi.org/10.1177/2051677019859423.

Tymoczko, Maria. *Enlarging Translation, Empowering Translators*. Manchester: St. Jerome, 2007.

The Ujamaa Centre for Community Development and Research. "Doing Contextual Bible Study: A Resource Manual." Resources of Ujamaa/Manual, May 2015. https://ujamaa.ukzn.ac.za/cbs-manual/.

Waard, J. de, et al. *Biblia Hebraic Quinta: Fascicle 18: General Introduction and Megilloth*. Stuttgart: Deutche Bibelgesellschaft, 2004.

West, Gerald O. "Accountable African Biblical Scholarship: Post-Colonial and Tri-Polar." *Canon and Culture* (2016) 35–66.

———. "African Biblical Scholarship as Post-Colonial, Tri-Polar, and a Site-of-Struggle." In *Present and Future of Biblical Studies: Celebrating 25 Years of Brill's Biblical Interpretation*, edited by Tat-siong Benny Liew, 240–73. Biblical Interpretation Series 161. Leiden: Brill, 2018.

———. "Contextual Bible Study in South Africa: A Resource for Reclaiming and Regaining Land, Dignity and Identity." In *The Bible in Africa: Transactions, Trajectories, and Trends*, edited by Gerald O. West and Musa W. Dube, 595–610. Leiden: Brill, 2000.

———. "Interrogating the Comparative Paradigm in African Biblical Scholarship." In *African and European Readers of the Bible in Dialogue: In Quest of a Shared Meaning*, edited by Hans de Wit and Gerald O. West, 37–64. Studies of Religion in Africa 32. Leiden: Brill, 2008.

———. "Moffat's seTlhaping Translation as Invasion: Re-Translation Resources for Decolonisation." *HTS Teologiese Studies/Theological Studies* 79 (Dec. 19, 2023) 8.

———. "Redaction Criticism as a Resource for the Bible as 'A Site of Struggle.'" *Old Testament Essays* 30 (2017) 525–45.

———. "Scripture as a Site of Struggle: Literary and Socio-Historical Resources for Prophetic Theology in Post-Colonial, Post-Apartheid (Neo-Colonial?) South Africa." In *Scripture and Resistance*, edited by Jione Havea, 149–63. Theology in the Age of Empire. Lanham, MD: Lexington, 2019.

———. *The Stolen Bible: From Tool of Imperialism to African Icon*. Biblical Interpretation Series 144. Leiden: Brill, 2016.

West, Gerald O., and Musa W. Dube. "An Introduction: How We Have Come to 'Read With.'" *Semeia* 73 (1996) 1–16.

West, Gerald O., and Beverley G. Haddad. "Boaz as 'Sugar-Daddy': Re-Reading Ruth in the Context of HIV." *Journal of Theology for Southern Africa* 155 (July 2016) 137–56.

8

Echoing Forward, Echoing Back
Thick Translation, the Song of Songs, and the Performance of Cultural Exchange

BECKA MARA MCKAY

"The process of reading other people's readings
of individual texts has no end."[1]

Introduction: On Thick Translation and the Secular Jewish Translator

Every translation is a performance of the original text[2] for its reader: the language written by the translator re-creates the experience of readers of that original much as actors on a stage re-create a playwright's work via both dialogue and stage directions. The words in the actors' mouths are the same words the playwright committed to paper, but are illuminated

---

1. Hermans, "Cross-Cultural Translation Studies," 382.

2. Like many translators, I am ambivalent about the word "original": most texts are a continuum, a compilation of ideas and language that begins in the mind of one or more authors and through labor and collaboration becomes fixed, however briefly, on the page. For the purposes of this chapter, I am treating the word "original" as a way to denote the text that the reader of the translation has no access to.

for the audience by the apparatus of the theater: sets, lighting, costumes, and vocal modulation all work together to create a world out of the text.

In 1976, Kwame Appiah published the article "Thick Translation," an exploration of his theory that translation, too, needed an apparatus that could salvage some of the losses of translation—not only linguistic, but also cultural, historical, and sociopolitical:

> A translation aims to produce a new text that matters to one community the way another text matters to another: but it is part of our understanding of why texts matter that this is not a question that convention settles; indeed, it is part of our understanding of literary judgement, that there can always be new readings, new things that matter about a text, new reasons for caring about new properties.[3]

In other words, translators should use all the tools at their disposal to provide not only content but context for the readers of the translation: "A thick description of the context of literary production, a translation that draws on and creates that sort of understanding, meets the need to challenge ourselves and our students to go further, to undertake the harder project of a genuinely informed respect for others."[4]

Rather than thinking of the performed text as being weighted down or interrupted by the apparatus of a thick translation (footnotes, forewords, and other paratexts), Appiah's ideas, when put into practice, suggest that readers should be encouraged to think of the translation as a multidimensional experience inside the original text—a guided tour of sorts, or perhaps, to coin a term, a "thick performance." In 2003, Theo Hermans adapted Appiah's ideas in his essay "Cross-Cultural Studies as Thick Translation." Hermans saw Appiah's ideas as a way to interrogate the field of translation studies and locate a richer, more flexible vocabulary and methodology:

> "Thick translation" seems to me a line worth pursuing if we want to study translation across languages and cultures. This translation, as a form of translation studies, has the potential to bring about a double dislocation: of the foreign terms and concepts, which are probed by means of an alien methodology and vocabulary, and of the describer's own terminology, which

---

3. Appiah, "Thick Translation," 816.
4. Appiah, "Thick Translation," 818.

must be wrenched out of its familiar shape to accommodate both alterity and similarity.[5]

In this chapter, I aim to take Appiah's and Hermans's ideas a step further: What is translation of the Hebrew Bible if not a cross-cultural exchange, and what is that cross-cultural exchange if not a performance? In the translations that I will examine below, I will demonstrate how the translators of Song 1:5–7 use the tools of thick translation to perform the past for present and future readers, and might even allow readers to perform the past for themselves. These "thick performances" of the text keep it vital and relevant.[6]

On Discovering Thick Performance

My first experience with Bible translation as an adult[7] occurred nearly twenty years ago, as I was finishing up my coursework for a PhD in comparative literature. I took a Biblical Hebrew class at my university. When she learned of my interest in translation and Hebrew, the rabbi who taught the class invited me to join the Hebrew Bible translation group at the local synagogue in Iowa City. Every Wednesday morning we met around a pile of Bibles, reference books, concordances, lexicons, and dictionaries. Some of us were students, some of us were professors, some of us were retirees. What we had in common was our deep fascination with the language and the meaning of the Hebrew Bible. This happened so long ago I cannot even remember what book we were translating, although I believe it was either the first or second book of Samuel. We always followed the same pattern: Each of us—with varying degrees of fluency—would read a verse aloud, and then we would set to work translating each word. Our aim was not to create a perfect or even a working translation, but to work

---

5. Hermans, "Cross-Cultural Translation Studies," 386.
6. I must give credit to Anne Carson's book-length poem *NOX* for introducing me to the possibilities of thick translation for its own sake. Carson creates an elegy as a both a literal box of artifacts and a series of poems and translations for her late brother. The book's pages fold out of a book-shaped box and appear as somewhat hazy reproductions of various bits of text and photographs. She begins by reprinting Catullus's poem 101, which is also an elegy for a brother. For each word in the poem, Carson offers a kind of lexicographic exegesis that begins as literal translation and evolves into a more personal revelation. It is as if she is the archeologist of her own grief, using her skills as a classicist to sift through the bones of language and find new meaning.
7. I grew up studying Hebrew and the Hebrew Bible, in part as preparation for my Bat Mitzvah.

through translation to understand what we could about the language and circumstances of the text. To understand the history of the words so that we might understand the motives and intentions of the redactors who put it together. I do not think it is a stretch to say that together we made translation into performance: with the rabbi as our stage manager and director, we read out our lines and then interpreted them, creating a dialogue with each other as well as with the text. As we pried more context out of the resources piled on the table in front of us, we refined our understanding and expanded our dialogue to include the redactors who'd first written these words many centuries earlier.

This communal, collaborative atmosphere gave me the resources and a system to first practice thick translation. My doctoral dissertation consisted of a collection of approximately one hundred poems that I translated from Modern Hebrew into English, along with a critical introduction to the collection. The writers of these poems came from every era of Modern Hebrew poetry, roughly one hundred years of poets spanning most of the twentieth century and the beginning of the twenty-first. Each poem contained some kind of biblical allusion: Some of the poems were written as dramatic monologues in the voices of biblical characters. Some were written as contemporary responses to God's promises. Some reimagined various scenes from the text, such as the binding of Isaac or Lot's wife looking back at Sodom. My goal—and my challenge—was to explore the process of translating these allusions out of the language they were born in. How would I re-create the experience of reading a poem whose language, metaphors, and/or speakers and characters were so intrinsically related to the language it was written in? The very act of translation would remove these poems from their geographic, historical, religious, and cultural contexts. As a poet myself, who always preferred to have an unmediated experience of poems that I read in translation, I had always resisted the idea of footnotes, which felt disruptive and even manipulative. Yet I saw no other way to fill in the gaps I was creating through the act of translation. Endnotes seemed like a good compromise: the tiny superscripted numbers that I thought I would hate came to seem like little jewels that could activate further explication for readers who wanted to flip to the back.

Though I was skeptical when I began this process, I soon grew to love it. These notes—sometimes quite extensive and sprinkled with Hebrew language and biblical citations—felt like little glimpses I could offer readers of the entire process of translation. I could explain my choices and offer insights and resources for the curious. Here is the first section of a poem I translated by Shimon Adaf, a poet who uses biblical allusion somewhat subtly, as this poem demonstrates:

Icarus Remembers

1. In this place
Was it ever autumn here?
Seven wicked birds
gaunt as pins
stitch sky to asphalt,
gnawing on the light's last
crumb.
Inside the trees, the rising stops
like love.
Some of the heart's great silences
entered me, a terrible trembling
in this place.

My endnotes for this section:

In this first section of the poem, Adaf takes a known story from the Tanakh and cloaks it in language that nearly obscures it. The line about the birds recalls Pharaoh's dream, which Joseph interprets (correctly) as seven years of impending plenty followed by seven years of famine: "And Joseph said to Pharaoh, 'Pharaoh's dreams are one and the same: God has told Pharaoh what he is about to do. The seven healthy cows are seven years, and the seven healthy ears are seven years; it is the same dream. The seven lean and ugly cows that followed are seven years; it is the same dream.'"

The Hebrew that Adaf uses to describe the thinness of the birds in this poem, in fact, is taken directly from the Tanakh: *harakot v'haraot* (הָרַקּוֹת וְהָרָעוֹת). Unlike the following example, in which I used the language of the King James Bible to stress a reference to the story of the prophet Elijah, here I chose to more freely translate the selection.

And here is the last section of the same poem:

In this place June is becoming a barrage of longings.
Childhood blindness replaces
nightfall.
A tooth, late and unexpected,

> in the hollow mouth of Sderot.
> What belongs to me I collect and I break
> like heat
> in the wings of a fan.
> The blades of small birds
> bruise the horizon's flesh.
> What is prone to change never changes.
> A permanent balcony. Mother's gaze is delayed. Lost
> on the way to those trees, this garden.
> What the light patiently erodes is fastened here
> by hard nails, the streets
> motionless. Evening. They die
> like grass,
> like all of summer's
> leaping growth.
> "If you only knew this abyss, this complicated air
> that lets me come
> and go."
> I know, but I am
> less than desire, less
> than eternity. More than
> ignorance. More than this ignorance
> of pardon's impossibility.
> Even now
> when everyone I've loved
> remains beneath the burning heavens,
> trapped inside the lungs, a great and strong wind rends the mountains.
> Slowly
> Do I breathe.[8]

And my note:

> Near the end of the fifth section of the poem, Adaf embellishes his poetry with language found directly in the Tanakh, rather than draw directly upon stories from the Tanakh as metaphor or to offer a revisionist view. The line "a great and strong wind rends the mountains" comes directly from the story of the prophet Elijah—the story in which God more or less relieves Elijah of his prophet duties—He fires him.

When read with my endnotes—the apparatus of thick translation—these translations became miniature performances of my actions

---

8. From Adaf, *Mah she-khashavti tzel hoo ha-goof ha-amiti* (*That Which I Thought Shadow Is the Real Body*), 11–17.

as translator of biblical allusion: here was where I faithfully quoted the Tanakh, here was how I chose which Bible translation should guide me, here was where I listened to the ideas of my predecessors and applied them accordingly. I include the following list of notes from a poem I translated about Job simply to demonstrate how much information a footnote can contain and the picture it can create even if the poem isn't visible:

1. This image of Job's earth-caked face seems to be a direct reference to Job 38:38, "Whereupon the earth melts into a mass / and its clods stick together."

2. As if to further mock Job's decline, this word for the worm's headrest, *m'roshot* (מראשות), is the same word used in Gen 28 to describe the stone that Jacob uses for his head on the night God speaks to him for the first time.

3. Job 16:8, "You have shriveled me / My gauntness serves as a witness"

4. Job 16:10, "They open their mouths wide at me / Reviling me, they strike my cheeks"

5. Bones appear many times in the book of Job, as a symbol of mortality. Job 33:21, "His flesh wastes away until it cannot be seen / And his bones are rubbed away till they are invisible." The words that I've translated as "his bones" here, *atzmotav* (עצמותיו), means corpse or remains in modern Hebrew—this is just one of several places in the poem where the words Weichert chooses are particularly charged because they resonate in both the modern and biblical usage.

6. In modern Hebrew, the word I've rendered as grass, *chatzir* (חציר), usually means hay. But because of the appearance of this material in Job 8 and Job 40, I've kept the text closer to the Tanakhic meaning. 8:12, "While still tender, not yet plucked / They would wither before any grass." 40:15, "Take now behemoth, whom I made as I did you / He eats grass, like the cattle."

7. The word that I have translated as crocodile, *tanin* (תנין), appears in Job 7:12: "Am I the sea or the *Dragon* / That you have set a watch over me?" Other English translations render this word as sea monster, whale, or sea serpent. I chose to use the word's modern

Hebrew translation because the image of the mocking crocodile is very clear; however, readers of the original would probably make the connection with the appearance of the *tanin* in the Job story.

8. Weichert chooses a somewhat unusual word for friend; it has the same spelling as the word for evil.

9. When Job responds to the arguments of his friends in Job 13, the word for idol or false deity, *elil* (אֱלִיל), appears (Job 13:4), though it has a slightly different meaning: "Ye are all forgers of lies; ye are all *physicians of no value*" (KJV). (Jewish Publication Society uses the word "quacks.")

In rereading these translations and my endnotes while preparing to write this chapter, the thought occurred to me that while these poems are not biblical poems per se, their language descends directly from Biblical Hebrew, like new residents of an ancient dwelling. They are, in translation, a *performance* of the Hebrew Bible. When I point out in note 5 above that the poet is choosing words that resonate in both languages, I am essentially acting out the effects of the original poem for the reader of the translation. Without my notes—without thick translation—the poem's multiple layers of meaning are absent in English.

This brings me to the project at hand—a thick performance of the Song of Songs. My challenge this time was to bring the same kind of explication and interpretation to poetry straight from the Hebrew Bible itself. As a mostly (but not completely) secular Jew, I found myself in the strange position of wondering whether I was transgressing somehow by attempting to translate the Hebrew Bible directly for its own sake, rather than as a tool to help readers understand translations of Modern Hebrew poetry. This odd, internal battle between my Jewish self, my academic self, and my poet self resulted in my choice to work with the Song of Songs—one of only two books in the Hebrew Bible that do not mention God (the other is the book of Esther). By examining a wide number of vastly different translations of the Song and focusing on several "secular" translations in particular, I found a starting point for a study of this enigmatic text and the performances that emerge from them.

On Choosing the Song

As Robert Alter points out in his 2015 translation of the Song of Songs,[9] "the erotic nature of the Song constituted a challenge for the framers of the canon, both Jewish and Christian, and their response was to read the poems allegorically—in the case of the early rabbis, as the love between the Holy One and Israel, and in the case of the Church fathers, as the love between Christ and the Church."[10] In her book *The Song of Songs: A Biography*, Ilana Pardes traces changing interpretations of the Song over centuries, including these competing Jewish-Christian readings: "The Jewish-Christian dialogue concerning the Song in late antiquity is surely tense, but it also reveals a fruitful cross-cultural borrowing and a shared belief that allegory is the true way of reading the biblical love poem. The only question that keeps lingering—not a minor one—is what kind of allegory."[11] The translators whose work I've chosen to examine in more detail in this chapter—Robert Alter, Marcia Falk, and Chana and Ariel Bloch—are less concerned with finding the "right" answer to this question and much more concerned with the text as both a cultural and linguistic object. All three translations, with their extensive notes on sources and methodologies, are examples of thick translation. Each translation attempts to animate the text by creating a performance of the ancient metaphors for love, desire, and longing.

My first experience with translating the Song, however, came not from encounters with any of these scholars or even with my interactions, as a mostly secular Jew, with the Hebrew Bible. Instead, I had a student who wanted to translate it for a project in my graduate translation workshop. One of the steps she took in her translation was to pick apart some of the denser or loftier metaphors in the text, including the first verse of chapter 4: "Behold, thou art fair, my love; behold, thou art fair; thou hast doves' eyes within thy locks: thy hair is as a flock of goats, that appear from mount Gilead."[12] Wanting to understand how the comparison of hair to

---

9. From this point forward I will refer to it as the Song per scholarly tradition.

10. Alter, *Strong as Death Is Love*, 3. If it seems I cite Robert Alter to excess in this chapter, it is due to his pioneering translations, which—dense with notes providing welcome insight into the lives of the people who created the text as well as useful linguistic information—set a high standard for thick translation.

11. Pardes, *Song of Songs*, 57–58.

12. Song 4:1 (KJV). I choose this translation here because it was the one my student was working from.

goats could possibly be complimentary, she went to YouTube to search for videos of wild goats. Finding a clip that showed goats bounding down a hillside, she saw that the goats' movements might indeed resemble the movement of curly hair bouncing down a woman's back.[13]

I include this example because of the way it shows how the language of the Song performs itself for the reader, and how metaphor is the primary language of the Song. While there is no consensus among scholars about the author(s) of the Song or when it might have been written, most agree that it is at its heart a series of love poems. As translator Marcia Falk explains, "the Song exhibits all the properties of oral verse. Songlike not just in its title but in its lyric style—replete with sound plays, repetitions, refrains, and other musical characteristics—it has been a part of postbiblical oral tradition for centuries."[14] My student wanted to create a translation that valorized the role of metaphor in elevating the pleasures of the senses. She continued to seek out visual representations of these metaphors to incorporate into her translation. This, too, I consider thick translation—and thick performance.

In addition to the translations of Alter, the KJV, the Jewish Publication Society, and Marcia Falk, I spent a lot of time with Ariel and Chana Bloch's 1995 translation, which they undertook, in part, to correct what they saw as a series of translational wrongs:

> The Shulamite's lively presence has been obscured by two millennia of translations and interpretations that, for the sake of propriety, have presented her as a sweet young thing, chaste and demure and properly bridal. In most translations (the King James is a notable exception), she wears a veil, a reading not supported by the Hebrew. That incongruous veil, like the fig leaf of Renaissance painting and sculpture, is a sign of the discomfort of the exegetes. When we lift the veil from her face, the Shulamite is revealed as a passionate young woman, as spirited and assertive as Juliet.[15]

Here, the Blochs are calling out previous "performances" of the text as being too consumed with prophecy and purity to actually see the text. In their goal of eliding the sexual/gender politics, religious schisms, and

---

13. In a footnote regarding this same line, Alter says (with, I think, much less visual imagination), "The hair of the goats would be black, like the hair of the beloved cascading over her shoulders" (Alter, *Strong as Death Is Love*, 23).

14. Falk, *Song of Songs*, xv.

15. Bloch and Bloch, *Song of Songs*, 3.

linguistic developments of those "two millennia of translations and interpretations" they lay out a good deal of evidence that the lovers in the text (the Shulamite and her male companion) must have consummated their relationship—a relationship that thrived outside of the bonds of marriage. Unlike Alter's focus on the linguistic-historical aspects of the text, or Marcia Falk's compressed love lyrics, the Blochs have created a text that places a narrative—and a sexually liberated one at that—front and center. This is a performance that prioritizes character and story arc along with detailed attention to the rich, sensuous metaphors.

On Chapter 1, Verse 5

One reason I chose the Song to study for this chapter has much to do with my recent involvement in the Decolonial Pedagogies Project (DPP), an interdisciplinary faculty working group at my university charged with reimagining nearly everything about higher education in order to separate it from its roots in hierarchical, top-down colonial structures. This group has challenged me to rethink everything I know, or thought I knew, about higher education and colonialism. My colleagues in the DPP and I have spent many hours over the last three years trying to bridge the gap between our understanding of the consequences of colonization and our desire to decolonize our classroom practices. This chapter represents in part my desire to demonstrate a decolonized practice of scholarship by tracing the far-reaching effects of certain language in the Hebrew Bible—namely, Song 1:5, which in particular has always fascinated and confounded me because of the wide variety of approaches I have found in its translations.[16]

Here is the original Hebrew:

---

16. I am far from alone in this pursuit. In a recent keynote address to the Society of Biblical Literature, Musa Dube challenged her colleagues to seriously consider a much larger picture of the field of Bible translation: "Do contemporary biblical studies have the courage to look upon the tomes and tons of translated bibles lying upon the surface of Mother Earth? What responsibilities and opportunities do these tomes and tons of the translated biblical corpus lay upon academic biblical studies? What research questions, challenges, and opportunities for collaboration do they open? What are the pedagogical obligations and implications of taking cognizance of the translated global biblical corpus? In other words, what does faithfulness and unfaithfulness to the translated biblical corpus entail, imply and demand?" (Dube, "Behold, the Global Translated Bible(s)!," 5).

שְׁחוֹרָה אֲנִי וְנָאוָה, בְּנוֹת יְרוּשָׁלָיִם; כְּאָהֳלֵי קֵדָר, כִּירִיעוֹת שְׁלֹמֹה.

Here, I've created a literal translation (brackets indicate words I added for sense):

> Black I [am] and lovely, daughters [of] Jerusalem; like Kedar's tents, like Solomon's curtains.

Here is the same line from the King James Version:

> I am black, but comely, O ye daughters of Jerusalem, as the tents of Kedar, as the curtains of Solomon.

From the New International Version:

> Dark am I, yet lovely,
> daughters of Jerusalem,
> dark like the tents of Kedar,
> like the tent curtains of Solomon.

From the Jewish Publication Society:

> I am dark, but comely,
> O daughters of Jerusalem—
> Like the tents of Kedar,
> Like the pavilions of Solomon.

From Alter's translation:

> I am dark but desirable,
> O daughters of Jerusalem,
> like the tents of Kedar,
> like Solomon's curtains.[17]

From Falk:

> Yes, I am black! and radiant—
> O city women watching me—
> As black as Kedar's goathair tents
> Or Solomon's fine tapestries.[18]

And here is the Blochs' translation:

> I am dark, daughters of Jerusalem,
> and I am beautiful!

17. Alter, *Strong as Death Is Love*, 9.
18. Falk, *Song of Songs*, Song 1:5.

Dark as the tents of Kedar, lavish
as Solomon's tapestries.[19]

What strikes me most when simply comparing these translations is not the most obvious difference—the choice to translate the vav in וְנָאוָה as either *and* or *but*, but the choice of both Falk and the Blochs to add an exclamation point—a move they seem to make deliberately *in addition to* choosing "and" instead of "but." While the addition of punctuation is standard for any translation of the Hebrew Bible, it seems as if the Shulamite of Falk and the Blochs takes a little extra pride in her appearance: the darkness of her skin—whether from sun exposure or her natural complexion—might be, as the Blochs suggest, another aspect of her beauty cherished by her lover: "The Shulamite's need to account for her dark skin sounds apologetic; on the other hand, since her dark skin may have contributed to her singularity and attractiveness, she may be boasting, not apologizing."[20] Alter, in his annotation, doesn't mention race. He explains that "the point of the line is precisely its paradox: I am as dark as a nomad's tent but as desirable as the lovely curtains of a king. This would be an especially effective rejoinder to the elegant urbanite daughters of Jerusalem who might mock her for her suntanned skin, the sign of a peasant."[21]

What are we to make of this line in the twenty-first century? I won't offer the standard explanation of "isn't about race," when, like many translations and mistranslations of the Bible, damage has been done by these words. In his article "'I Am Black and Beautiful': A Black African Reading of Song of Songs 1:5–7 as a Protest Song," Robert Kuloba Wabyanga reads this passage as a protest against the gaze of racism:

> From the perspective of Song of Songs 1:5–7, protest against injustice is the responsibility of the oppressed. The oppressed in the Song of Songs is not contained. She is assertive! She uses the music podium to sing of her worth with pride. She is boastful; she is black and beautiful. That statement, "I am black and beautiful," is important in protests in contexts where beauty is understood from a white perspective that regards the black colour, hair and face or figure as ugly.[22]

---

19. Bloch and Bloch, *Song of Songs*, 47.
20. Bloch and Bloch, *Song of Songs*, 140.
21. Alter, *Strong as Death Is Love*, 9.
22. Wabyanga, "'I Am Black and Beautiful,'" 603.

Wabyanga uses the lens of African Biblical Hermeneutics to demonstrate how the text performs this protest, the speaker's voice echoing forward through the centuries to offer validation and support. In a broad but incisive examination of the effects of white settler colonialism on black Africans and the African diaspora, he creates a lineage of such protests, all the way to the 2020 demonstrations after the murder of George Floyd. Wabyanga's translation performs antiracism as antidote to the centuries of performed racism that inhere to translations such as the KJV, the NIV, and the JPS.

Of course, even more than the passage's focus on the speaker's skin tone, it's that single letter, ו (vav), meaning *and* or *but*, that is the sticking point. In Hebrew this letter never even stands on its own, but must be attached to other words. (Oceans of ink have been spilled about this word and its grammatical significance in the Hebrew Bible.) I translated it as *and* even if it means ignoring the paradox intended. In doing so, I freely admit that I am influenced by my decolonial training as well as by the ugliness made apparent through an antiracist reading of the text. The Blochs' approach is to split the difference, neither ignoring the possibility of discrimination present in the text nor employing it for a separate social agenda.

The translators I am looking at here can all be considered contemporary, creating their works in the last thirty years or so. The books that these translations appear in are sold in bookstores and the translations themselves are not primarily meant for inclusion in religious services. Their performances remain on the page to bloom in the mind of the reader—a reader who might first read a verse or a chapter of the Song and then flip to the back of the book or glance down at the footnotes for further contextualization, picking up interesting tidbits of information about the rituals and habits of an ancient people. From the Blochs, we learn that "tents of nomadic Bedouins in the Middle East are typically woven from the wool of black goats."[23] From Alter, we understand what he has chosen to translate as "desirable" (נָאוָה) comes from "the verbal stem '-w-h, 'to desire,' and given the erotically fraught world of the Song, that meaning is probably activated here."[24] These translations are rich with this cultural knowledge, but the performance is something created between the text and the reader. As can be gleaned from the divergent yet

---

23. Bloch and Bloch, *Song of Songs*, 140.
24. Alter, *Strong as Death Is Love*, 9.

harmonious voices in this book, there are easily as many ways to define "performance" as there are to read a sacred text. Peter Perry defines performance as "a communication event re-expressing traditions before an audience"[25]—a definition I do not disagree with. In the case of a secular Jew like me—my desk strewn with copies of the Hebrew Bible, translations of the Song, and a backbreaking array of dictionaries and lexicons—the text is a performance for an audience of one. This performance changes every time I read the text because I change every time I read the text. The world changes. Translation remains a negotiation between the known and the unknown that I show up for again and again, as both performer and audience.

A Literal Performance of the Text: A Brief Case Study

In 1940, a Zionist theater troupe in Mandatory Palestine put on a production of *Love as Strong as Death*, a Hebrew-language play based on the Song. In their article about the play, Yair Lipshitz and Naphtaly Shem-Tov explain the importance of the Hebrew Bible to the Zionist movement:

> Hebrew theatre took part in reclaiming the Bible for the sake of Zionist nation-building through various plays that dramatized key biblical stories and made the Bible live again on stage. Of the many biblical texts that inspired Zionist culture, the Song of Songs was particularly fundamental, mainly due to its elaborate descriptions of landscapes and nature and its liberated celebration of the body.[26]

Lipshitz and Shem-Tov go on to demonstrate how the production used Yemenite actors as a way to "physically embody the biblical world."[27] Yemenite Jews, as natives of the Middle East, were seen as closer to the literal source of the Hebrew Bible. They spoke a more "original" Hebrew, with an accent thought to be reminiscent of the ancient Israelites. At the same time,

> the Hebrew Zionist culture constructed the Yemenite Jew's image in terms of the orientalist stereotype. The Yemenite was presented as inferior, primitive and chauvinistic, but also as industrious, "content" and suitable for agricultural work. This

---

25. Perry, "Biblical Performance Criticism," 5.
26. Lipshitz and Shem-Tov, "'Why Were Our Yemenite Brothers Insulted?,'" 51.
27. Lipshitz and Shem-Tov, "'Why Were Our Yemenite Brothers Insulted?,'" 57.

justified not only their low wages and meagre living conditions, but also their employers' patronizing and condescending attitudes toward them. This attitude included the allotment of land for building agricultural settlements only to Ashkenazi pioneers who became, in time, the heroes of the meta-Zionist narrative ... In contrast, the Yemenites were relegated to the margins of the Zionist narrative where they attained neither actual capital nor the prestigious labelling as pioneers and national leaders.[28]

All of this tension plays out on the stage, particularly when the actress playing the Shulamite speaks her first lines from offstage before making her entrance: "Do not stare at me because I am dark, because I am darkened by the sun."[29] Of course, the speaker's entreaty to her lover not to notice the darkness of her skin is ironic: not only is the reader (and, we imagine, the lover) bound to immediately imagine the speaker's sun-darkened skin, but in a theatrical production the audience will be acutely aware of it before them: "In this particular performance, Shulamite's labelling as 'black' highlights the extent to which the casting here differs from traditional casting and from Hebrew–Ashkenazi theatre's customary 'whiteness' at the time."[30] In fact, the entire production was overlaid with a Yemenite flavor, from the costumes to the music to the set design. Yet these contributions were barely mentioned in the production notes that Lipshitz and Shem-Tov researched.[31] One review of a later production of *Love as Strong as Death* treats the sight of Yemenite theatergoers as an unusual spectacle: "Even if well-intentioned, the enthusiastic tone in which [critic] G.Z. writes about the play is deeply grounded in a paternalistic viewpoint in which Western theatre is cast as the white redeemer

---

28. Lipshitz and Shem-Tov, "'Why Were Our Yemenite Brothers Insulted?,'" 53–54. A more detailed examination of the ongoing tensions between Jews of Arab heritage (Mizrahim) and Ashkenazi Jews of European ancestry is beyond the scope of this chapter, but certainly important to keep in mind, especially when considering the racialized reading that has been attached to Song 1:5–7.

29. Lipshitz and Shem-Tov, "'Why Were Our Yemenite Brothers Insulted?,'" 56. This is the authors' translation of the playwright's Hebrew.

30. Lipshitz and Shem-Tov, "'Why Were Our Yemenite Brothers Insulted?,'" 56.

31. Lipshitz and Shem-Tov, "'Why Were Our Yemenite Brothers Insulted?,'" 56. Interestingly—though unsurprisingly—the authors of this article note that the Yemenite Jews involved in these aspects of the production received almost no credit for their work.

whose role is to shed light, if only momentarily, upon dark Yemenite existence."[32]

Conclusion: What Is Performed and What Is Exchanged

Every time I teach translation, my students have a moment where they ask, in one way or another, *can I do that?* As if they might dishonor or injure or otherwise ruin the text they are translating. This often happens when I or one of their classmates has made a suggestion that seems too bold, too "creative," too *something*. Translation, like writing, is a series of choices, but one choice that new translators often need to be told about explicitly is that they can take ownership of their translation. If they can support the decision they make—be it word choice, omission of words, addition of words, rearrangement of sentences, change in punctuation—they have permission to make that decision. Not permission from me, although I am usually the one granting it. Not permission from the author, whom my students for many reasons have likely not contacted. But permission in the larger sense of the word. Permission from St. Jerome, maybe—the patron of translation. Permission from their inner critic. Permission from the text itself to decide what it means.

I have found both poetry and danger in claiming to understand the word of God, which offers the hope of knowing. There is poetry in the layers of meaning revealed when I read the text again and again in its first written form and then in translation. All of the juxtapositions, interpretations, losses and gains—the whole apparatus that I perform when I read the Hebrew Bible—have gifted me with both a vocabulary of and an instinct for sacred language. All of the crossing back and forth between languages—Biblical Hebrew to Modern Hebrew to English—as I both translate and write has (and this may be a terribly unscholarly claim) blessed my ears and given me so much to work with.[33] And yet any work that so freely and boldly crosses between sacred and secular does feel dangerous to me. There is danger, perhaps, in believing that reading this sacred text creates the same pact between me and the page and that any act of reading creates. As I've mentioned, the Song of Songs contains no mention of God, which has confounded and challenged translators and scholars for centuries (and did not keep St. Bernard of Clairvaux,

32. Lipshitz and Shem-Tov, "'Why Were Our Yemenite Brothers Insulted?,'" 61.

33. Indeed, as a result of the research and writing of this very chapter, I have so far written 35 poems of a planned 117-poem cycle based on each verse of the Song.

medieval monk and mystic, from writing eighty-six sermons about them and how they were meant, in his view, to bring people closer to God). By examining the performative and cultural potential of the Song of Songs through these translations (and subsequently through my own poems), I am trying to do exactly what I've been telling my students to do for years: give myself that permission to take ownership of the text. To make decisions based on what I believe the author intends. But what author? Or, should I say, whose God?

Bibliography

Adaf, Shimon. *Mah she-khashavti tzel hoo ha-goof ha-amiti* [*That Which I Thought Shadow Is the Real Body*]. Jerusalem: Keter, 2000.

———. *That Which I Thought Shadow Is the Real Body*. In *Kaleidoscope: Three Hebrew Poets*, 89–92. Oakville, ON: Mosaic, 2014.

Alter, Robert. *The Book of Psalms*. New York: Norton, 2009.

———. *Strong as Death Is Love*. New York: Norton, 2015.

Appiah, Kwame Anthony. "Thick Translation." *Callaloo* 16 (1993) 808–19.

Bloch, Ariel, and Chana Bloch. *The Song of Songs*. New York: Modern Library Classics, 2006.

Dube, Musa W. "Behold, the Global Translated Bible(s)! Research and Pedagogical Implications." *Journal of Biblical Literature* 143 (2024) 5–25.

Falk, Marcia. *The Song of Songs*. Waltham, MA: Brandeis University Press, 1993.

Hermans, Theo. "Cross-Cultural Translation Studies as Thick Translation." *Bulletin of SOAS* 66.3 (2003) 380–89.

Lipshitz, Yair, and Naphtaly Shem-Tov. "'Why Were Our Yemenite Brothers Insulted?' Love as Strong as Death as a Prequel to Mizrahi Presence in Israeli Theatre." *Theatre Research International* 49.1 (2024) 50–69.

Pardes, Ilana. *The Song of Songs: A Biography*. Princeton: Princeton University Press, 2019.

Perry, Peter S. "Biblical Performance Criticism: Survey and Prospects." *Religions* 10 (2019) 1–15. https://doi.org/10.3390/rel10020117.

Wabyanga, Robert Kuloba. "'I Am Black and Beautiful': A Black African Reading of Song of Songs 1:5–7." *Old Testament Essays* 34.2 (2021) 588–609.

9

Performance in Sign Language Bible Translation

ISELA TRUJILLO

Introduction

Performance criticism in Bible translation studies proposes a theoretical and methodological model[1] where Deaf[2] translators can find a path that fully understands their communication codes, and that allows them to deepen and legitimize their Bible translation work. I emphasize legitimizing because the translation of the Bible into Sign Languages has often been seen or dismissed as a translation that transgresses the basic principles of "fidelity," since the entire "form" of the written biblical text is transformed into a visual-gestural "form" that is, among other things, essentially performative.

We must begin by emphasizing that Deaf people are visual people, who see and understand the world through signs, images, drawings, metaphors, and dramatizations. However, being a visual person in a world of hearing people has never been easy. One of the most dominant ways of perceiving Deaf people is based on the view of deafness being

---

1. Rhoads, "Emerging Methodology," 1–36; Maxey, "Expanding Dialogue," 1–2; Perry, "Performance Criticism," 1–15.

2. We capitalize Deaf as a convention suggested by the Deaf movement which states: "We adopted the convention of using the capitalized 'Deaf' to describe the cultural practices of a group within a group. We use the lowercase 'deaf' to refer to the condition of deafness, or the larger group of individuals with hearing loss without reference to this particular culture." Padden and Humphries, *Inside Deaf Culture*, 1.

an impairment, disability, or disease, for which reasons one must try to "normalize and cure" Deaf people through their oralization. This approach considers verbal expression and lip reading as the only true form of human communication.

Those who know the art of performance and its extraordinary potential for communication would be alarmed by the shocking statements of the Second International Congress on the Education of the Deaf in Milan (1880) and which, although old, has had a tremendous impact on the education of Deaf people in many countries to the present day. In this congress, they affirmed the following:

> Considering the indisputable superiority of the word over the gesture because of the integration of the deaf-mute and to facilitate a better knowledge of the language, the Congress declares that the oral method is preferable to the sign method in their education ... Considering that the simultaneous use of gesture and word has the disadvantage of impairing speech and lip reading as well as the precision of ideas, the Congress declares its preference for pure oral methods.[3]

This oralist perspective on Deaf people has permeated many areas, not only educational but even religious, including many people's ideas about translating the biblical text. It is still common to equate the written form with the word of God in such a way that it is thought that the word of God can only be transmitted in verbal communication codes.

In the same way, the words of the apostle Paul taken literally as "faith comes by hearing" have had a strong impact on Deaf people, since such point of view has led them to consider that the "official" language of God is an oral language, like that of hearing people. This literal interpretation would imply that deafness and everything related to them, such as their Sign Language, is immoral, since they are the product of sin.[4] It is not by chance, then, that to this day there is a significant lag in the development of Bible translations into Sign Languages.

However, from a sociocultural perspective, quite contrary to the oral approach, Deaf people make up a community with its own culture, language, and identity. For several decades now, Deaf people from different countries have been fighting for recognition as a linguistic minority

---

3. Saizarbitoria, "Sistema de Comunicación," 154–57; the translation of the text into English is mine.

4. Broesterhuizen, "Deaf Liberation Theology," 5.

that possesses cultural traits that can be described and equated to those of any other linguistic and cultural group.[5]

Deaf communities are characterized by having an eminently visual culture, which implies a way of knowing and conceiving of the world in a different way from that of hearing people. This way of thinking about the world is extraordinarily well conveyed and symbolized through Sign Languages, through which they name the world and transmit ideas, thoughts, values, emotions, etc., giving rise to Deaf culture in its multiple manifestations.

In many contexts, the translations of the Bible that Deaf people create are only understood as a work for people with "disabilities," which have nothing interesting to contribute to biblical studies and the field of translation. The present study is not only developed from a sociocultural perspective on Deaf communities, but rather we maintain that a sociocultural view is crucial for a good understanding of the process carried out by Deaf translators and the impressive visual creativity they use to communicate the text of the Bible through Sign Languages.[6]

Linguistic Characteristics of Sign Languages

There is evidence that human beings have communicated using their hands and gestures since immemorial time, but throughout history, for Deaf people, these seemingly peculiar forms of communication have led others to consider them to be mentally ill, possessed by the devil, idiots, etc. The first educators of Deaf people, who used to be religious, were those who observed the form of communication that Deaf people developed among themselves, tried to systematize their observations, and made some proposals for communication with the use of their hands. An example is the first publication of the manual alphabet in 1620 or the works of the famous Abbot L'Epée.[7]

It was not until the mid-twentieth century, when Stokoe published his ground-breaking paper on Sign Language Structure, that Sign Language began to acquire relevance and interest in the field of linguistics. Stokoe and his Deaf collaborators,[8] against all currents of the time,

---

5. Lane, "Ethnicity," 291–310; Padden and Humphries, *Inside Deaf Culture*, 1–10.

6. For discussion on intercultural dialogue and the interpretation of the Bible with Deaf communities, see Tamez and Trujillo, "Diálogo Intercultural," 44–61.

7. Castres, "L'Epée," lines 14–16.

8. Stokoe, *Sign Language Structure*, 1–78.

attempted to describe the features of what would later be recognized as American Sign Language. His work constitutes a milestone in the history of Sign Language linguistics, Deaf education, Sign Language teaching and interpreting. It has had a profound impact on many of the Deaf communities throughout the world, since it demonstrated, from scientific and linguistic criteria, that Sign Languages are not simply disjointed or only mimic forms of communication, but on the contrary, they are actual languages with their own syntactic and grammatical structure.

After Stokoe's work, numerous investigations have been carried out, demonstrating and analyzing the linguistic universals of these languages, equating them to the functioning of spoken languages, but also discovering and describing their linguistic characteristics as visual languages.[9]

Sign Languages have grammatical rules that can be described in a similar way to any of the structural levels of spoken languages, such as phonological (keriological), morphological, syntactic, semantic, and pragmatic levels. For example, there are different parameters that are observed and analyzed in the formation of signs. Most analyses describe the signs based on six criteria: (1) configuration of the hand and fingers, (2) orientation of the hand and arm (palm up, down, in front, etc.), (3) location of the sign (in relation to the body, arm, head, chest, etc.), (4) type of movement, (5) direction, (6) non-manual markers. Each of these criteria must be considered since the change in only one of these traits can generate important differences in terms of meaning.[10]

Facial expressions (non-manual features) such as eye gaze, eyebrows, the movement of the head, shoulders, mouth, and the position of the body, have the function of marking the accentuation, the transmission of emotions, and various aspects of what one wants to express. These characteristics can't be ignored because they are part of the grammar. Various adverbial forms are marked with manual speed (slow/fast), and at the syntactic level, space management is essential to structure communication.

In Sign Languages, the transmission of meanings at a semantic level is very interesting because it follows multiple and varied strategies, closely linked to performative expression. Roughly speaking, we can observe three great pillars or routes to communicate an idea, thoughts, or things: conventional signs, classifiers, and performance. These three strategies

9. Klima and Bellugi, *Signs of Language*, 7–67; Taub, *Language from the Body*, 19–35; Sandler and Lillo-Martin, *Linguistics Universals*, 503–8.

10. Martínez, *Manual de Gramática*, 6–10.

are performative because they use fingers, hands, face, eye gaze, and body movement as expressive support to represent and name the world.

Conventional signs are lexical items which are represented visually with hands/gestures/movements, which have been conventionally and consensually established as the representation of those things, concepts, or ideas in a determined context and recognized by a specific group of users. These types of signs are usually unique to a given Sign Language and may not be understood by people who are fluent in other Sign Language. These are the signs that we will normally find in the dictionary of a local or national language. Some of these signs are formed with one hand, others are formed with two hands, others can be formed with either one or two hands.

Classifiers are a special type of configuration of the hands that will allow the communication of many other meanings related to the shape, size, consistency, and location of things. Likewise, classifiers can represent a class or group of referents (people, animals, and objects) with an important number of hand configurations.

In Sign Language, performance refers to dramatization and personification. That is, to the acted representation of the things and actions that are to be communicated, and to the incarnation of the characters who do those actions. This strategy integrates the movement of the head, the body, the use of gestures, eye gazes, and their direction, including the management of space.

Deaf people, according to what they want to communicate and to whom they want to communicate it, will select the communication strategy, using the conventional sign, classifiers, performance, or a simultaneous combination of all these strategies. For example, an action such as running can be communicated with a conventional sign, with the use of a classifier, in a dramatized way, or with classifier and dramatization simultaneously.

When a Deaf person who is fluent in a Sign Language meets another Deaf person who is fluent in a different Sign Language, to communicate, they will prioritize the use of classifiers and performance over the use of lexical (conventional) signs.

In the translation of the Bible into a Sign Language, Deaf translators play with these strategies and make decisions about how to best express the meaning they are trying to communicate. For this reason, expecting to find a conventional sign for each of the words or concepts that we find in the Bible text would reveal a total ignorance of how a Sign Language works, since it is likely that many of these ideas or concepts are expressed with classifiers or in dramatized form.

The Process of Translating the Bible into a Sign Language

Deaf translation teams and their churches often face a paradigm shift since, to begin with, a Sign Language Bible is not presented on paper but through a video. This fact alone confronts many Christian traditions strongly rooted in the Bible as a book. So, the first thing that must be understood is that a Sign Language Bible not only responds to the principles of an interlinguistic translation (between languages) as is the case with spoken and written languages but is also an intersemiotic translation.[11]

Tamez, who is a biblical scholar and Sign Language translation consultant, has emphasized for some years that when we talk about translating the Bible into a Sign Language, we are talking about an intersemiotic translation. This is true because we go from a translation of a written discourse system of an oral language, which is linear, to a visual, gestural, performative, spatial, iconic, and simultaneous discourse system.[12]

Publishing a Sign Language Bible translation video implies a lot of previous work at different stages in the translation process. There is no single work path, as each project and team of Deaf translators face different challenges according to the reality of their contexts. Below, I will only roughly present some of the stages that take place "behind the scenes" and the main challenges related to the intersemiotic perspective and performance.

Exegesis of the Text from Deaf People's Perspective[13]

As in all translation work, the first stage of the process begins with the exegesis of the text. In the exegesis that Deaf people develop, the type of questions they ask the text, the type of answers they find, and how they internalize the translation to sign it in their Sign Language are where we can better understand that we are dealing with another semiotic system

---

11. On this topic it is suggested to read Hodgson, "Cultura y Medios."
12. Tamez, "Bible and Performance," 211–345.
13. It is up to Deaf people to describe the exegetical process they make of the biblical text. However, as a translation consultant with experience in checking Bible translations into Sign Language, I want to share here my experience and observations of working with Deaf translators.

and involved in a dialogue between verbal and linear discursive forms versus visual-gestural discursive forms.

In response to the questions that Deaf translators ask about the biblical text and reviewing video drafts of the translation in different Sign Languages, I observe that there is a strong link between enunciation strategies and performative needs that Sign Languages present. Therefore, they frequently ask questions related to the information they need to visualize the actions of the biblical event that is to be narrated or presented.

For example, Deaf people inquire about the place where events take place (the "setting"), about the characters that appear in the events, who they are, their character or attitude and their relevance (protagonistic, antagonistic, secondary), about the shape, size, and qualities of the objects that are mentioned. They analyze if there are displacements or movements of the characters, and they review the chronology of events and other contextual elements to understand the situation. In short, the visual information that must be inferred to set the scene and reenact the event. I will not stop at this moment to give more details of these aspects, as this will be taken up more precisely and exemplified in the analysis section of this article.

Storyboard, Self-Recording, Glosses

As part of the process of the semiotic leap that Deaf translators will take to go from the written biblical text to a Sign Language Bible text, I observe different methodological strategies that vary according to the preferences of each translation team. Broadly speaking, we can say that there are three main strategies: the storyboard, self-recording, and glosses.

Some teams prepare a storyboard, that is, a series of illustrations that the translators prepare as a guide to understand and remember the story, to pre-visualize it according to the sequences they have chosen and focusing on the most important aspects of the story. Other teams analyze the passage and divide it into small units that they will provisionally film and then later film the entire passage. Finally, other teams, especially those with the most knowledge of the oral language of their community, create glosses. Glossing is a transliteration system wherein words form a spoken language are used as labels to represent each sign, classifier, and some of the non-manual features, respecting the grammatical order of the Sign Language.

The translators use one of these strategies as an aid to prepare the first draft video of the translated text in Sign Language. It is a crucial step, in which the semiotic leap is finally made from the written text to the text now presented in Sign Language as a visual language. From this point on, the translators will continue working from a visual perspective.

Deaf Community Check

Once the translation team has polished their translation drafts, they present them to the Deaf churches and communities for whom they are translating and which are represented in the translation project.

Checking with the Deaf community is a very important stage for the acceptability of the translation, and it has to do with the acceptability not only of the translation itself but also of the "signer" of the translation. Unlike a written translation, where the translator can remain anonymous, in a Sign Language, the translation has been embodied by a signer,[14] whose identity is known and visible to the entire Deaf community.[15]

The visibility of the identity of the on-screen signer links the translation with the acceptability or unacceptability of the Deaf person chosen to sign, which can be evaluated in terms of age, gender, personal and ecclesial testimony, Sign Language fluency, etc. For this reason, several of the translation teams work in advance to come to a consensus regarding the on-screen presenter(s) for the project to help ensure the acceptability of the translation.

During the community checking stage there will be a dialogue primarily about aspects related to the clarity and naturalness of the signing and the consensus on signs proposed or created by the translation team.[16]

Bible Checking by the Translation Consultant

Bible translation projects into Sign Language usually have a translation consultant, who is responsible for answering questions from the translators, providing information, and making observations or comments

---

14. Later we will define and exemplify what we mean by embodiment or incarnation.

15. There are some projects that have decided to hide the identity of the signer through animation. However, so far animation has not become widely accepted in the field of Sign Language Bible translation.

16. The proposal or creation of new signs is part of Deaf culture.

on the translation video related to biblical languages, the sociocultural background of the texts, and exegetical or translation problems. The Deaf translators dialogue with the consultant until the problems that were observed are resolved, then they prepare a new draft video of the translation, which is usually the pre-final draft that will serve as a kind of prompter for the signer of the final video.

Final Filming and Editing

The final filming for a Sign Language Bible video is typically done in a video recording studio that has been specially designed for Sign Language recordings. In addition to a high-quality video camera and good lighting for the face, hands, and upper body, typically three to six monitors are placed in various parts of the signer's visual field. A green chroma key background is often used.

Unlike a film studio for spoken language videos, where the speaker(s) may use teleprompters containing text, Deaf translators cannot rely on a single monitor, because the direction of the signer's gaze indicates their perspective and the location of characters in a narrative. Thus, multiple screens which are simultaneously showing the approved draft of the Sign Language translation function as a teleprompter while allowing the signer to maintain natural eye gaze throughout the performance.

Sign Languages are characterized by having a signing space, which is the area on and around the signer where the signs are formed. The size may vary slightly from one Sign Language to another, and even from one signer to another, but generally signs need to be articulated on and around the upper part of the body. In the filming of Bible translation videos, it is customary to use a single camera setting which is set up so that the signer's hands remain in the frame. The signer is always filmed from the front without any adjustment to the camera's zoom.

For the final filming, the Deaf translators also decide on various visual aspects related to the type and color of clothing that the signer will use, the amount of makeup, the colors of the background, etc. All these decisions will impact the final presentation of the translation.

Deaf people who are dedicated to artistic production and have a lot of knowledge and experience in handling the camera, lenses, lights, zoom settings, makeup, etc., have shown impressive results in terms of what can be achieved with technological effects, increasing the impact that Sign Language complemented with these effects can have. It may be that in the future this type of creativity can also be brought to the field of Bible translation.[17]

Once the final "official" filming of the translation video has been completed and the footage has been carefully reviewed, the next step is final editing. In many cases the video editing includes the incorporation of illustrations, maps, and/or computer graphics, titles in written language and/or Sign Language, verse references, subtitles in a written language, etc. Once the editing is complete, the video is carefully checked.

Multimodality and Multidimensionality in the Sign Language Bible Translation

Translations into Sign Languages are essentially multimodal, not only because Sign Languages internally use different strategies to communicate meanings, but also because elements belonging to other semiotic communication systems such as illustrations, maps, genealogies, written texts of the oral language, etc. are often included in the videos.

Sign languages are characterized by being three-dimensional and by having more than one articulator (two hands, a face, and a body), so individual signs can be sequential or simultaneous, and the signer can also simultaneously convey information spatially and/or through non-manual markers. This means that although many signs and their components are presented one after the other, some one-handed signs and/or classifiers can be articulated simultaneously, and in the same spatial frame around the signer, with or without a simultaneous non-manual marker articulated by the face or body.

As an example, let's look at the following phrase taken from the passage of the "Poor Widow" in Luke 21:1–4, "two small coins of very little value" in one screen shot:[18]

---

[17]. As an example, see the "fish" video created by a Deaf artist "fish" (Virnig, "Deaf Man's ASL Storytelling").

[18]. This image is a screenshot of a draft video in Ecuadorian Sign Language. The signer has given permission for the author to use her image in this chapter.

Performance in Sign Language Bible Translation 213

The signer with her right hand indicates that it is a coin, with her left hand that it is small, and with her face indicates that they have very little value.

In this other example from Gen 1, let's see again in a single screenshot the formula that is repeated in several verses "and God saw that it was good":[19]

19. This image is a screenshot of a draft video in Dominican Sign Language. The signer has given permission for the author to use his image in this chapter.

The signer is incarnating God, with his left hand he is holding the creation, with his right hand he is looking at the creation, and with his face he indicates that he liked it, that it was good.

In addition to this three-dimensional way of communicating in Sign Language, in many Bible translations, it is customary to accompany the signing with elements that come from other semiotic systems, such as illustrations, maps, and/or written text.

For example, an illustration or drawing is often shown before presenting the story or passage translated into the Sign Language. This provides visual information on what is going to be signed. Illustrations can also appear at any time during the translation to exemplify some cultural object or just to clarify a scene. In some translations, a text written in the oral language appears at the beginning to indicate the title of the story, and also may appear throughout the translation where the spelling of names or places is given, or when the presenter uses signs that are not widely known.

There are various reasons why translators incorporate these elements, but most have to do with the goal of achieving greater clarity in the translation. It is thought, for example, that this multimodality will help Deaf people who do not have a broad or sufficient knowledge of the Sign Language, due to isolation, linguistic deprivation, or oralization, to understand the passage. Translation teams have found that is indeed the case. However, since Deaf people are so visual, even fluent signers often appreciate the inclusion of illustrations and maps, which help them to better visualize and remember passages. Many fluent signers also appreciate a link between a biblical term or name and the corresponding sign(s), so that they will better understand their written Bible.

Performance Analysis in Sign Language Bible Translation

To understand the functioning of the semiotic system of Sign Languages, as hearing people we must begin to deverbalize ourselves and try to think of the world in images, visual concepts, metaphors, and performance.

As mentioned above, Sign Languages convey meanings not only through lexical (conventional) signs, which often do not have a one-to-one correspondence with the words of a spoken language, but also through visual concepts, and the use of an infinite variety of classifiers, leaps toward personification or incarnation of characters, the dramatization of events, ever present facial expressions which indicate emotions, and the intensity and tone with which an event or situation must be understood.

We must emphasize here that "performance" is an incredibly important strategy for transmitting meaning in Sign Languages, and it is an intrinsic part of the visual-manual modality. That is, any Deaf person who knows a Sign Language will make use of this strategy. The signer does not need to be an "actor" or to have studied "acting" to perform it; rather it has been internalized as a natural form of communication.

There is a wide spectrum between "performance" that is executed naturally, as an innate part of the signed modality, and "performance" in an artistic or theatrical sense. The latter can include makeup, zoom effects, lights, changes or graduations in the direction of the camera to impact the audience, etc. For artistic "performance," the signing space, the size of the signs, the movements of the body, and the other non-manual features may be expanded or intensified. It is important to note that there are important cultural differences between different Deaf communities in the world when determining the degree of "performance" or volume which is considered part of their natural form of communication versus amplification for theatrical purposes.

In Sign Language Bible translation, when it is done naturally, the visual-gestural characteristics of Sign Languages are respected, and the performance is the axis or pillar of its entire realization. Unfortunately, I have observed that, whether due to the dominance of the hearing culture, or due to a theological perspective more attached to the "form" of the Bible, sometimes Deaf translators feel pressured or do not feel confident in using "performance" fully or freely. This leads them to make decisions that go against the visual naturalness of their own forms of expression. They opt for the simple use of lexical signs, considering that by doing this, their translation can be more "faithful" to the biblical text, and at the same time widely satisfy hearing people[20] and Deaf oralists.

Other things that can reduce the use of performance are the lack of access to Sign Language from early childhood (linguistic deprivation), or the strong oralization in the education of Deaf people, to the detriment of acquisition of the Sign Language, which many Deaf people experience throughout the world. As a result, many Deaf people do not know, or have not fully mastered, the Sign Language of their community. Due to

---

20. I mean hearing people who don't know or are unaware of the important function of performance in Sign Language, or are conditioned by their own theological perspective of the biblical text.

this lack of knowledge, "performance" is seen only as a kind of "mimicry," or disarticulated language.

Fortunately, the above factors are changing little by little in countries or regions where Deaf people have a strong identity, organize themselves in Deaf communities, and affirm their culture with great confidence, so the trend will be to intensify the "performance" of the language. In a Sign Language Bible translation, this will be reflected by incorporating all the dramatic and gestural elements that are required, even occasionally beyond the "natural" or "grammatical" limits. As they say, to "turn up the volume." They do this so that their translation is clearer and more vivid for Deaf people, even for those who are not fluent in the local Sign Language.

The characteristics of Sign Languages and their beauty and creativity can only be fully seen, understood, and appreciated in all their splendor when those who know these languages see the actual signed performance. However, since this is an article that is not only for Sign Language specialists, I will try to verbalize and illustrate, with the help of some images, concrete examples of some of the strategies that I have found by analyzing a Bible "text" which was translated and produced by Deaf people.

Performance in a Sign Language Translation of Luke 13:10–17

In the performative analysis that I present, I will show what happens in a Sign Language through four aspects that I have called "Incarnation of the Characters," "Scenery," "Dramatic Actions" and "Context." As an example, I have analyzed the translation of the Bible text "The Stooped Woman," from Luke 13:10–17, translated and published by the Mexican Sign Language Bible Translation team (BLSM).[21] The signer of this passage is the Deaf translator Alfredo González.[22]

Incarnation of the Characters or Embodiment

Incarnation of the characters or embodiment refers to personification, that is, when the signer takes on the role of, represents, or "becomes"

---

21. I recommend a prior reading of this biblical passage to better follow the analysis presented below.

22. The analyzed video can be accessed through the following link to the Mexican Sign Language Bible page: Biblia LSM, "Lucas 13:10–17."

the characters mentioned in the narrative. A signer can take on any role: boys, girls, men, women, the elderly, animals, Jesus, God, or even the devil himself.

In Sign Language Bible translation, Deaf translators tend to approach the biblical characters in a more personal way than spoken language translators do, because they need to understand them much better. This is because the signer is going to give life to each character and must visually differentiate them through non-manual components such as head and body position and eye gaze to communicate their position relative to other characters. Other non-manual markers are also included which express linguistic elements. Affective or attitudinal non-manual components must also be incorporated, such as facial expressions, and the non-manual components which are part of the performance, including their posture, manner of movement, and all the gestures that give life to each character. This process is very similar to the way in which an actor studies his character from different angles and references to understand and portray him.

In the story of "The Stooped Woman" in Luke 13:10–17 the signer embodies the narrator and several characters: Jesus, the stooped woman, the spirit, the leader of the synagogue, the people gathered, the opponents, and the ox or donkey. Let's see in images how the Deaf translator has incarnated each one of them.[23]

---

23. These are screenshots of the publicly available video translation, https://biblialsm.com/lucas-13-10-17.html. The translators and signers have given permission to the author for their images to be used in this chapter.

All the characters are perfectly identifiable throughout the narrative by the non-manual components that the signer has assigned to each of them. There are innumerable variations of facial expressions used throughout the story. Just as a sample, I have presented a single screenshot of each one of them, so you can appreciate the gestures and head and body positions created by the Deaf signer to differentiate each character.

The narrator is easy to identify in Sign Languages, since one of the main characteristics is his gaze is always directed toward the viewer. However, his performance is very important because he has the challenge of telling the story, of capturing or attracting the audience and keeping it attentive to the series of actions that will take place. As narrator, the signer not only introduces the characters but links the sequence of actions.

Scenario (Place, Location of the Characters, and Perspective)

To sign a Bible narrative, Deaf translators must create a scenario, that is, visualize in the signer's frame the place or places where the events and their sequence take place. The visual scenarios are interactive, they can change as many times as necessary, and you can create momentary or secondary scenarios.

Once the location of the events has been visualized, the signer will also begin to spatially distribute each of the characters mentioned in the narration so as not to overlap them or needlessly position characters in one location.

An interesting pattern that has been observed in some Sign Languages consists of placing the important characters, protagonists, or those who represent good to their right, while those who are antagonistic, or secondary, are placed on their left.

The location of the characters in the Bible passage will give the signer a "perspective" of the scene and will allow him to refer to, personify, or lead the characters by shifting his head, shoulders, and upper body to the right or left side, and his eye gaze up or down, straight ahead or to the right or left. There is a cultural component to how accentuated or visible these movements are. In some Sign Languages it is very marked, while in others it is more subtle.

In Sign Language Bible translation, it is crucial for the signer to establish people and places in the signing space, because that is the natural way to express who is speaking with whom, and who is responding to whom without having to repeat the character's name each time. It also allows the presenter to avoid signing words such as "and he said," "and he answered," or "he warned him." In some Sign Language verbs, the location where the sign is formed or the direction of the sign indicate who does or receives an action.

Deaf people, when signing the scenarios of a biblical narration, depending on their creativity and curiosity and, if the biblical text indicates it, often like to be clear if the event being narrated is in an interior or exterior space. For example, if it is in a town, on the road, in the city, in the Temple of Jerusalem, in what part of a house, if the place is small or large, on the banks of the Jordan River or the Sea of Galilee, in a flat or mountainous place, etc. Essentially, they want to answer the question of what the place looks like so that they can better visualize the scene and thus sign more naturally and accurately.

If the Bible text does not provide this information, Deaf people will often try to search in extra-biblical sources for some visual data. If after that there is still no information about the place where the scene occurs, the signer will often have to make a visual decision about what the scenario is like to bring staging to life.

In the analysis of the translation of the Stooped Woman, of Luke 13:10–17, the signer has indicated at the beginning of the narration that this story takes place inside a synagogue. Analyzing from the perspective of the viewer, gathering all the characters in the synagogue in a single shot, we would place them as follows:

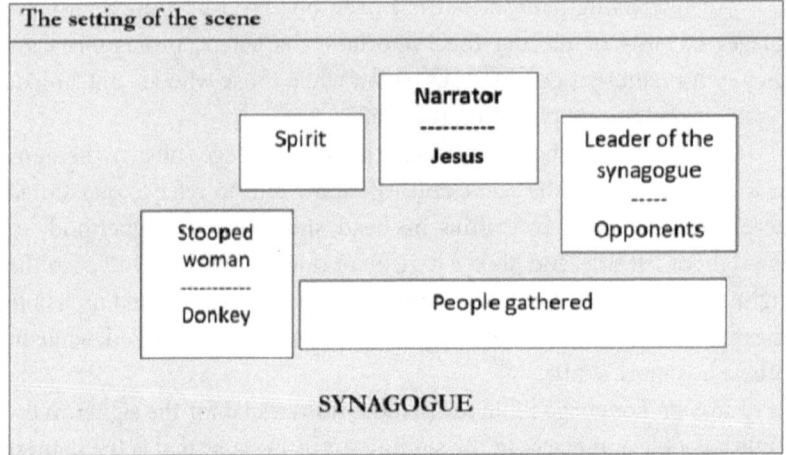

However, if we analyze sequence by sequence, we will see that there are movements in the signer's perspective that allow the creation of momentary scenarios or specific characters and actions to come the foreground. In other words, it can be compared to the moment in which a film director turns his camera and approaches a certain character or action, forgetting for a moment the rest of the scene.

It is interesting that the narrator and Jesus have the same position in the center, but they are distinguished by the direction of their gazes and facial expressions. As I mentioned previously, the narrator's gaze is always directed forward, toward the viewer. Whereas in this case, when the signer takes the role of Jesus, he will move his shoulders and look to the left or right, depending on who he is interacting with. It is also notable that at different moments in the narrative the Stooped Woman, the leader of the synagogue, and even the donkey have been personified in the foreground. This allows the viewer to give them the necessary attention during the narration.

Performative Actions (Dramatization)

The performative actions refer to the moments in which the signer, when personifying, executes the actions in an embodied way, that is, as if he were living them at that moment. This strategy can appear at any time and does not respond to the narrative or expository structures of oral languages. That is to say, as soon as the Deaf person sees an opportunity to dramatize, they can make use of it, even if the oral language does not imply dramatization.

It is not possible in this work to expose in detail each and every one of the sequences and dramatic actions carried out by the signer in the passage of Luke 13:10–17; I only highlight some crucial and emotional moments of this passage. The signer has placed these moments in the foreground precisely because of their importance.

The moment of the encounter between Jesus and the stooped woman when he heals her is key at the beginning of the narrative. Let's see some details of how these events are dramatized. In Luke 13:12–13 I highlight two moments. In the first, the woman comes to the fore as "Jesus lays his hands on her":

In the second moment, the stooped woman is the focus, and it is dramatized as the woman straightens up and begins to praise God.

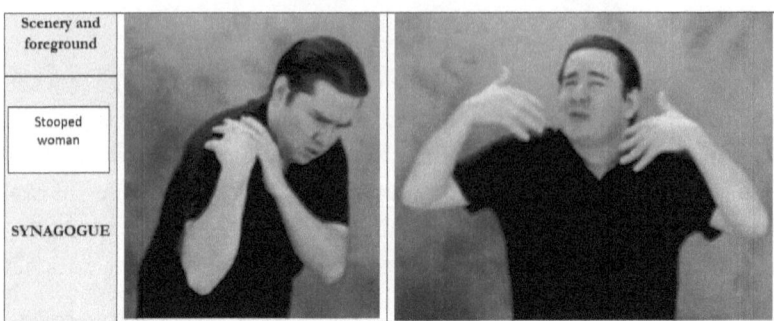

Another crucial moment is in Luke 13:14, when the synagogue leader gets angry with Jesus and gives a speech about the Sabbath to the assembled people, for which he comes to the fore or center of attention:

At the end of the narrative in Luke 13:17, the signer highlights the dramatization of the embarrassed opponents versus the people who marvel at the miracle of Jesus.

Context (Inferences)

Sign Languages are high-context languages, that is, they require sufficient visual information to convey speech or narration. To supply this information, inferences are used, and information that is implicit in a written text of a spoken language is made explicit. The written biblical text, from the perspective of a Deaf person, has many visual gaps, which a signer will need to fill in one way or another to make his narrative natural and understandable. Otherwise, it would seem to be truncated or visually incomplete.

The same logic and thought process needed to dramatize a story is used to show the elements that must be filled in visually in a Sign Language translation. This can sometimes involve looking for more contextual information to allow the signer to complete the scenes. Many times, this can be accomplished by consulting information before or after the passage or in other parts of the Bible, by summarizing previous actions, by looking for extra-biblical information about the culture or geography of the Bible, or simply by using their creativity or common sense.

Let's see some contextual elements provided by the signer in the passage from Luke 13:10–17.

Example 1

In this unit the original Greek text tells us that there were people gathered in the synagogue. The English translation cited in footnote 10 says "the crowd" (v. 14) and "the entire crowd" (v. 17), but the Greek doesn't specify their position or location they were in relation to Jesus.

In Sign Languages, to give us a visual context, the signer does not start the narration already inside the synagogue with the gathered people, but takes us to a previous moment, where a crowd of people enter the synagogue, and who arrange themselves in a semicircular way to receive happily the teaching of Jesus.

The signer has chosen to visually present us with a synagogue that was packed with people. He gives us this context, possibly based also upon what was indicated in several previous passages, which refer to the fact that the crowds crowded behind Jesus.

In the original Greek and spoken language translations nothing is said about the assembled people until they are mentioned in v. 14, and we are also not told where the people were located relative to Jesus. In a translation into a Sign Language, it is necessary to visually locate these people from the beginning since it would not be logical visually for Jesus to be teaching without them already being there. It has also been inferred that these people are in a semicircle around Jesus to receive his teaching.

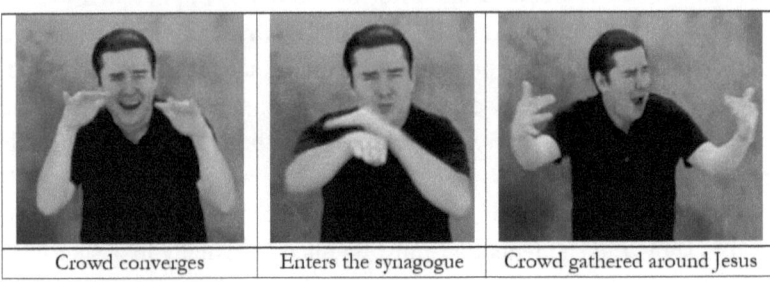

| Crowd converges | Enters the synagogue | Crowd gathered around Jesus |

Example 2

Another contextual element that the signer brings us in this translation, and that gives emotion to his narration, is not only the location of the stooped woman over among the people, but a dramatic moment in which the stooped woman looks disconsolately at Jesus.

In 13:12, the passage indicates that "Jesus saw her, called her and said to her." The signer makes a beautiful visual recreation of this whole moment, creating a small scene where he puts the woman looking inconsolably at Jesus, a Jesus who realizes her presence and pauses his teaching to look at her with compassion, calls her, asking her to come closer to him, and she walks toward him. At no time does the Bible passage say when the woman saw Jesus or when she walked toward him. It is an implicit detail which is made explicit by the signer because it is necessary visually to give the scene logic and emotion.

| Stooped woman looking at Jesus | Jesus looking the stooped woman | The stooped woman walking towards Jesus and Jesus looking at her |

Example 3

In Luke 13:15 Jesus asks the synagogue leader the following question: Does not each of you on the Sabbath untie his ox or his donkey from the manger, and lead it away to give it water? The Deaf signer creates a momentary scene where there is a corral with an ox or a donkey. Later he personifies the donkey, with a rope tied around its neck, desperately straining against the rope because it is thirsty and needs water. Then, some person (located in the place of the opponents), seeing how the animal suffers and nevertheless knowing that it is the Sabbath, very discreetly approaches and unties one end of the rope. He takes hold of the rope and leads the donkey, which plods along thirstily. The donkey then sees a dish filled with water and drinks vigorously.

The signer has creatively inferred and reconstructed the entire scene in such a way that it is possible to clearly see how, due to the suffering of the donkey, a person is moved to take it to drink water, even though it is a Sabbath.

Donkey trying to untie for thirst

A person discreetly untying the donkey

Donkey drinking water very thirsty

These three examples show much needed contextual information which has been inferred by the Deaf translators and incorporated into the translation of this passage to recreate the scene in a logically coherent way. Sign Languages, as visual and performative languages, require these elements to fully comply with the rules of their languages and to transmit of the full meaning of the text. Without these elements, the translation would not only be flat, but would not be an integral transmission of the Bible message.

Conclusion

Deaf people in a hearing world suffer many different types of oppression, and one has to do with their forms of visual-gestural communication. Many times, there is a tendency to disdain this form of communication, giving primacy to a kind of manual copy of the linear forms of oral languages. This tension is particularly reflected in the work of Bible translation, since the issue of what we consider fidelity to the word of God is also involved.

In this chapter I wanted to highlight how insights gleaned from the field of performative criticism are very important in the work of translating the Bible into Sign Languages. This is an approach that, by its nature, can contribute not only to a comprehensive understanding and recognition of the validity of the natural forms of communication that Deaf people use to transmit meanings, but it can also provide them with strategies for the study and translation of the biblical text in a clear, accurate, natural, and acceptable way.

Linguistic studies of Sign Languages are very important, as they have shown that these languages have a structured linguistic system and follow the universal principles of all human communication. However, for the work of Bible translation, the analysis of other components of Sign Languages is essential, such as performativity, multidimensionality, simultaneity, etc. That is, not only as another language, but as another semiotic system.

In the translation of the Bible into Sign Language based on the performance approach, I consider it essential to analyze how the signer personifies or embodies the characters, how he creates the settings and manages perspective in the location and movement of the characters, the moments and manners in which he decides to use the strategy of dramatization, the facial expressions and gestures that he uses to express emotions, and how context will be added to fill the visual gaps in the text to be translated, among other elements.

The analysis I have carried out of the Luke 13:10–17 passage translated into Mexican Sign Language has been based on a biblical text with a narrative style where the discursive strategies of performance are very evident. However, performance, being a constitutive part of the forms of communication of Sign Languages, can be found in the translation of any literary style or genre of the Bible. For this reason, there is still a lot of research that remains to be done with this type of approach to the Sign Language Bible translation process.

If we focus only on the level of grammatical analysis, syntactic order, and the structure of the signs used, we will be far from understanding the great communicative richness of Sign Languages that Deaf people can and should use when preparing the translation of the biblical text. In the worst case we will also be limiting translators in their abilities to comprehensively bring the biblical text to the world, the thinking, and the extraordinary forms of cognition of Deaf people.[24]

Bibliography

Biblia LSM. "Lucas 13:10–17." N.d. https://biblialsm.com/lucas-13-10-17.html.
Broesterhuizen, Marcel. "Deaf Liberation Theology and Deaf Teología Indígena." Paper presented at symposium "Deaf and Other Lives: Living in Multiple Cultures," September 25, 2008, Amsterdam. https://theo.kuleuven.be/fckupload/file/Amsterdam.pdf.
Castres, Olivier. "Carlos Miguel de L'Epée (1712–1789) y el arte de enseñar a hablar a los sordomudos de nacimiento." 2007. https://cultura-sorda.org/carlos-miguel-de-lepee-y-el-arte-de-ensenar-a-hablar-a-los-sordomudos/.
Hodgson, Robert. "Traducción de la Biblia en la cultura y en los medios de comunicación." https://www.um.es/tonosdigital/znum9/portada/tritonos/bibliahodgson.htm.
Klima, Edward, and Ursula Bellugi. *The Signs of Language*. Cambridge: Harvard University Press, 1979.
Lane, Harlan. "Ethnicity, Ethics and the Deaf-World." *Journal of Deaf Studies and Deaf Education* (2005) 291–310.
Martínez, López, et al. *Manual 3 de Gramática de la Lengua de Señas Mexicana*. México: Mariángel, 2016.
Maxey, James A. "Biblical Performance Criticism and Bible Translation: An Expanding Dialogue." In *Translating Scripture for Sound and Performance: New Directions in Biblical Studies*, edited by James A. Maxey and Ernst R. Wendland, 1–21. Biblical Performance Criticism 6. Kindle. Eugene, OR: Cascade Books, 2012.
Padden, Carol, and Tom Humphries. *Inside Deaf Culture*. Cambridge: Harvard University Press, 2005.
Perry, Peter. "Performance Criticism: Survey and Prospects." *Religions* 10 (2019) 117.
Rhoads, David. "Performance Criticism: An Emerging Methodology in Biblical Studies." https://www.sbl-site.org/assets/pdfs/rhoads_performance.pdf.
Saizarbitoria, Ramón. "La elección del sistema de comunicación en la educación de los niños sordos." *Zerbitzaun* 27 (1999) 154–57.

24. I greatly appreciate the valuable comments and observations for the improvement of the writing of this article made by colleagues Elsa Tamez, Shelley Dufoe, and Alyssa Shelamer, who know well the Sign Languages and the Bible translation process. I also want to thank Dr. Maxey for his valuable comments and suggestions in the development of this article.

Sandler, Wendy, and Diane Lillo-Martin. *Sign Language and Linguistics Universals.* Cambridge: Cambridge University Press, 2012.

Stokoe, William. *Sign Language Structure: An Outline of Visual Communication System of the American Deaf.* Buffalo, NY: University of Buffalo Press, 1960.

Tamez, Elsa. "Sign Language, Bible and Performance." *The Bible Translator* 66 (2015) 211–345.

Tamez, E., and I. Trujillo. "Diálogo Intercultural en el Proceso de Lecturas Bíblicas." In *Nuevas aproximaciones al texto bíblico: Métodos exegéticos y hermenéutica en el siglo 21*, edited by N. Míguez, 44–61. Buenos Aires: La Aurora, 2022.

Taub, Sarah. *Language from the Body: Iconicity and Metaphor in American Sign Language.* Cambridge: Cambridge University Press, 2004.

Virnig, Dack. "Deaf Man's ASL Storytelling, 'Fish.'" YouTube video, July 12, 2015. https://www.youtube.com/watch?v=DR4HF6S_hzo.

10

Translating What Is (not)(un)Said

Richard W. Swanson

My title is perhaps a little precious, but it touches an important complexity that attends all translation, especially translation from another millennium, another continent, another culture. Any text, even a simple one, is a mix of things explicitly said and things left unsaid, perhaps because they simply did not need to be said, perhaps because they are hinted at in a way that draws the audience into a dance of complicity in deriving the meaning of the text. Sometimes the creator of the text leaves things unsaid in an act of refusal, defiance, or resistance. And sometimes things that are apparently unsaid (at least so far as we in our millennium and culture can tell) would have sounded like shouts in the ears of the original audiences. These complexities need to be felt and explored in any act of translation, any act of "carrying across" a text from one world into another.

Of course, the word "translate" comes out of Latin and hands us the metaphor of physically carrying physical things across from one place to another. The physical reality of this act is important. Trans-lating[1] texts does not involve blowing the gas of meaning into a new set of words.

---

1. I use the hyphen in "trans-lating" to call attention to the matter of physically carrying the elements of ancient texts into contemporary worlds. I will not render the word with a hyphen every time, but only when the physicality of translation (translation) needs extra emphasis.

Texts are physical objects with roots sunk deep in a physical world. And that rootage brings its own kind of complexity.[2]

The task of this essay is finally to explore how these complexities can be carried across in the process of multimodal translation. To that end, I will work (eventually) with a single biblical text, a scene out of the Gospel of Mark. In fact, I will finally focus on one particular moment in the scene involving the woman who had for twelve years lived with a flow of blood.

But before I tighten the focus down to that particular moment, I need to begin with wider considerations about the task of carrying texts across the chasms that separate us from their place and time of origin.

You Gotta Know the *Techne*[3]

The most important thing I have learned (and re-learned) as a translator is that the first task is always to get clear what it is, exactly, that you are translating.

If you are translating a handbook, or an instruction manual, or a technical document, your translation has to render and respect the use to which the document will be put. If it is a handbook, it has to work while being held in hand in the midst of performing a discrete task. If it is an instruction manual, it has to give instructions. And if it is a technical document, it has to be detailed in the way technical tasks are detailed.

At the same time, it has to engage the *techne* that is being performed. You have to translate knowing that those who already know the *techne*, the art, may glance at your translation, but only to see if you also know the art, and then they will simply perform the art on their own. You have to translate, further, so that someone new to the *techne* can learn the art by performing the techniques you have translated.

But that means that even the translation of documents that are merely technical manuals needs to attend to carrying across the function that the original document laid open. It also means that you have to translate so that those who know the art, the *techne* behind the mere technique, will recognize not just the details of the task, but more importantly the

---

2. For a thorough, and provocative, exploration of the physical work of translation, see *Experiencing Translationality: Material and Metaphorical Journeys* by Piotr Blumczynski.

3. With apologies to the musical *The Music Man*, which makes it clear in its opening song, "Rock Island," that "you gotta know the territory."

integrity of the art. Both of these are part of the function of the original document. The very nature of such a manual therefore requires a careful weaving together of saying and not saying. If the manual says too much, those who know the *techne* will reject the manual since it does not respect their knowledge. If it says too little, it will not be usable for those who do not know the art in question. The manual must connect with both kinds of users since both are intended audiences. This connecting is accomplished especially through the matter of word selection. The technical terms in the translation must reveal respect for the *techne* involved without shutting out the non-specialists in the intended audience.

The Techne of a Board Game

I first learned this during my years in graduate study. I spent a summer studying German at the Goethe Institut in Prien am Chiemsee. In 1988 the FX Schmid game company had its headquarters in Prien. The year before one of their games, *Auf Achse*, had won the "Game of the Year" award. In the game, the players traveled back and forth across Europe driving trucks and delivering freight and paying tariffs, hopefully making profits. The company was planning to create an American version of the game. Among the people studying at the Goethe Institut was a small group of Americans, and they enlisted us to help them with the translation. They had worked up a preliminary translation and they wanted us to tweak it for release in the States.

We first pointed out that there are no lorries in the States. There are trucks and there are 18-wheelers. There ensued a longish discussion about which term was an appropriate translation in the game. Some of the group thought that a truck is a truck. Some of us who knew actual truckers pointed out that every trucker we knew had a truck (a pickup, to be specific), but referred to their rig as an 18-wheeler. Unless they were talking to another trucker, in which case they only called it a rig. People who knew the *techne* knew what they meant.

And then there was the matter of the title of the game. *Auf Achse* means "on axle." That makes perfect sense to German truckers, but means nothing to Americans. So should the title be kept untranslated (since the German title was part of the *techne* of game playing), or should it be carried across in some technical trucking term recognizable in the States? And if we should choose a technical term, which one? We played with "Over-the-Road Truckers," since that named the kind of long-haul trucking that the game presupposed. That title had too many hyphens in the opinion of the company representative. Those of us who knew over-the-road truckers noted that several of them had favorite songs related to trucking, especially "Six Days on the Road"[4] or "White Line Fever."[5] Maybe those song titles could be part of the name of the game. The rest of the group had never heard of those songs and thought that our efforts at technical specificity had gone too far. Someone mentioned that Willie Nelson's "On the Road Again,"[6] while not about trucking (at all), was a favorite song of many truckers. Most of the group had heard that song. Maybe we could call the game *On the Road Again*. The company had translated the title as "On The Move," which made no sense to any of us, but we suggested that maybe *On the Road* would catch American ears, truckers and non-truckers.

I don't think FX Schmid ever published an American version of *Auf Achse*, but I came away with a deeper understanding of what it meant to carry a rulebook for a game across the gap between (sub)cultures and languages. Translation required us to consider how people that knew truckers would react to the language we came up with to carry the game across the ocean. And this required us to pay careful attention to what was said, and what was left unsaid. Of the two, the matter of what is unsaid is often of more importance. Things left carefully unsaid establish alliances with audiences. Such hints let audience members feel that they are included in the circle of those who know the art.

The Techne of the Medea

I encountered this issue again when I began to translate ancient Greek tragedies for the theatre department at the university where I teach.

For over twenty years I have created translations for the theatre, translations explicitly created to be performed. Most of these translations have been of biblical texts, texts carried across from Hebrew or Greek into English, but in that time I have also translated ancient Greek drama for performance. I began by translating Euripides's *Medea*, a task that required me to bring to life a character who has been put in boxes, coffins in some cases, by millennia of translators.

---

4. Written by Earl Green and Carl Montgomery, and recorded by Dave Dudley.
5. Written and recorded by Merle Haggard.
6. Written and recorded by Willie Nelson.

The task of translating biblical texts is of course different from the task of translating Euripides. The genre is different, of course, but even the language itself is different. The Greek of the Gospels is often structured more like biblical Hebrew than like the Attic (or sometimes Doric) Greek of the *Medea*. But as I worked through the *Medea* I found a commonality it shared both with biblical texts and with the rulebook for *Auf Achse*. In some real ways, all three sets of literature function as books of instruction, at least as they have been translated and used by the receiving audience.

At first glance this seems, at least, counterintuitive. In our work with *Auf Achse*, we were simply translating a rulebook, a manual for use with the game. The *Medea*, however, is a play, a performance piece, not a rulebook, and biblical stories seem quite distant from both ancient Greek drama and manuals of any sort. But more attentive examination reveals more connection and more complexity.

To begin with, it is easy to find readers of biblical narrative who view these documents as "manuals for living." It is even easy to find deeply informed Jewish interpreters who hear Torah as instruction.

There are multiple interesting issues here. First of all, if Torah is instruction (and the word itself, in Hebrew, implies that this is precisely what Torah might be) what is the lesson being taught? There is also a prior question: what exactly is meant by Torah? Whether it encompasses the first five books of Jewish Scripture, the entirety of Jewish Scripture, or all of Jewish teaching and life, Torah is wildly diverse. Torah (even if it is limited to only the Pentateuch) is so diverse that every reading and reflecting community creates its own "canon-within-the-canon" to simplify the diversity. This hermeneutical tool tames the text, renders it compliant with the aims and ethos of the receiving community. But that means that the task of translation involves carrying the receiving community's ethos and aims across even when the text itself seems to suggest a different lesson. If the text is a vehicle for the lesson valued by the receiving community, then the text is not the object of translation. What has to be carried across is the community's plan of instruction.

So if the text is a vehicle for instruction, that supposes the existence of an ordered curriculum. A curriculum is larger than a message, to be sure. It is even larger than any individual plan of instruction. A curriculum establishes the canon of what will be read, what will be held as valuable. A curriculum encompasses all individual plans of instruction; it both expresses and inculcates the culture of the receiving community.

A curriculum, therefore, limits and focuses what will be interpreted, and at the same time specifies what interpretive results will be judged to be licit. The current conflicts over matters of curriculum in the United States make it clear that curricula are tools used by interested communities to transform the wild stuff of life and history into a global understanding that the controlling community wants transmitted. Close attention to this ongoing wrangle makes it clear that curricular decisions are always the site of battles for control. No matter what side(s) you find yourself on, you have interests and you seek to control what is carried across as the message of the text, the tradition, the wild stuff of life and history. To ignore the impact of interest on all sides is at least disingenuous. It is surely cynical and counterproductive.

But what about the *Medea*? It is a play. Is it in any sense also instruction for life? My work in translation has taught me to get clear exactly what it was that I was translating. If the *Medea* is in any proper sense a manual for living, it embodies a truth, a message that I will be expected to carry across in my translating. And if I am carrying across a message, then my task would be to allow my work to be controlled by a curriculum, by an interested community that had decided ahead of time what the message of the text was, what it could even be allowed to be. If my work is governed by an imposed curriculum, then my task would be to submit to that curriculum, to welcome that control, and to find in the text only what the community had already authorized interpreters to find. That, and nothing else.

Even a cursory review of the history of translating the *Medea* provides abundant examples of controlled translation, governed by a curriculum. In translation after translation, the woman, Medea, is controlled by being carried across as a "typical woman" (a viewpoint that would gladden the heart of her dullard of a husband). She becomes a tool in the hands of patriarchy to demonstrate that women are wildly emotional, magically dangerous, and that they are transformed into monsters whenever they violate their duties as child-rearers and care-givers.

Particularly telling was the version of Medea created in the mid-twentieth century by Jean Anouilh.[7] This is not a word-by-word translation, but it is still a carrying across of the story from ancient Greece to twentieth-century France. The characters in Anouilh's version are

---

7. Anouilh, *Medea*, in *Plays*.

engaged in a Freudian struggle between lust and reason. In that struggle, Medea sees herself as wounded, maimed.[8]

This rightly celebrated version is deeply settled into the ethos of its time, as well. Medea is made into a thoroughly modern woman, thoroughly at home in the French twentieth century, most powerfully aware of herself in sensuality and sexual submission. In Anouilh's retelling, Jason is solid and rational and Medea is dangerously passionate. The curriculum is clear and easily read.

Even more intriguing is the recent version created by German novelist Christa Wolf. This also is a version, not a word-trading translation perhaps (Wolf herself calls it a "re-telling" in that it retells the story without picking up the original words), but still Wolf also carries the story across, trans-lating it (as it were) for a new century and a different world. The nature of this act of trans-lating is made clear by philosopher and sociologist Elisabeth Lenk, whose words are the epigraph for Wolf's *Medea: Voices*. Lenk writes:

> Achronism is not the inconsequential juxtaposition of epochs, but rather their interpenetration, like the telescoping legs of a tripod, a series of tapering structures. Since it's quite far from one end to the other, they can be opened out like an accordion, but they can also be stacked inside one another like Russian dolls, for the walls around time-periods are extremely close to one another. The people of other centuries hear our phonographs blaring, and through the walls of time we see them raising their hands towards the deliciously prepared meal.[9]

The physicality of the link between Lenk's epochs matters. It matters even more that Lenk has identified this trans-lating as "achronism," and not "anachronism." As she argues: the walls around time-periods are extremely close to one another. We can hear from one side to the other. In fact, we not only can, we must. This sheds important light on the ways that the curriculum functions in the task of translating. The stories we carry across are, as it were, thin places (to borrow an image from Celtic spirituality), places where the realities of separate worlds come perilously close to each other, places where we go to encounter both the peril and the insight that comes with it. We go to the *Medea* because the matter of how women and men interact is crucial to us. And because this matter

---

8. Lyons, "Ambiguity of the Anouilh 'Medea,'" 317–18.
9. Elisabeth Lenk, Epigraph to *Medea*, by Christa Wolf.

is crucial, this becomes the ground on which community curricula assert themselves. Wolf embeds this insight in a chapter devoted to Jason's voice. Wolf has Jason report the words of Medea:

"At the end she said, 'They've made what they need out of each of us. Out of you, the Hero, and out of me, the Wicked Witch.'"[10]

"They've made what they need . . . ." This need reveals the required curriculum that governs the way the characters are interpreted.

This is not a new phenomenon, as is made clear by Donald Mastronarde in his notes to the Cambridge critical edition of Euripides's *Medea*. Mastronarde notes with care that "Euripides's own portrayal of Medea is complex and finely nuanced," but that later Hellenistic and Roman philosophers were fixated on her "passionate emotions and violence" and tended to ascribe her actions to "her 'otherness' as Colchian and sorceress."[11]

From the beginning the *Medea* has been trans-lated as if it had a message, a truth about women and men that had to be carried across from the ancient world to the contemporary world. In each of these instances of "carrying across," the wild story of Medea, the woman, is controlled by making the play into a story about the men. And that is the only thing that the *Medea* is not. This translational re-creation of Euripides's play was shaped and controlled by the curricula of patriarchal communities. It seems to me, however, that the wildness of the story is more essential to Euripides's play than is the controlling interests of translating communities.

---

10. Wolf, *Medea*, Jason's voice, 40.

11. Mastronarde, *Medea*, "General Introduction." See his detailed discussion in which he notes that "the word *barbaros* itself appears only four times in the play, uttered only by Medea . . . or by Jason . . ." "[I]t is important to note that Jason's claims of Greek superiority in the *agon* have been undercut by his own action." *Medea*, 15. And further: "On the whole then Euripides has been rather restrained, and also partly ironic, in exploitation of the Greek-foreign contrast. This conclusion is borne out by two further points. First, within the play Medea is portrayed as worshiping and invoking the same gods as the Greek characters . . . Second, if Euripides' treatment is compared to subsequent versions of the same story, one can see clearly how the motif of foreignness is intensified or exaggerated by later authors." *Medea*, 24.

The Techne of Performance, as Experienced in Production Meetings

If the first task in translating is to get clear about what it is, exactly, that you are translating, we ought to note that the *Medea* is a play, a performance piece.

Much of what I know about performance pieces I have learned from production meetings. In production meetings professionals from the multiple fields that make theatre work gather to dream, plan, and realize what will become the performance. Costume designers explore fabrics, flow, fit, and allusions that will create the visual character that audiences will experience. Scenic designers consider what various settings would add or subtract from the show. And in all of this, the director and the dramaturg listen and respond to the dreaming and planning, shaping the shared imagining of the production team so that the emerging shared vision is physically realized on stage. It is a complex process, loaded with theoretical considerations and practical realities. The script unites the entire process, but the process reveals the complex problems embedded in the script.

In the case of the *Medea*, the final scene contains a particularly complex problem, and therefore especially exemplifies the interlocking modalities that go with translating the play from the page to the stage.

In the lead-up to the final scene, Medea has been promised safe haven in Athens, provided she can get to Athens on her own. Other characters have urged her to accept any means available: horse, cart, or on foot. But none of these other means are available to her, and she stands on stage with the bloody corpses of her children, confronting her blustering and faithless husband. Euripides, having reminded us that she is the granddaughter of the Sun, provides her with an escape in a flaming golden chariot. The question on the table at the first production meeting was: How in the world will we get her off the stage? The problem is sometimes solved by having Medea fly off, but that option was not available to us: the stage at our university is not equipped for flying, and none of the students are certified flyers. The scenic designer imagined that she could build a chariot, but the chances that it would look hokey were too high. Of course ancient dramaturgs faced the same problem. Ancient Greek theatres did not have flying capability and if a chariot was provided, it would have looked like a cart, however golden. But ancient Greeks had an advantage that we could not count on: the audience knew the story and had grown up imagining Medea as the granddaughter of the Sun. Ancient dramaturgs could count on the audience to supply imaginatively what the scenic designers could not build. At the first meeting the director and dramaturg made it clear: our audience would not know the story until we told it to them. If they saw a cart, they would see it as a cart, not a flaming chariot of gold capable of flying to the sun. Or, perhaps worse, even if we succeeded in making a glorious chariot that somehow rose above the fray onstage, the audience would see it as a circus trick, as a cheap escape from trouble that made Medea immune to the trouble that was brought on her by her husband and the city that gave her refuge but not a home.

In the end, the designers decided to forgo the chariot and to create an escape on the plane of the stage. Medea was thus not above it all, but was still able to contrive an escape. They designed a wall of the set that could be lit to glow like the sun, and when it glowed, it opened to Medea. She exited and the wall closed behind her and the light faded back into ordinary illumination. It worked admirably, but I learned a lot about translation as I listened to the designers and the director work through the difficulties. This was not merely a matter of technical difficulties. The entire point of the play was at stake. If at the end Medea is Othered, if she is made into a magical being who was never at risk, then her identification with the women of Corinth earlier in the play was a lie, a pretense carried out by a wicked schemer. And if Medea is finally made into an Other, then we have collaborated with Jason and Creon (and with the centuries of translators) who have made her into a dangerous barbarian, a witch, an Other who must be subdued as must all women. But at the start of our conversation the director and I made it clear: Euripides had given Medea the most elegant Greek in the entire play. If anyone sounds barbarous, it is Jason and his idol, Creon. The task at hand was therefore at heart multimodal translation: How do we carry the character across the millennia and onto our stage so that Euripides's daring story is rendered adequately?

Translating Messages v. Carrying Across Provocations

My years of working with actors, directors, and audiences have taught me to distrust any performance that begins by imagining that it has a distinct message to share. First of all, such a beginning threatens to make performance merely didactic, merely ideological. Ideological theatre is dull because everything is preprocessed. Any "surprises" come out of a can shipped from an approved warehouse and opened on cue. Even the dullest audience already knows what will come out of the can. You could read it on the ideological label.

Years of working with the theatre have taught me that theatre is about moments of actual surprise, not canned pre-processed surprises. Theatre is provocation and provocation refuses to be controlled. George Tabori says it well: "Catastrophic expectation is the essence of the performing arts, the silent assumption that in spite of all our best-laid plans, something will go wrong, that Othello may, in fact, strangle his lady."[12] As Anat Feinberg points out, "Tabori—like other innovators such as Brook, Chaikin, or Richard Schechner—calls for the 'presence' of the actor who produces life instead of reproducing art."[13] Feinberg notes that for Tabori, "The actor is an honest provocateur."[14]

In that vein, the ideological curricula of those who translate the *Medea* are instructive. The wild life of the woman at the center of the story provokes translators to find a way to control her. Somehow. The desperation is instructive. It flags the actual provocation that is the heart of Euripides's wild play. The question then is how do you translate a provocation? The efforts to smooth over the provocation are instructive. Those efforts make clear the heart of the play, the heart that must be carried across. The question is, how?

Even in plays that are not so wild as the *Medea*, provocation is central. The stage is full of actors who inter-act.[15] The director with whom I have worked closely through these years, Jayna Gearhart Fitzsimmons, works vigorously to avoid stabilizing the inter-action. She works with the actors to foster intense reciprocal awareness. They see each other. They hear each other. They respond to each other, and in responding they create surprises. Things happen on opening night that have never happened before. Sometimes this is because of the presence of the audience. But Fitzsimmons sets the moment of surprise on a deeper foundation. She works with the actors to treat the surprises themselves as the stuff of the

---

12. Tabori, quoted in Feinberg, *Embodied Memory*, 53.
13. Feinberg, *Embodied Memory*, 60.
14. Feinberg, *Embodied Memory*, 62.
15. The unexpected hyphen in the middle of this word is important. On stage one expects acting, and interacting is an ordinary aspect of life. But when the acting on stage is powerfully inter-active, something beyond easy prediction and control happens, both for the actors and for the audience.

play. Actors are onstage to inter-act, to listen and respond to each other, alive in the wild moment when anything could happen.

But that means that the play is not a set-piece that is rolled onstage every evening at 7:30 when the curtain opens. It is not a message, not a curriculum. That means that what happens onstage, what the actors and the audience experience, is a play of provocation. Close study of deconstruction has taught me that written text is wildly diverse and uncontrollable. Closer attention to what happens onstage has confirmed what deconstruction theorizes. The lines are the same every night, but living theatre is different every time. The task of the actors is to see and hear each other in the wild freedom of the moment and to be provoked in living and unpredictable ways. The result is that the audience is provoked as well, and the play provokes transformation.

When I translate a piece for performance, this is what I am translating: a provocation, a transformation, a set of words that sit unstable on the page. It is the instability that must be carried across, not the tamed curricular message that the controlling community has decided is safe enough to let loose in public.

As I noted at the outset, my biblical translations have also been created for the theatre. That has taught me to distrust the notion that my task is to carry across a pre-processed message, no matter how palatable or "gospel-centered." Performance is provocation. Performance, therefore, will always destabilize ideology, always shake the foundations of any power structure that seeks to control the message of the text.

Translating a Destabilizing Touch

For the remainder of this study I will test this notion on a particular moment of a complex scene in the Gospel of Mark, specifically Mark 5:21–43. Jesus is hurrying through a pressing crowd, rushing to heal a young woman, twelve years old, who is at the point of death. And a woman, twelve years in a flow of blood, comes up behind him and touches him.

For customary interpretation and translation, the woman who touches Jesus does so in order to allow him to deliver a message. She is a tool used to that purpose and as such she enters from nowhere and returns there when she has been used. Once Jesus saves her, we are done with her. Having come from nowhere, she vanishes into nothingness.

For performance translation, the woman has to come from somewhere, and she has to have a reason for leaving where she was and coming into the crowd behind Jesus. Yes, she came to be healed, but her understanding of this will have been complicated and the actor playing her will have to find those complications in order to play the scene. And she cannot simply vanish when the scene concludes.

The Problem of the Vanishing Woman

Well, actually, she could. When the gospel is performed by a solo performer (which is the norm in biblical storytelling), the performer clicks between the distinct episodes in the larger scene. Jesus gets out of the boat and is greeted by Jairus, a father whose daughter is dying. He departs immediately on a mission to save the daughter. Click. First episode completed. Then we meet the woman with the flow of blood. We learn her history. We learn her intentions. She carries out those intentions and knows that she is healed. Jesus hunts for her and she comes forward. Jesus announces what she already knows: she is healed. Click. Second episode completed. And then messengers come from Jairus's house. The daughter is dead. Jesus proceeds to the house, denying the fact of death. He grasps her hand and speaks to her in Aramaic and the daughter rises from her deathbed. The girl walks around; the people are amazed; Jesus suggests that she might be hungry. Click. And thus the third episode, indeed the entire scene, is completed. Solo performers often tell the story of the first episode, then turn fifteen degrees and tell the second, and turn fifteen degrees yet again and complete the story they had originally begun to tell. The episodic nature of Mark's story provides them with cues as to when to click from episode to episode, when to turn and tell the next separate piece of the scene. At the conclusion of the longer scene, the episodic narrative provides a cue to make a bigger turn and click into the next scene in Mark's story.

Solo performance is the norm in biblical storytelling, and it has made both audiences and performers strongly aware of the physical and relational reality of these stories. Clearly the stories were born in a world that knew and valued performed narratives. But solo performance also can obscure provocative moments in the stories that have to be carried across for the story to be fully translated. And solo performance is susceptible to treating the story as a message, a gospel truth that the performer delivers to the audience as part of a community curriculum. That is why I have done my work with ensembles, not soloists. When members of the ensemble inter-act, wild life happens.

Even ensemble performance has to confront the extremely episodic nature of Mark's story. When episodes end, everyone vanishes. But in this particular scene, the storyteller has created a provocation that an ensemble must find a way to trans-late. The woman touches Jesus. She knows she is healed. Jesus feels his potency leave him, and he turns and turns around in the crowd looking for the woman who has done this. It is a beauty of Greek pronouns that the storyteller can let us know that Jesus knows it was a woman who touched him and drained his potency. He finds her when she lets herself be found, and he tells her that her faithfulness has rescued her. Whatever that means.

And then the storyteller says, "While he was still speaking . . ."

The Woman Is Still Onstage

This means that the report from Jairus's house comes while the woman is still standing there. If Jesus is still speaking, she is still listening, still interacting, still hearing. But if she is still hearing, she hears that the child has died because of Jesus' delay.

The actor playing the woman must hear that her character triggered the delay. Yes, it was Jesus who created the delay when he dithered in the crowd, perhaps seeking a means to deliver the message that the controlling community wanted him to deliver. Yes, if Jesus had not needed to tell the woman what she already knew: she was healed, the delay would not have occurred and the child would not have died. But the actor knows that her character chose to come up behind Jesus in the crowd and touch him. Even if she made that choice in order to avoid any possible delay, and maybe especially if she made that choice because she had heard that Jesus was rushing to heal another woman, the actor will have to navigate her character's sense of complicity. Her touch triggered the delay. From that recognition it is a small step to concluding that her touch had caused the delay and had therefore also caused the death of the daughter at the point of death. The actor will have to choose how her character will react to this surprise, this provocation. Whatever the actor chooses, the audience will see it, hear it, and incorporate it into their construal of the scene. The provocation, however it is performed, is integral to the scene and must be translated, carried across for the translation to be fully effective.

The provocation, however, makes it clear that this scene cannot be boiled down to a message. Yes, Jesus is a healer and goes two-for-two in this scene. But in the middle of the scene the woman who touches him has to respond to the result of his dithering. The daughter died, not because the woman touched Jesus (though the actor playing the woman would have to come to terms with this understanding), but because Jesus turned and turned around in the crowd looking for the woman who had touched him.

How Do You Trans-late a Woman Who Refuses to Disappear?

Here is the most important translational task. What ways might the woman respond to Jesus' dithering? And how does Jesus respond to her reaction? The storyteller has handed us this provocation, and our preference for a curriculum in which Jesus the healer can do no wrong cannot remove our responsibility to carry across this provocation.

In fact, as translators we are responsible to carry across a full range of possibilities. This reveals one of the crucial complexities of translation for ensemble performance. When a complete performance is developed, each actor will have made choices that limit what any individual scene will mean. As these choices interact with each other onstage, anything can happen, but the choices constrain each other even as they provoke each other. At the same time, however, an embodied trans-lation must facilitate, even fund, all of the performative possibilities. The woman could be crushed by guilt at having caused the delay, which would leave Jesus to respond to this crushing. He could be annoyed by the woman's action, which would increase her sense of guilt. Jesus could want to relieve her of her guilt, but he still has to hurry on to Jairus's house so he has to tear himself away from doing anything to relieve the woman who had touched him.

The woman could be irritated, or even angry, with Jesus because he dithered when he need not have delayed. The storyteller has informed us that the woman is healed, so Jesus does not need to stick around to complete the job. His delaying is gratuitous.

The storyteller might even have given us a more complicated provocation to trans-late. The scene involves a woman who is bleeding. We are not told that this is menstrual blood, but if this unsaid bit of the scene is something we are intended to understand, the provocation becomes even more revealing. Ancient patriarchal culture surrounded menstruation with taboo. Paula Fredriksen is surely right: there were no purity police who hunted down menstruating women so as to exclude them from public life,[16] but texts from that approximate time reveal that men thought that a menstruating woman could sour milk at a distance. And, more relevant to the scene at hand, a touch from a menstruating woman could render a man impotent.[17] Notice that in the scene Jesus feels *dunamis* go out from him and proceeds to hunt for the woman who had done this. *Dunamis* is typically (and appropriately) translated as "power," but it could also be rendered as "potency." In fact, it is precisely the right word in ancient Greek for male potency, and the loss of that "power" is exactly how impotence would be expressed. So how does the woman react if she sees that Jesus is worried about being impotent just because she touched him? The actor will have to experiment with a range of fascinating possibilities. The storyteller has intensified this provocation by having Jesus tell her, in the presence of the crushing crowd, that the woman is healed from her *mastigos*. The translators of the New Revised Standard Version render this word as "disease," which again is a perfectly workable meaning for *mastigos*. But the word has a metaphorical root in the tool used in flogging prisoners, and thus is well-translated as "scourge."

They Hear Our Phonographs and the Woman Knows That We Are Disturbed

Elisabeth Lenk pointed out that any act of trans-lating will, of necessity, be achronic. As she argues, the walls between historical eras are very thin and the people on the other side "hear our phonographs blaring." If they can hear our phonographs, the woman in the scene can hear in the word *mastigos* the ways some women in my generation (but not in my family) were taught to speak of menstruation: some called it their "scourge." If that is what the woman hears in Jesus' choice of words to name her bleeding, the actor will have an even more complicated task. Does she accept this word that implies that menstruation is somehow a punishment? Such an acceptance will show itself physically. Or is she desperately tired of the patriarchal habit (suddenly shared also by Jesus) of imagining this basic experience of women as somehow evidence that she had to be punished? This choice will also be visible physically, but will carry the associated problem of directly challenging Jesus' response to her bleeding. And no matter which option the actor chooses, she will also

---

16. Fredriksen, *Jesus of Nazareth, King of the Jews*, 67–68.
17. See Amy-Jill Levine's "Discharging Responsibility," 70–87.

have to decide what it means for this word to come out of a male mouth. I remember realizing that even though some women I knew in my youth used this word, it was not a term to be used by men. The border between those who bleed monthly and those never will is marked by words that can be said by some of us, and must be unsaid by the rest. What if the scene reveals a messiah who does not realize that his words are transgressive? If this is the embodiment of the scene that is carried across, this scene will be linked for the audience with the scene in Mark 7 in which Jesus calls a mother a dog.

What matters for faithful trans-lation is the recognition that the scene contains not a message but a provocation. Multimodal translation of this scene makes it clear that any controlling curriculum has just been destabilized by the embedded provocation. It also makes it clear that any printed translation will have the responsibility to render words in ways that signal the presence of a provocation. Even more importantly, the provocation in this scene (and in so many other scenes, especially in Mark's story) makes it clear that any adequate trans-lation of this scene will require multiple performances, performances that destabilize each other. To put it plainly, any stable translation that bows to and serves any controlling curriculum erases the provocation, and is therefore a mistranslation. The provocation is essential to the scene.

The Woman Bleeds and the Messiah Is Murdered

This is, perhaps, what we ought to expect in a story of a murdered messiah. Perhaps we ought to see this as finally consonant with the larger story that promises a resurrection, but tells a provocative story in which no one, not even the reader or audience, ever sees Jesus raised from death. This particular provocation sparked the creation of four alternate endings to the story, each of which obviously served a community curriculum in which Jesus rolls death back and fulfills all the promises that hang on the notion of a messiah.

I once attended a performance of Mark's story that promised to take the original ending (16:8) seriously. The actor spoke the final words, looked frantically about, and ran off stage. I was impressed. But then he came back. He said, "That is how the story ends. But I like to think that the original performer came back onstage and answered all the questions the audience must have had. Yes, Jesus was raised . . . ." He went on for quite a while. Before he finished, he had done all four of the additional endings. He blunted the very provocation that he had promised to take seriously. It was an astonishing testimony to the power of the provocation that I argue is essential to the scene in Mark 5 and to the whole of Mark's very odd story. I find myself imagining (achronically) that Christa Wolf (if she had worked with Mark instead of with Medea) would have had Jesus say, "They've made what they need out of each of us. Out of you, the audience that understands everything, and out of me, the well-tamed and well-mannered mascot that so many Christians seem to want."

This scene, like all of Mark's story, leaves many things unsaid in ways that refuse to be tamed. In the end, Mark's messiah is as wild and uncontrolled as Euripides's Medea. Any attentive audience is left with questions that demand answers as the result of a performance that refuses to calm its audience. Perhaps as a result, Euripides's play did not take honors when it was performed, but finished third in the competition. Perhaps as a comparable result, Mark's Gospel was labeled as chaotic and incomprehensible in ancient times and was added to the regular rotation of the preaching lectionary only relatively recently. I would argue that it is time we carried the provocation across. The times in which we live make it clear that the order we imagined to be fixed and eternal is in fact imposed and partial. Perhaps it is time that our privileged daydreams be destabilized so that we can begin to learn how to think about our life together in ways that don't involve simple reliance on power and privilege.

Bibliography

Anouilh, Jean. *Plays*. New York: Hill & Wang, 1967.
Blumczynski, Piotr. *Experiencing Translationality: Material and Metaphorical Journeys*. New York: Routledge, 2023.
Feinberg, Anat. *Embodied Memory: The Theatre of George Tabori*. Iowa City: University of Iowa Press, 1999.
Fredriksen, Paula. *Jesus of Nazareth, King of the Jews*. New York: Knopf, 2000.
Lenk, Elisabeth. Epigraph to *Medea: A Modern Retelling*, by Christa Wolf. New York: Doubleday, 1998.
Levine, Amy-Jill. "Discharging Responsibility: Matthean Jesus, Biblical Law, and the Hemorrhaging Woman." In *A Feminist Companion to Matthew*, edited by Amy-Jill Levine, 70–87. Feminist Companion to the New Testament and Early Christian Writings 1. Sheffield: Sheffield Academic, 2001.
Lyons, Charles L. "The Ambiguity of the Anouilh 'Medea.'" *French Review* 37 (1964) 312–19.
Mastronarde, Donald J., and Euripides. *Euripides, Medea*. Cambridge: Cambridge University Press, 2010.
Wolf, Christa. *Medea: A Modern Retelling*. New York: Doubleday, 1998.

www.ingramcontent.com/pod-product-compliance
Lightning Source LLC
Chambersburg PA
CBHW031726230426
43669CB00007B/261